The Dynamics
of Urban Growth
in Three Chinese Cities

The Dynamics
of Urban Growth
in Three Chinese Cities

HT
384
.C6
Y87
1997
West

Shahid Yusuf
Weiping Wu

PUBLISHED FOR THE WORLD BANK
OXFORD UNIVERSITY PRESS

Oxford University Press

OXFORD NEW YORK TORONTO
DELHI BOMBAY CALCUTTA MADRAS KARACHI
KUALA LUMPUR SINGAPORE HONG KONG TOKYO
NAIROBI DAR ES SALAAM CAPE TOWN
MELBOURNE AUCKLAND
and associated companies in
BERLIN IBADAN

© 1997 The International Bank for Reconstruction
and Development / THE WORLD BANK
1818 H Street, N.W.
Washington, D.C. 20433, U.S.A.

Published by Oxford University Press, Inc.
198 Madison Avenue, New York, N.Y. 10016

Manufactured in the United States of America
First printing August 1997

The findings, interpretations, and conclusions expressed in this study are
entirely those of the authors and should not be attributed in any manner to
the World Bank, to its affiliated organizations, or to members of its Board of
Executive Directors or the countries they represent. The boundaries, colors,
and other information shown on any map in this volume do not imply on the
part of the World Bank any judgment on the legal status of any territory or the
endorsement or acceptance of such boundaries.

Cover: Detail from a Chinese scroll, courtesy of the Freer Gallery of Art,
Smithsonian Institution, Washington, D.C.

Library of Congress Cataloging-in-Publication Data

Yusuf, Shahid, 1949–
   The dynamics of urban growth in three Chinese cities / Shahid
Yusuf and Weiping Wu.
      p.   cm.
   Published for the World Bank
   Includes bibliographical references and index.
   ISBN 0-19-521113-8
   1. Urbanization—China—Case studies.   2. Industrialization—China—
Case studies   3. Shanghai (China)—Economic conditions.   4. Tientsin
(China)—Economic conditions.   5. Canton (China)—Economic
conditions.   I. Wu, Weiping.   II. World Bank.   III. Title.
HT384.C6Y87   1997
307.76'0951—dc21   97-2013
                                                                 CIP

Contents

Tables

Figures

Preface

This book would not have been possible without the assistance and support of many individuals and organizations. First, we want to acknowledge the contribution of two authors of an earlier World Bank report from which we drew a considerable amount of information: Shekhar Shah (World Bank) and Barry Naughton (University of California at San Diego). Shekhar Shah also made valuable suggestions about the outline of the book. We are also grateful to the anonymous referees, who reviewed both the previous report and the manuscript of this book, for their constructive criticisms and suggestions.

Several individuals and groups deserve special thanks. Gary Jefferson (Brandeis University) and I. J. Singh and Dilip Ratha (World Bank) were extremely generous in providing access to large data bases on China's industrial enterprises. The Consortium for International Earth Science Information Network (CIESIN) provided us with base maps of China at no cost and with valuable technical assistance. Within the World Bank, the Asian Technical Department and the cartography unit helped with geographic mapping. William Easterly, Andrew Hamer, Rajiv Lall, Vikram Nehru, and Robert Taylor provided help and information for the book. We also want to thank those who assisted us technically, including Larry Austin, Les Barker, Charlene Hsu, Jeffrey N. Lecksell, Julia Li, and Min Zhu of the World Bank, Liu Chuang and Jack Evans of the CIESIN, John Zhao of Brandeis University, and Scott Kennedy of the Brookings Institution.

We are very grateful to the Policy Research Department of the World Bank, which provided us with a wonderful working environment. Special thanks go to the director, Lyn Squire, who supported our effort; to

Sushma Rajan, whose invaluable help improved every aspect of the book; and to Robert Akl and Maria Elena Edwards, who offered technical support.

We would also like to thank the following persons for invaluable assistance with the production and publication of this book: Paola Brezny, James Feather, Kathryn Dahl, Elizabeth Forsyth, Rebecca Glenister, Sherry Holmberg, William O. Lively, Barbara Malczak, and Jason Peaco.

Both of us have survived the sweet, protracted agony of authorship more or less unscathed because of the care and support lavishly provided on the home front. Weiping Wu thanks Michael Crowley for love and encouragement that eased the final and most taxing stages of revision. Behind Shahid Yusuf there stood Natasha, Nadia, and Zain. Their enthusiasm for the project ensured that the manuscript never languished and that the year of writing was lived joyfully.

Abbreviations and Data Notes

FBIS-CHI	Foreign Broadcast Information Services—China
FDI	Foreign direct investment
GDP	Gross domestic product
GNP	Gross national product
GVIAO	Gross value of industrial and agricultural output
GVIO	Gross value of industrial output
R&D	Research and development
TEU	Twenty-foot equivalent unit
Y	Yuan

Market exchange rates, Chinese yuan/U.S. dollar, 1964–96 (IMF, *International Financial Statistics Yearbook,* February 1997)

1964–71	2.46	1984	2.80
1972	2.24	1985	3.20
1973	2.02	1986–88	3.72
1974	1.84	1989	4.72
1975	1.97	1990	5.22
1976	1.88	1991	5.43
1977	1.73	1992	5.75
1978	1.58	1993	5.80
1979	1.50	1994	8.45
1980	1.53	1995	8.31
1981	1.75	1996	8.30
1982	1.92	1997	8.30
1983	1.98		

The Dynamics of Urban Growth: Location, Size, Structure, and Reforms **1**

Gazing a few decades into the future, optimists see China moving steadily to the top of the economic league. For example, several sources forecast that China will be the world's second largest economy by 2005 (Australian National University 1995) and the world's largest economy by 2020 (Australia 1997; OECD 1997). Although China's per capita income might still trail behind that of some Western economies, in the aggregate China's domestic product will be the largest. Many skeptics are not persuaded that the recent high growth rates will persist for long. In their view, a variety of systemic forces, some already apparent, will increasingly constrain China's expansion in the years ahead. Both the optimists and the skeptics base their assessments on an evaluation of China's urban economy, which is the principal driving force. This book should be of interest to both camps. Its theme is the interplay of geography, size, and industrial structure in determining the industrial vigor of cities. Its message, which is abundantly illustrated by the experience of three Chinese cities, is that turning each of these factors to the city's benefit requires sound policymaking. Unless initiatives are taken to exploit inherited capabilities and to approach comparative advantage in a dynamic framework, a strong production base can start to decay, pulling the city into a vicious, downward spiral.

Reforms: Background and Framework

Reforms began inconspicuously in the mid-1970s. Farmers in a handful of China's poorest agricultural counties demanded to be released from the commune system and returned to the autonomy of household production. At first the central government resisted, but then, in the face of

1

agricultural stagnation and rural unrest, it cautiously permitted experiments in Anhui, Guangdong, and Sichuan.[1] By 1978 these stirrings of change had acquired sufficient political backing and economic credibility for the government to announce a reform program at the plenary session of the Eleventh Party Congress, held in December. The congress signaled a break from the past and committed China to pragmatically exploring pathways to modernization (see Fewsmith 1994 and Riskin 1987 for excellent accounts of the circumstances leading up to this decision). It was the beginning of the end of an era in which ideology was an arbiter of institutional acceptability and a touchstone for policy.

What was initially a limited mandate for reform has grown with each passing year to cover all facets of economic life in China. The Four Modernizations Program, launched in 1978, was pragmatic and experimental in outlook. Its ambitions for the economy were pitched high, but its scope and the degree of institutional change anticipated initially were rather narrow. They grew wider as reforms proved successful and generated "imbalances," which could only be smoothed away by further changes (see Lin 1994). In the earlier years, agriculture was the principal beneficiary, and expansion in farm output accounted for about half of overall economic growth. Agriculture, which until 1983 included rural industry, grew at an average annual rate of 7 percent between 1978 and 1984 and was responsible for 30 percent of overall growth. Thereafter, growth declined, averaging 4 percent annually for the remainder of the 1980s.

After 1983 the spread of reform brought industry to the forefront. Since then, the urban industrial economy has been largely responsible for China's nonpareil industrial growth (which averaged 12 percent a year between 1978 and 1995). This is a considerable departure from trends that emerged shortly after the communist government came to power. Maoist policies were colored by the earlier persecution of communists in cities such as Shanghai. With its antiurban bias, the Maoist vision considered cities to be parasitic and strived to contain "nonproductive," mainly service-related, activities (see Buck 1978; Murphy 1980; Chang 1994). One tenet that was never pursued aggressively was to unite city and countryside. Others that were implemented to varying degrees called for dispersing industry, building regional self-sufficiency so as to enhance defense capabilities, and curbing the growth of the urban populace. The Third Front policy, whose genesis was the perceived threat to China following U.S. involvement in Vietnam, transferred some heavy industry from the coast to the interior provinces and absorbed between a third and half of all gross investment between 1966 and 1973 (see Naughton 1988; Bramall 1993; Zhao 1996).

Urban industrial change in China since the early 1980s has followed a circuitous path, and the next step is still being teased forth (see Shirk 1993; Fewsmith 1994; and the commentary in Yang 1996b). Inevitably, the story emerging is complex, but its principal elements are now falling into place. First, China's reforms do not constitute the unfolding of a grand design; rather at each major juncture they have been a hedged and extensively brokered response to emerging contingencies.[2] For instance, once the government eased controls on agriculture, permitted rural markets, and encouraged collective industry to expand, the resulting dynamic generated pressure to allow urban industrial enterprises to face the new competition from rural producers. Thus each round of reforms has carried the seeds for future actions.

Second, China's size and its long history of decentralized management within a unitary framework have meant that reforms are interactive (with the initiative shifting between central and local players), defined in broad terms, interpreted variously, and implemented unevenly. At the outset of the reform era, the balance of power might have favored the center. But with central leaders having to build coalitions (or factions) composed of party, provincial, and People's Liberation Army leaders to shore up their own positions, power has tended to become more diffused (Dittmer and Wu 1995 discuss the importance of personal relationships and factions in Chinese politics). The prosperous coastal provinces have acquired a bigger say in the conduct and pace of reforms under the decentralized regime. While retaining the role of key decisionmakers, central government leaders have had to listen, negotiate, compromise, and occasionally retreat in their dealings with other national stakeholders. Increasingly they have had to respond to the demands of the "selectorate," a term Shirk (1993) uses to describe the key central and provincial players.

Third, gradual administrative decentralization since the late 1970s, the rise of rural industry, and price reform have all influenced fiscal decentralization. The last, in turn, has profoundly increased the incentives to introduce new changes. Administrative decentralization has transferred more autonomy to China's 30 province-level units (prior to 1997, when the city of Chongqing was added as the 31st province-level unit), which have delegated authority to the 2,166 county- and lower-level units. Rural industrialization has provided local governments with additional tax revenue and off-budgetary sources of income. And industrial price reform has drastically eroded the profitability of state enterprises and the revenues derived from these profits. The upshot of all these is a diminution of central administrative and fiscal capacity, which, in turn, has moderated the central government's ability to manage the course of reforms or to take major initiatives. On balance, the course of fiscal change favored the provinces and very likely induced rapid growth, at least in the coastal region. But tax reforms introduced after 1994 reflect a cross-provincial agreement that too much decentralization, by fiscally impoverishing the center, would be detrimental to macroeconomic stability and national development.

Fourth, nationwide growth and the double-digit rates at which rural industry has expanded in many provinces have brought out two important characteristics of the Chinese economy: the extraordinary sense of place and the magnitude of social capital accumulated by China's local communities (*social capital,* a term coined by James Coleman, refers to community organizations, associations, and networks). Local networks, associations, and kin-based ties help generate resources, the institutional arrangements to minimize entrepreneurial risk, and the capacity to provide effective governance, all of which are necessary for development (see Keating 1995). To an unusual degree, history and tradition have equipped China for decentralized development.

Fifth, from the very start, industrial reform has been a carefully circumscribed process, which has kept pace with other reforms. In addition, because ownership of state enterprises is distributed across the central, provincial, and municipal governments, all parties have had an interest in proceeding cautiously. They have been forced to do so because enterprise reform in China affects well over 100 million workers, who constitute the most powerful political bloc in the country. Furthermore, a very large proportion of China's industrial capital is tied up in the state sector, and any radical moves to impose market-based solutions on the public sector would quickly bankrupt between a third and a half of all state enterprises.

This brings us to the final point. China's transition to the market has been successful and prolonged for several reasons. It has succeeded because decentralization mobilized local governments to provide the administrative infrastructure needed to ignite and sustain the growth of industry and the elaboration of markets. It has been prolonged because all the principal players want to reform the state sector gradually. In this way, they minimize the risks of potential upheaval and the costs for the urban workforce. This does not mean that the social costs have been dissipated, only that they are being shouldered by the dynamic segments of the economy.

China's Urbanization

If we examine the pattern of urbanization in China from the start of the century to the present day, the first four decades saw rapid urban growth with a concentration of population in port cities and in cities strategically located along major transport arteries. War and dislocation during the 1940s interrupted the process, which resumed once the communist government restored order in the early 1950s. That is, a normal tendency apparent worldwide reemerged, with more and more people gravitating toward cities, especially those in the coastal belt. Urbanization crested in 1960, with about a fifth of the population residing in cities.

Thereafter, China diverged sharply from the normal pattern.[3] The share of the urban populace actually fell, and the growth of major cities, such as Shanghai, was curbed as some manufacturing plants and workers were shifted to smaller cities in the deep interior. Until the 1970s, severe restraints on mobility, enforced mainly through the *hukou* (household registration) formally introduced and implemented since 1958, checked the flow of people to cities (see Ma and Fan 1994). The hukou determined access to housing, basic foodstuffs, and urban services such as education and health care. Use of the hukou to limit rural-urban migration and even movement within cities, together with the transfer of several million city youth to rural areas, helped to maintain the level of urbanization at a nearly constant 19 percent between 1960 and 1980 (Zhou 1991). Step by step, however, these restraints have been scaled back and the antiurban bias erased. The result has been a surge in rural-urban migration (Chang 1994 notes that 117 million people migrated to urban areas during 1979–90, most of them on a temporary basis; also see Goldstein 1990; Gui and Liu 1992). Because development has been most rapid in the coastal provinces, cities along the eastern seaboard have attracted the largest number of migrants. Once a rarity, throngs of visitors and migrants are now commonplace in the coastal cities. Their presence, which is especially visible around railway stations, is evident throughout the cities, and they contribute significantly to the workforce on construction sites, in some service activities, and in certain assembly industries.

This reversal in urbanization policies has restored the "normal" pattern of urban growth. According to estimates by the State Statistical Bureau, China's urban population, which was 134 million in 1980, was 478 million in 1994, or roughly a fifth of the total for developing countries.[4] It is growing at close to 6 percent a year, which is among the highest rates for developing countries. Kojima (1995) estimates that the adjusted rate of urban population growth during 1982–91 was 6.2 percent a year, which has no precedent in economic history. The number of cities rose from 223 to 622 between 1980 and 1994. In 1994 China had 32 megacities, 42 large cities, 173 medium cities, and 375 small cities (see the appendix to this chapter for definitions). Currently, China's urban economy—industry plus services—is the source of two-thirds of gross domestic product (GDP). If current trends persist, the number of urban dwellers will have doubled by the turn of the century, and all but a fifth of national output will be generated by urban areas.

For these reasons, an analysis of China's urban economy that adopts a geographic perspective and is informed by historical trends extending to the beginning of this century can be profitable in three ways: first, attention to geographic and historical angles can enrich the economic analysis of recent development in China; second, concentrating on the urban industrial sector, which is the hub of economic activity, makes it easier to apprehend the interplay between reform and growth; third, a well-honed sense of urban dynamics is critical to appreciating China's future economic prospects and to understanding what further reforms will be required to deal with old problems still unsolved and new ones lying in wait.

Selecting Three Cities

There are several alternative methods of analyzing China's urban economy. It can be done on a macro scale using a broad brush and composing a picture from aggregate trends and the pattern of urban development seen on a national scale. At the other extreme, a single industrial subsector can provide insight into certain aspects of urban change. For the armature of our story, we have juxtaposed the macro and the subsectoral experience of three major and strategically situated cities: Guangzhou, Shanghai, and Tianjin (see figure 1.1). These cities were selected for several compelling reasons. First, they are among the most important urban centers in China, and two of them enjoy the status of provinces.[5] The State Statistical Bureau puts their combined industrial product at 9.9 percent of China's industrial output in 1994.[6] Second, they share certain similarities—each is a major industrial center with a coastal location, a rich hinterland, and a privileged place in China's urban and industrial history. Third, the differences among them are also significant, and their industrial structure varies considerably—it is most diversified in Shanghai and narrowest in Guangzhou—but there are signs of convergence, as Shanghai and Tianjin have begun to concentrate on fewer core activities and have joined with Guangzhou in emphasizing the development of producer services. Examining their experience can help to uncover the forces driving this convergence. Fourth, all three cities have been active reformers, but their reform programs have differed in timing and scope and in the determination with which they have been implemented. A comparison across the three cities highlights the efficacy of reforms in overcoming obstacles and in exploiting advantages.

Modern industrial development commenced in Shanghai in the late nineteenth century, and the city has remained China's foremost industrial center. Shanghai's hinterland, which encompasses the lower Yangtze valley, is the richest in resources and one of the most densely populated regions of China. Tianjin, with its fine deepwater port, initially gained significance from its proximity to Beijing and the industrial cities of Liaoning Province. From being a transport hub, it has grown into a leading industrial center. Guangzhou's industrial presence is of a more recent vintage. An old administrative and trading center of the Pearl River delta region, Guangzhou acquired a modest manufacturing base in the 1960s and 1970s. However, the extraordinary acceleration of economic

Figure 1.1 Three Cities and Their Hinterlands, China

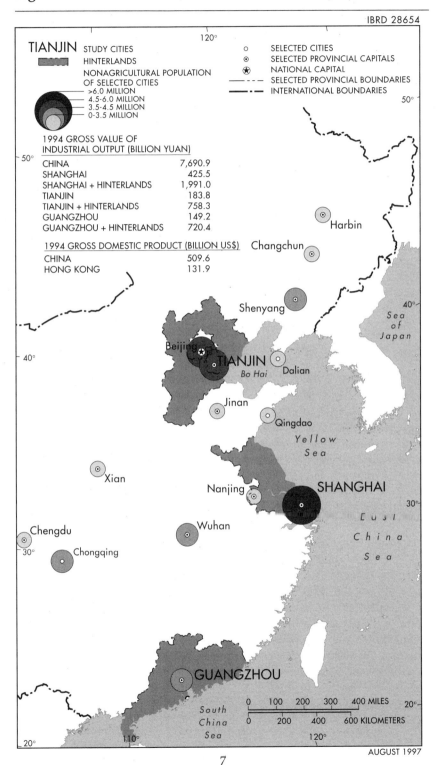

activity in Guangdong Province since the start of reforms has transformed Guangzhou into the principal industrial node for southern China, a region whose economic strength rivals that of the lower Yangtze valley.

Examining growth and industrialization in these three cities illuminates the process of change, underscores its diversity, and enables us to perceive the complex interplay between reforms and economic forces. This approach is valuable at several levels: it demonstrates how a specific geographic locus can affect the course of industrialization; it reveals how China's cities are reversing decades of neglect and adapting to a new, more competitive environment; and it informs future policy not just in China but also in other countries confronting development imperatives of equivalent urgency.

It is the theme of this book that at any point in time the economic prospects of a city are determined by location, historical traditions, and momentum derived from past development and the available production base, which is composed of infrastructure, physical facilities, human capital, and administrative capabilities. These givens define an initial menu of possibilities, but no city is bound by them. The set of options can be enlarged, comparative advantage can be reshaped, and development paths can be redirected by suitable action, which takes history as a point of departure but then uses policy to augment the resource base, exploit locational benefits, solve systemic ills, and improve the functioning of the city as a dynamic organism.

To define and explicate concepts central to this theme, we weave together strands from economic geography and growth theory as well as issues arising from the "urban life cycle." In particular, economic geography is the source of two important building blocks that directly affect the resource base and productive efficiency of a city's economy: neighborhood effects and agglomeration effects. Growth theory offers a framework for incorporating the consequences of externalities arising from industrial structure and of policies affecting spillovers of agglomeration (see Mills and McDonald 1992). At a heuristic level, it also permits treatment of conditions that are "growth creating" or "growth diverting" in a manner analogous to the analysis of trade creation and diversion in a customs union framework. Last, bringing in the notion of an urban life cycle, it is possible to treat more explicitly the question of production costs that are associated with characteristics linked to age. Some of these have to do with the labor market and with safety nets for retirees; others relate to the state of infrastructure. Olson (1982), for instance, has drawn attention to strong, entrenched organizations and interest groups, such as the tenured urban labor force and party cadres, that affect the pace of change (see also Mueller 1983). But age is also associated with the depth of institutions of learning, which can provide ideas along with some of the motivation to innovate.

Factor Supplies and Their Efficient Use

Industrial growth of cities, much like that of the economy as a whole, is ultimately reducible to flows of capital and labor, the efficiency with which they are allocated across production activities, and the rate of technical change. Although the primary factor inputs, especially capital, have been shown to account for a third to half of aggregate growth, the literature on growth accounting has underscored the contribution of human capital—measured most commonly by education—and a variety of elements that affect the productivity of factor combinations (see Denison 1967, 1983; Romer 1989, 1993). The four elements that are most meaningful in the urban context are scale economies, industrial organization, the diffusion of ideas, and services that manage the flow of information and, through it, the efficiency of markets. Thus the larger the urban market, which includes the city as well as its immediate hinterland, the easier it is for industries to achieve economies of scale. Organizational structures, which maximize learning, adaptive flexibility, innovation, and effective networking among firms, have an important bearing on micro-level productivity and the capacity to exploit economies of scope. The ready diffusion of ideas within the urban system and the ability to attract and harness relevant knowledge from other industrial centers will stimulate growth as well as efficiency. Last, producer services that generate and diffuse market information have a large hand in determining the quality of allocative outcomes. (The role of institutions, particularly in transition economies, has attracted intense attention, especially the matter of property rights; see Poznanski 1992; Weitzman and Xu 1994.)

Each city has production and cost functions that are unique in certain respects. The uniqueness derives from the geography and size of the city, the composition of industry, the use of land, and the state of infrastructure. Aside from geography, none of these givens is immutable; they can all be modified by policies, although an underlying inertia places limits on the rate of change. The interesting point is that specific characteristics or legacies associated with institutions (for example, those associated with socialist planning and even with geographic circumstances) will affect the readiness to grasp the reform nettle and, thereby, the speed with which reforms begin to work.

Our intention is not to specify and empirically estimate production functions but to use the "new economic geography" and growth theory to explain urban development, proceeding on the premise that the relevant attributes of a city and policies modifying these features impinge on factor supply, the efficiency of utilization, and the (endogenous) generation of knowledge. We make eclectic use of the standard neoclassical growth theory that stresses factor inputs, as well as endogenous growth theories that emphasize scale econo-mies and the generation of operationally usable knowledge through the application of human capital.

Neighborhood Effects: The Impact of Location

Neighborhood or spillover effects refer to the advantages and draw-backs of a particular location (see Porter 1990; Romer 1990; Ayal 1992; Glaeser and others 1992; Hughes and Holland 1994). These can be either growth creating or growth diverting. Growth-creating effects refer to scale economies obtained when industries in an advantageously located city have access to a wide market in the surrounding region through a multiplicity of forward linkages. The size of the market will be deter-mined by population, income levels, industrial structure, effectiveness of the distribution system, and transport infrastructure. Growth-creating effects also arise from backward linkages to regional sources of factor supply and the provision of knowledge. A rich hinterland with a large population can provide labor, skills, and investable resources for industries within the city. In addition, there can be important knowl-edge spillover effects, some of which might be embodied in capital, while others might be communicated by way of technical assistance. Invest-ment in urban industry originating from other parts of the country or overseas can bring technology with it. Knowledge of production prac-tices, coming in the wake of capital, can further enhance productivity. This can be transferred by word of mouth, but the circulation of manag-ers, technicians, and workers is probably of greater importance. Net-working with industry in the region, which permits subcontracting and shares the fruits of research and greater specialization, can also enhance growth through its influence on organization and allocation. As the tech-nological complexity of industry increases, the development and pro-duction of new products require more team effort between specialized manufacturers, who can collectively harness the skills and research and development (R&D) resources. Hence the significance of networking (see chapter 6). City governments, in collaboration with industry, are in a position to maximize growth-creating effects through policies that develop infrastructure; attract capital, skills, and labor to the city; and cement alliances with producers in surrounding areas. In this manner, the advantages of location can be drawn on to the full. The rich litera-ture on industrial districts refers to the resource-augmenting and capacity-building activities that have been markedly successful in north-ern Italy, parts of Germany, the Republic of Korea, and Taiwan (China) (Brusco 1989; Piore and Sable 1984; Markusen 1995; Pyke and Sengenberger 1992; Schmitz and Musyck 1994).

The presence of other strong industrial and financial centers in the vicinity can be a source of fruitful competition, but such contenders can also divert growth by acting as alternative poles of attraction for resources (Krugman 1991; Storper and Walker 1989). The presence of strong competitors, who might benefit from an early start, have a better developed infrastructure, or use policy incentives more aggressively, can negate some of the neighborhood effects that an individual city might enjoy. Competition between large cities in a region can be a positive sum game, as in the Kanto plain of Japan, but it may not be if a dominant player is determined to enlarge its share. In some developing countries, primate cities such as Bangkok and Seoul have inhibited the growth of alternative foci of industrial activity in the surrounding area because their accumulated advantages exert an irresistible pull on resources.

Agglomeration: Size, Economies of Scale and Scope, and Externalities

The consequences of agglomeration work through some of the same channels as neighborhood effects, but there are several significant differences as well. Chief among the benefits are scale economies from a larger market and efficient use of lumpy, urban infrastructure. Large agglomerations gain from externalities associated with industrial diversity, faster diffusion of knowledge brought about by face-to-face interaction, and strong demonstration effects.[7] They give rise to concentrations of labor skills that lower entry barriers to new firms and permit industrial deepening (see Krugman 1991). Agglomerations support arrangements between firms that permit the greatest degree of choice in how production is organized within and between companies. For instance, just-in-time production scheduling and tight management of inventories are most feasible when all suppliers are located within a short radius of the main firm. In many cases, city size is correlated with the diversity of the industrial base, which allows multiple areas of specialization and scope for responding quickly to new challenges. Large agglomerations are generally more successful in setting up financial markets to mobilize local and regional capital than smaller ones. They can also be more innovative in devising mechanisms of delivery, such as venture capital companies that improve access to finance. In addition, they can enjoy a competitive edge, for reasons linked to history and culture, in producing human capital through a system of universities and associated capabilities in R&D (Luger and Goldstein 1991).

Agglomeration economies are advantageous not so much because they exercise direct effects on factor supply but because they increase factor productivity by multiplying the avenues for organizational flexibility and by giving fuller play to scale effects. Scale effects are multiplied by feedback effects, with one round of expansion sowing the seeds for second and subsequent rounds. However, a negative side to agglomeration offsets many of the gains (see Wheaton and Shishido 1981). Although urban diseconomies of scale are difficult to test empirically, bigger cities often suffer from congestion, environmental pollution, and problems of governance that raise production costs. For example, governance problems can most directly manifest themselves by way of fiscal imbalances, which in turn make it difficult to supply the desirable volume of essential services. Viewed through the lens of growth theory, agglomeration economies can lower the efficiency of capital because stringent pollution controls might be required, because security concerns may entail the unproductive use of labor, or because congestion, which is a growing problem in Chinese cities, means that more funds are tied up in transport equipment.

Another dimension of agglomeration diseconomies prominent in China, but also encountered in many other developing countries, is the presence of a large state-owned industrial sector in major cities. When publicly owned firms incur losses, they can impose direct costs not only on the central government's budget but also on the finances of the municipal economy. Beyond that, their organization and labor policies give rise to deleterious externalities that have challenged reformers and strongly influenced the course of change not only in China but also in the transition economies in East Europe and the former U.S.S.R. Inefficient labor practices and the suboptimal wage structure in state firms can spread to private and collective enterprises, compromising their productive efficiency and inflating their costs. The preferential access to financial resources that state enterprises frequently enjoy can have serious, localized "crowding out" effects, which not only starve private companies and, through such misallocation, reduce factor productivity but also saddle publicly owned banks with what can turn out to be nonperforming assets. Furthermore, where state enterprises are vertically integrated, as is invariably the case in China, they are likely to produce many items in small lots at an excessive cost. Depending on the size of the public sector, this will inhibit the emergence of a more efficient production system based on a hierarchy of specialized manufacturers linked through subcontracting arrangements.

As in the case of neighborhood effects, municipal government policies can enhance the benefits of agglomeration while minimizing the drawbacks. Urban infrastructure is the key to realizing scale economies and also to maximizing gains from the hinterland (see Button and Pearce 1989; Eisner 1991). How well a city fares in the provision of, say, transport services depends on proper planning, fiscal policies, and pricing of services. The development of financial markets will depend, to a considerable degree, on action at the national level, although local initiative and the ability to create a conducive environment are by no means insignificant. Balance with respect to policies as well as to the provision of municipal services is also critical for an environment in which institutions of higher learning can take root and flourish. A city can enhance its locational advantages by means of policy action. Other cities can strengthen their hand by using policy incentives more aggressively to bring about change, remedy deficiencies, and put the local economy on a firmer footing.

Urban Life Cycle and Costs

Life cycle effects can take a number of forms, but of most relevance for the purpose here are those that influence production costs. Three tendencies associated with a city's life cycle can affect the costs of doing industrial business (see Downs 1979; Branbury, Downs, and Small 1982; Porter 1990). First, older cities in which natural population growth has stagnated and migration has not reshaped the population pyramid are, on balance, likely to have an older workforce and to have a high percentage of retirees. This phenomenon is particularily noticeable in China because of very low population mobility and an enterprise-level social security system that requires firms to support retirees with housing, pensions, and social services. This problem is exacerbated by the relatively low age of retirement (50 for women and 55 for men) for workers. This has several implications: the average wage is greater, labor may be more set in its ways and more accustomed to practices that are dysfunctional, interest groups are likely to be more numerous and obstructive, and as Olson (1982) and others have noted, their questioning of change and protective attitude toward the existing regime of entitlements often make it hard to implement policies that depart from established arrangements. Where these tendencies exist, the burden of social security payments is heavier on both individuals and businesses. Under the socialist system, China's state and collective enterprises were and in large part continue to be responsible for the bulk of services, including pensions. They have served as "total institutions," taking responsibility from the cradle to the grave.

Second, population density and patterns of land use are likely to raise the leasing costs and periodic fees for serviced land. This has been starkly apparent in cities such as Tokyo for some time and is a rapidly emerging problem in China (on Japan, see Hill and Fujita 1993).

Third, the infrastructure of a city, the distribution of housing, and the space available for commercial use evolve gradually over time. As a city ages, it can lose flexibility. Its structure at any time is likely to be optimized for conditions suitable to an earlier pattern of living, technologies, and land use. This does change under the pressure of new forces, but it inevitably does so quite slowly. For instance, many new production technologies are best accommodated by a single-floor rather than a multifloor plant. The location of factories in downtown areas, as was prevalent in China, can become singularly inefficient from the perspective of land use or commuting (Gaubatz 1995). In older cities, conveniently located, large factory sites are difficult to find and expensive to lease.

All of these handicaps can be overcome, and enough old cities have revitalized their industries to suggest that enlightened policies, success at raising finances, and determined implementation do produce results (Sassen-Koob 1986; Fox-Przeworski, Goddard, and de Jong 1991; Sassen 1991). Although greenfield sites away from an existing center are more attractive for companies establishing new plants and wishing to take advantage of cheaper land and a younger workforce without the baggage of industrial traditions, mature industrial centers also have their attractions. Workers may be older on average, but they are likely to be more experienced, which has a counterbalancing effect on costs. In addition, cities that have created an infrastructure of training and research provide an environment hospitable for skill- and knowledge-intensive industries and a rich source of externalities. Migration to the city—encouraged by housing policies, social services, and a reputation for sound management—can enlarge the pool of workers and lower its average age. Efficient administrative practices can ensure that municipal services are less costly than elsewhere, which would make it easier for employers to accommodate higher average labor costs. Because older cities will have amortized more of the physical plant supplying urban services, prices might be lower than in cities at an earlier stage in the life cycle.

The mature, diversified, industrial city can have a head start in accumulating learning, which will have a direct bearing on current productivity and the potential for future growth. The ability to accumulate learning will depend on the past stages of industrialization and the interaction among industrial growth, infrastructure building, and the increasing level of skills. Henderson, Kuncoro, and Turner (1995, p. 1069) show that "new high-tech industries are more likely to take root in cities with a history of industrial diversity." But once projects have taken root, they are more likely to thrive in relatively specialized cities where the localization economies are more prominent. If we move from cities to regions, according to the U.S. experience, specialization is on the decline, and diversity seems to be the more hospitable industrial environment (see Kim 1995).

The cumulative experience that enables a city to graduate from less to more sophisticated industries involves a process of layering. A first round of basic manufacturing activities must be followed by successive rounds of industry building in an upward spiral, which puts in place a hierarchy of technological capabilities. Firms are more likely to invest in ascending levels of manufacturing activity if the associated infrastructure is created, as has been attempted fairly successfully in Singapore. Advanced industries are far more demanding in their need for transport and communications. Their skilled workers expect a range of physical amenities. Hence cities that invest continuously in the improvement of urban facilities create a milieu conducive to industrial deepening (creating "smart" and "sustainable" cities is the challenge that municipal administrators and all other stakeholders must tackle; see Serageldin, Barrett, and Martin-Brown 1995; U.S. Congress, Office of Technology Assessment, 1995).

Much of the embedding of skills and the acquisition of tacit knowledge of production processes occurs on the job or through training provided by firms themselves. But the learning that promotes transition to higher-order manufacturing activities also rests on training and research that codify and assimilate formal knowledge of new technology. When this formal training is combined with on-the-job experience, the stage is set for the upgrading of industry. Learning, therefore, is related to the methodical pursuit of industrial layering on an ascending curve over an extended period of time. The experience of Singapore's electronics industry aptly illustrates the process. Hobday (1995, p. 1188) notes that firms in Singapore were "engaged in a painstaking and cumulative process of technological learning [rather than a] leapfrog from one vintage of technology to another." Much of the learning occurred in the preelectronic areas such as mechanical, electromechanical, and precision engineering. Competencies tended to build upon each other incrementally. Singapore's progress in electronics required the development of capabilities in plastics, moldings, machinery, assembly, and electromechanical interfacing; in acquiring the skills needed to manufacture small precision motors; and in increasing the supply of qualified engineers. Indeed the historical evidence testifies to the importance of gradual technological accumulation.

In any event, if finances can be found, there is little to prevent a city from radically changing land use and upgrading infrastructure so as to seize a new range of industrial opportunities—to stake its claim to new lines of comparative advantage—whether it is exploiting spillover effects, neutralizing agglomeration diseconomies, or coping with ripe maturity; the readiness to use the full range of policy tools so as to sustain industrial advantage comes through very clearly both from experience worldwide and from the particular experience of cities in China. The greater the competition is between cities—and regions—the more urgent it is continually to seek the possibilities inherent in location or size, to anticipate and solve problems even as they appear, and to capitalize on the advantages of a long industrial tradition rather than fight a rearguard action so as to combat urban sclerosis arising from old age.

Outline of the Book

The book is divided into seven chapters. Chapter 2 provides the historical backdrop to economic geography in the three cities extending from the early years of the century to the eve of reform. It also describes the course of urban and industrial development in China and situates the three cities within the national context. Chapters 3, 4, and 5 explore the salient features of development in Shanghai, Tianjin, and Guangzhou, respectively, employing elements of the framework described above and relating the efforts of each city to enhance its industrial strength through the effective deployment of reforms. Chapter 3, on Shanghai, applies the framework most comprehensively. The approach with respect to the other cities is more selective and emphasizes only those angles that bring out important similarities or contrasts between the cities. In other words, the chapters differ in structure and are tailored so as to test and illustrate the theme of the book to the fullest. Chapter 6 compares the experiences of the three cities and their strategies, relates these to restructuring efforts in other metropolitan areas of the world, and looks at the forces driving urban change in China. Finally, chapter 7 reviews the main messages emerging from the juxtaposition of theory and experience in the context of the three cities. It also examines the future strategic choices for these cities with respect to both reform and directions of sectoral development. In doing so, the chapter focuses on the choices for Guangzhou, Shanghai, and Tianjin. But through them it also looks beyond at the imperatives as well as the options for other major cities in China and the developing world.

Appendix: Definition of Cities and Hinterlands

The administrative structure of cities (*shi*) and counties (*xian*) changed significantly in the late 1970s. Prior to this time, cities, with the exception of those under direct control of central and provincial governments (*zhixiashi* and *shengxiashi*), and counties were administered by prefectures (*diqu*). The designation of prefectures was eliminated as a result of the change. Counties now are generally administered by major cities in their vicinity. Thus urban statistics are collected for two levels: the city proper (*shiqu*), including urban area and suburbs, and the city and counties (*diqu*), including counties administered by the city. For both levels, total population, which includes both agricultural and nonagricultural population, and nonagricultural population are also accounted for separately. Because of the urban focus of this book, we use the first level of accounting for the three cities, which excludes counties, unless otherwise specified. A pragmatic concern here is with the availability of statistical data, as industrial subsector–level data are rarely available for counties. For the same reason, village-run enterprises are also excluded in our statistical accounting.

One major confusion lies in the accounting of urban population. For the period 1964 to 1982, the official measure of urban population was "city and town" population—the aggregate of all nonagricultural population in the designated cities and towns. The 1982 census used a different methodology, which defined urban population as all noncounty population in all districts of cities, irrespective of agricultural or nonagricultural status. Because of the growing concern with the large proportion of agricultural population entering the urban count, the 1990 census used a more complex system, similar to that used before 1982 in principle (for details, see Kirkby 1994; Kojima 1995).

The current classification of city size in China is based on nonagricultural population in the city proper (excluding counties):

- Megacities have more than 1 million population.

- Large cities have between 0.5 million and 1 million population.

- Medium cities have between 0.2 million and 0.5 million population.

- Small cities have less than 0.2 million population.

The counterpart of what is called a metropolitan area in North America would then comprise both the city and counties administered by the city. Metropolitan population would include both nonagricultural and agricultural population in the city and counties.

There are two ways of defining the hinterlands of cities. The first, and narrower, one includes only counties that are administered by the cities. As mentioned above, the lack of industrial subsector–level data for counties makes this approach a poor fit. The second one embraces larger regions surrounding the cities, reflecting both economic and geographic boundaries. In our case, we define the hinterlands of Shanghai as the lower Yangtze River delta (including Jiangsu and Zhejiang Provinces); of Tianjin as the Tianjin-Beijing-Tangshan region (Jin-Jing-Tang, including Beijing and Hebei Province); and of Guangzhou as the Pearl River delta (Guangdong Province). This definition also allows us to demonstrate the emergence of secondary cities in these regions and their growing competitiveness relative to the three cities.

2 *China's Changing Urban Geography: The Rise of Three Cities*

To understand the pattern of urbanization in China we must reach into the past. This will enable us not just to uncover macro tendencies sweeping the entire country but also to enlarge our comprehension of how certain cities rose to the upper tiers of the urban hierarchy. Ever since the start of the contemporary era, roughly around the 1840s, coastal cities overtook such ancient inland cities as Kaifen, Luoyang, and Xian, which in earlier times had achieved prominence as dynastic capitals, to become centers of modern industrial and commercial development. A major impetus was the signing of several treaties with Western countries and the designation of a dozen or so coastal cities as treaty ports, which began to function as China's windows to the outside world. In particular, Guangzhou, Shanghai, and Tianjin dominated the urban scene for about a century, until the communists took over in 1949. Thereafter, their preeminence waned for close to three decades, only to be restored after 1979 when coastal cities were again recognized as the prime developing areas.

The level of urbanization in China at the start of the nineteenth century was fairly low. Between 3 and 4 percent of the populace resided in cities, or approximately 12 million out of a total of 350 million persons (Feuerwerker 1983; Rozman 1990). This is similar to the rates of urbanization in the United States and Russia (5 and 6 percent, respectively) but well below those in the United Kingdom and continental Europe as a whole (19 and 11 percent, respectively; see Bairoch 1988). Through the balance of the nineteenth century, the pace of urbanization was also much slower in China than in Europe and the United States. A hundred years later, only 17 million Chinese, or about 4 percent of the population, were living in cities. By comparison, a fifth of all Americans were city dwellers, as were 35 percent of Russians and two-thirds of the British. The slow growth of Chinese cities was largely a consequence of industrial backwardness. To thrive and expand, urban centers must export goods and services to pay for the purchase of food and other materials. In the absence of industry, cities must export administrative and commercial services. For most Chinese cities, the provision of administrative services was their mainstay (see De Long and Shleifer 1993 on the relationship between absolutist power and slow growth of cities). Hence growth was concentrated in the provincial capitals and a few commercial centers strategically located along the arteries through which flowed China's domestic waterborne trade.

The Urban World of Imperial China

At the start of the early modern era for China, six cities occupied the uppermost rung of the urban hierarchy: Canton (Guangzhou), Hankow (Wuhan), Nanking (Nanjing), Peking (Beijing), Shanghai, and Tianjin.[1] Peking drew its importance from the administrative functions associated with being a capital city. The others were primarily centers of China's nascent industry and trade, both between regions and overseas. The tug of the coast on urbanization clearly reinforced economic forces in the development of four cities—Canton, Nanking, Shanghai, and Tianjin—while Hankow's presence was a carryover from an earlier time when an insular, inwardly focused China oriented its trading activities along the Yangtze River.[2] Hankow's choice location along this economic lifeline made it China's largest city in the fourteenth century. Marco Polo described Hankow as "without doubt the finest and most splendid in the world." Idovic of Bordenone, who spent three years in Hankow in the 1320s, thought it was the world's greatest city (see Mackerras 1989, pp. 19, 21). Even after economic activity had begun gravitating toward the coast, Hankow retained, for a time, the distinction of being one of China's largest cities; as a place where tea, salt, rice, and medicinal herbs were actively traded, it was still one of the largest cities in the world in the nineteenth century (see Rowe 1984). But as modern industry and international linkages became the determinants of growth, Hankow quickly fell behind and, by the early twentieth century, was no longer near the top of the city hierarchy. This brings us to the factors responsible for the dominant position that industrial cities along the coast attained in the mid-nineteenth century.

Until the end of the eighteenth century, all external threats to China emanated from the steppe frontier extending in an arc along the western and northwestern parts of the country. At intervals, tribal confederacies became strong enough to send invincible armies of horsemen sweeping into China to wreak havoc and, on occasion, to topple the dynasty holding power. Thus China's military interaction, its diplomatic dealings, and its tributary relationships were principally with its nomadic neighbors.[3] The westward orientation of the commercial axis reinforced the tendency to concentrate on trade links along winding land routes connecting China with Asian countries to the west and south.

The absence of a threat from Japan and the limited scope for seaborne commerce meant that there were few coastal cities of significance. Amoy (Xiamen), Canton, Ningbo, and a handful of lesser centers flourished, but they were the exceptions. Until well into the nineteenth century, none of the forces responsible for the rise of coastal cities in the West was strongly evident in China. The occasional need to defend coastal settlements against pirates never compelled the government to construct and maintain a large naval fleet.[4] China's self-sufficiency, domestic politics that militated against the maintenance of a large oceangoing fleet after the mid-fifteenth century, and the relative backwardness of its eastern neighbors reduced the scope for trade. Furthermore, shipbuilding, small-scale manufacturing, and finance, which were the lifeblood of Western cities, remained small in scale. The rapid growth of the great port cities of the Atlantic can be attributed largely to the expansion of shipping, which enabled them to acquire significant manufacturing sectors, including the shipbuilding industry (see Konvitz 1994).

Officialdom, which rigorously administered the interior of China, especially the cross-provincial trade along the principal waterways and land routes, left the coastal areas largely to their own devices. By turning its back on the coast, the imperial bureaucracy gave towns and cities along China's maritime frontier a measure of administrative independence not enjoyed by urban centers situated inland. Fairbank (1983, p. 13) explains how the "continent facilitated bureaucratic government." To avoid this involvement, private enterprise flowed into coastal commerce and overseas trade. Such autonomy induced commercial initiative, allowed emigration overseas, and from roughly the eighteenth century onward facilitated the integration of ports in Fujian and Guangdong into trading networks spanning the South China Sea. The physical distance from the center of imperial power in Peking and the government's disinterest in the economy of China's eastern rim imparted a dynamic similar to the one experienced by European cities that spearheaded the revolution first in commerce and then in industry.

Canton

Among the cities dotting the coastline, Canton was by far the largest until the 1920s (see table 2.1). Its historical roots stretched back 2,000 years, but the growing importance of trade in silk, tea, and ceramics, starting in the latter part of the eighteenth century, brought a new round of prosperity. Standing at the intersection of two marketing hierarchies, Canton became the principal trading center of southern China.[5] Canton occupied this key position in the marketing system spanning southeastern China, but it was also a vertex in the trading network created by migrant Chinese communities who had settled in Indo-China, the Philippines, Thailand, and elsewhere (on the spread of Chinese immigrant communities, see Heidhues 1974; on cultural links between China and Vietnam, see Woodside 1971). Tea grown in Anhui and Fujian was traded, in part, through Canton (Gardella 1994). When porcelain exports to Europe, which also served as ballast for vessels carrying tea and silk, gained in significance, high-quality ceramics came from Jingdezhen 600 miles away in Jiangxi Province. By one estimate, ships of the East India Company carried 24,000 tons of fine porcelain to England between 1684 and 1791 (see Goodwin 1991). The goods were first brought by boat to Nanchang on the Gan River. They then traveled south down the Gan River to a point where they could be offloaded and carried over a mountain range to another river, which flowed to the environs of Canton. An alternative route led from Jingdezhen by river to Nanjing, then down the Yangtze to the coast, and thereafter by junk to the southern port city.

The means by which goods were brought to Canton highlights another factor of importance in the rise of China's major coastal cities. Difficult terrain and a limited road network made land transport exceedingly expensive. Difficult terrain was perhaps more important than poorly developed roads. During the late Han dynasty, China's road network, with about 35,400 kilometers of roadway, was comparable to that of the Roman Empire: approximately 8.9 kilometers per 1,000 square kilometers. Cotterell and Kamminga (1990, p. 197) describe the Chinese and the Romans as the most enthusiastic road builders of the ancient world. The road network diminished in size during the Tang dynasty, and more responsibility for construction and upkeep devolved onto local communities. But as late as the seventeenth century, Westerners expressed admiration for China's road system. From the mid-nineteenth century, decay set in as dynastic capabilities diminished (see Ronan 1995). Long-distance trade, especially of bulky products, moved mostly along inland waterways or depended on the availability of coastal shipping. Thus in the imperial era—and even after some rail services were introduced—only those coastal cities located at the terminus of a waterway network could sustain strong and continuous commercial links with market towns in their hinterlands and in adjacent market systems. Canton occupied an ideal location crossed by tributaries near the mouth of the Pearl River in the delta region. Not only did the rich agricultural economy of the delta produce a food surplus more than adequate to feed a large urban populace, but its tracery of canals, streams, and watercourses could support a trading center, which exported raw material and finished goods drawn from producers scattered across a radius extending several hundreds of miles inland.

Table 2.1 Population and Rank of Large Metropolitan Centers in China, Selected Years, 1922–93

City	1922 Population	Rank	1938 Population	Rank	1953 Population	Rank	1970 Population	Rank	1985 Population	Rank	1993 Population	Rank
Chongqing					1,772,000	5	2,400,000	7	6,512,000	4	15,036,500	1
Shanghai	1,500,000	2	3,595,000	1	6,204,000	1	10,000,000	1	11,805,100	1	12,947,400	2
Beijing			1,574,000	2	2,768,000	2	6,999,000	2	9,190,000	2	10,511,800	3
Chengdu							1,250,000	15	3,890,000	13	9,473,000	4
Yangzhou											9,338,900	5
Tianjin			1,223,000	4	2,694,000	3	4,000,000	3	7,779,000	3	8,877,300	6
Xuzhou											8,339,400	7
Shijiazhuang									1,069,620	37	8,273,100	8
Handan											7,817,700	9
Nantong											7,812,000	10
Wuhan			1,242,000	3	1,427,000	7	2,560,000	5	4,179,000	12	6,916,900	11
Qingdao							1,300,000	14	4,255,000	11	6,753,500	12
Tangshan									1,333,000	29	6,717,800	13
Shenyang					2,300,000	4	2,800,000	4	5,142,000	9	6,576,500	14
Changchun							1,200,000	16	5,754,116	5	6,510,400	15
Xian							1,600,000	11	2,940,000	17	6,309,100	16
Guangzhou	1,600,000	1	1,022,000	5	1,599,000	6	2,500,000	6	5,620,000	6	6,236,600	17
Hangzhou									5,280,600	7	5,871,000	18
Luoyang									2,501,475	19	5,836,500	19
Suzhou									5,274,107	8	5,692,800	20
Zhengzhou							1,050,000	20	1,424,000	28	5,677,000	21

City								
Changsha					2,403,500	21	5,554,200	22
Fuzhou					1,650,000	27	5,506,500	23
Jinan	1,163,000	8	1,100,000	17	3,246,000	16	5,335,300	24
Harbin			1,670,000	9	2,550,000	18	5,299,900	25
Dalian			1,650,000	10	4,720,000	10	5,270,900	26
Nanjing	1,092,000	9	1,750,000	8	3,612,000	14	5,147,400	27
Qiqihar					1,320,933	30	4,743,600	28
Jilin					1,071,000	36	4,192,800	29
Hefei					3,359,600	15	3,970,800	30
Yichang					1,215,600	32	3,949,300	31
Zibo					2,234,000	23	3,878,400	32
Nanchang			1,100,000	18	2,483,185	20	3,827,600	33
Kunming			1,050,000	21	1,990,608	26	3,670,700	34
Anshan			1,350,000	13	1,210,000	33	3,315,200	35
Taiyuan			1,450,000	12	2,220,000	24	2,713,500	36
Lanzhou			1,080,000	19	2,310,000	22	2,612,100	37
Fushun					2,059,600	25	2,242,200	38
Huainan					1,036,000	39	1,884,300	39
Baotou					1,042,000	38	1,787,600	40
Guiyang					1,277,000	31	1,602,400	41
Hohhot					1,149,000	34	1,419,900	42
Ürümqi					1,076,000	35	1,379,300	43

Note: The population account uses the broader definition, including city-administered counties and agricultural population. Data are listed only for cities where the population exceeds 1 million.

Source: Fan 1988, appendix A; State Statistical Bureau, *China: Urban Statistical Yearbook,* 1993–94.

Shanghai

Shanghai had all of Canton's advantages and then a little more. Located on the coastal periphery, it was spared the imperial bureaucracy's vise-like grip. Built along the Whampou (Huangpu) River in the Yangtze delta, it possessed a sheltered harbor, and the riverine environment eased the transport constraints on the city's development. Its rich hinterland was a source of raw materials for the textile industry. The city was reasonably well situated to handle the overseas distribution of tea and silk from provinces to the south and southwest when the Taiping rebellion of the 1850s interrupted the flow of these commodities to Canton.

Shanghai entered the pages of history as a fishing village in the tenth century. In 1074 it became a county seat and thereafter skillfully capitalized on its location and deepened its commercial services.[6] Merchant families from nearby Ningbo were instrumental in making Shanghai a part of the coastal trading system. In association with the famous Shanxi merchants, they laid the groundwork of banking services essential for a commercial center that was coming to dominate the regional marketing system (see Rankin 1986). As Shanghai's economic influence grew, Kiangnan (Jiangnan) silk merchants began trading through Shanghai, further bolstering the city's position not just as a center of regional commerce but also as a gateway of exports from the lower Yangtze valley to other parts of the country and overseas. By 1853 Shanghai had surpassed Canton as China's premier trading city, although the size of its population lagged behind that of Canton for almost another hundred years.

Tianjin

Although the Tianjin area was settled in neolithic times, the construction of the Grand Canal allowed an urban center to strike roots. Tianjin started out as a transshipment point at which grain and satin barged up one segment of the canal were transferred to another segment so as to continue their northward journey. The earliest recorded references date back to the mid-Tang period, in the eighth century. By the time of the Song dynasty, a fortified town had been established to protect the region and its valuable trade from raiders. During the Ming period, the city acquired its current name, which commemorates the crossing of the Hai River by the Yongle emperor: hence Tianjin, or Heavenly Ford. The city also consolidated its position as a prime transport node and a vital link in the defensive shield around Peking.

Much like Canton and Shanghai, Tianjin benefited both from being located at the point where five rivers draining the northern plains enter the Hai River and from being the most accessible port serving the North China plain. Even though the river network around Tianjin is frozen part of the year and the area is notoriously swampy, the importance of water transport added immeasurably to Tianjin's economic advantages.

Grain storage and distribution activities drew a nucleus of officialdom to Tianjin, and the number of government offices multiplied as the production and distribution of salt grew in importance. The shift of the government-run Changlu salt administration to Tianjin in the early years of the Qing dynasty stimulated commercial development, which in turn led to the growth of long-distance coastal trade. As in the case of Shanghai, this was financed through the system of remittances established by the Shanxi bankers. In the first half of the nineteenth century, Tianjin acquired yet another commercial function, when it became the entrepôt for opium entering north China. Over an 800-year period, Tianjin had progressed from being a transshipment node on the Grand Canal to being the largest port in north China and the center of the area's market system, combining commercial as well as administrative functions.

The Growth of Coastal Cities

The next stage in the development of all three cities was closely related to the growing presence of foreigners and their investment in industry, trade, and transport; the spread of manufacturing activities; the building of railways that substantially augmented a system largely dependent on waterborne traffic; and the strengthening of commercial links with the outside world. The succession of "unequal treaties" imposed on China by external powers—starting with the Treaty of Nanking of 1849, which ended the Opium War—led to the opening of treaty ports and enclaves along the coast and major waterways. Canton and Shanghai were among the earliest treaty ports. Tianjin became a treaty port after the Treaty of Peking was signed in 1860. At that time its population numbered some 60,000 (see Hershatter 1986). By 1920 almost 100 of China's most strategically placed cities and towns were part of the treaty network.

A form of proto-industrialization was taking place in China for well over a century. This was similar to developments observed in South Asia from the seventeenth century onward and was partly responsible for increasing European involvement in the subcontinent (see Perlin 1983). In China, treaty ports helped to catalyze the next stage of development. Small-scale, household-based manufacturing activities, which dovetailed with agricultural production, had a long tradition in many parts of China. Among these, cloth making, food processing, metalware, and woodworking industries were the most prominent. Proto-industrialization was most advanced in Fujian, Guangdong, Jiangsu, and Zheijiang because of climate, opportunities for trading, or agricultural constraints that forced farming households to seek supplementary sources of income. Thus the situation in some of China's coastal areas and the Yangtze valley region during the eighteenth and nineteenth centuries resembled that of Japan during the same period and Europe in the sixteenth and seventeenth centuries.

Modern industrialization, which began toward the close of the nineteenth century in Shanghai and Tianjin plus a few other treaty ports, was firmly grounded in a matrix of small-scale rural manufacturing. For instance, cotton cloth, widely traded in the nineteenth century, was produced by farming households and sold to merchants, who served as conduits for the transfer of goods from rural areas to towns and cities.

Although mechanized production in factories displaced a significant amount of cottage industry, urban and rural manufacturing evolved alongside urban production, which used putting-out arrangements to tap skills available in nearby rural households. This reduced the need to invest scarce capital in expensive Western equipment and, so long as the logistics of dispersed production were manageable, gave urban entrepreneurs flexibility in an uncertain environment. The rural-urban symbiosis allowed China's coastal cities to respond rapidly to the stimulus provided by modest doses of foreign investment and the growth of trade. This extensive mode of production, with its low overhead and skillful conjoining of modern industry to rural workshop, was a frugal, suitably labor-intensive, and technologically enlightened outcome.

As in other late starters such as Italy, Japan, and Russia, the state took the lead in experimenting with Western production techniques, although the waning administrative capabilities of the imperial government, the innate conservatism of senior mandarins, and grave fiscal shortcomings in the latter half of the nineteenth century prevented it from aggressively pursuing industrialization (see Gerschenkron 1968; on the contribution of official funding to the start of China's modern industry, see Feuerwerker 1977; on revenue constraints that circumscribed the government's capacity to promote development, see Rankin 1986). Nevertheless, the ambition of a new breed of administrator to make China "rich and powerful" resulted in several initiatives: first, to equip Chinese armies with weaponry comparable to that of their Western adversaries and, second, to create a production base in textile and metallurgical industries. Bureaucratic capitalism, albeit hampered by the lack of expertise, began building arsenals and shipyards starting in 1865. Shanghai's Kiangnan Shipyard employed 2,000 workers and was well stocked with machine shops and repair facilities.[7] Although its output and efficiency were far below expectations, the shipyard enabled the urban economy to acquire new skills, was the source of demonstration effects, and, through linkages, helped to launch other arsenals. A mix of government and local capital also brought into existence a modern cotton textile industry. In 1890 Li Hongzhang, an influential government official, built the Shanghai Machine Weaving Mill, China's first. Other mills, also under government sponsorship, sprang up shortly thereafter, not just in Shanghai but also in Canton, Hankow, and Tianjin.[8]

As in Japan, government action spurred wealthy local merchants to divert some resources from commerce to modern industry. The extraterritorial status of the treaty ports meant that industrial property owners could enjoy a measure of protection from the demands of the government and the at times unchecked rapacity of warlords and local officials. These two inducements, together with cost advantages accruing from foreign investment in rail transport after 1895, pulled local capital into industry. Much of China's railway system through the mid-1930s was funded by loans from Belgium, Germany, and the United Kingdom. Prior to 1911 Chinese engineers and contractors were responsible for only 10 percent of construction, but by the 1920s local capacity had expanded to dominate the construction and operation of railroads (see Chang 1993). On the eve of World War I in 1913, the modern industrial sector included 549 Chinese-owned manufacturing and mining establishments, a nucleus that grew rapidly over the next two decades.

Innovations in transport and communication, diffusing in from overseas, transformed China's economic landscape. Motorized water transport and railways significantly increased the volume and patterns of production and trade. For instance, the total volume of goods transported tripled between 1895 and 1936 (Rawski 1989). Improved transport reduced the costs of moving commodities, opened fresh trading routes, and induced the growth of new transportation hubs (including Chongqing, Hankow, Harbin, Shenyang, and Tianjin). The most drastic changes occurred in and around major urban centers, where virtually every new form of transport could be seen, such as railways, trucks, buses, steamships, and even aircraft. The first two passenger cars—Oldsmobiles from the United States—were registered in Shanghai in 1902 (Harwit 1995). Manchuria, or the northeastern provinces, for example, had close to a quarter of all railways in China (M. Howard 1990). In addition, the construction of the north-south railways reoriented domestic trading, which had been based on east-west river arteries. This underscored the growing importance of the eastern region, where many industries were now located.

Railways soon became the dominant form of transport in China. The first railway line, 15 kilometers long, was constructed by Jardine Mathison to link Shanghai with Wusong. The story of the first railway line is as follows: soon after the first half of the line opened on July 1, 1876, a Chinese man was hit by a train and died (see Hou 1965). Popular protest and opposition from conservative officials followed, and after tense negotiations Jardine agreed to complete construction, run the line for a year, and then sell it to the Chinese. The line began operating and immediately made a profit early in 1877. In November the line became the property of the Chinese, and on the orders of Shen Baochen, governor of Kiangnan, the tracks were uprooted and the rolling stock was shipped to warehouses in Taiwan (China). Except for the Tangshan-Hsukochwang (Xugezhuang) line, no more railways were built until China's defeat at the hands of Japan almost 20 years later, in 1894–95 (see Feuerwerker 1983; Hou 1965). Railway investment initially resumed in the northern and northeastern parts of the country but later spread from the eastern coastal cities. Major rail lines were built connecting Beijing to Wuhan in central China and to Guangzhou in the south. The rail system expanded fairly rapidly in the first half of the twentieth century, and by 1949 more than 20,000 kilometers of rail lines were in service (Rawski 1989, table 4.7). Priority was placed on developing a network connecting cities lying in the eastern region.

Foreign presence in the treaty ports widened China's trading horizons and shifted the economic focus of the country to the coastal regions. Foreigners also laid the groundwork of legal institutions that gave private Chinese capital a modicum of property rights, which are widely perceived as the basis of a modern market economy. After the first phase, which lasted until 1913, foreign investment increased in volume and diffused beyond commerce and finance into railways and industry, a shift that accelerated urbanization by adding industrial muscle to the economies of coastal cities. Because food processing was the dominant industry in China's coastal cities during the early period, most foreign investment in manufacturing was channeled into the preparation of tea, mainly in Foochow (Fuzhou). The manufacture of brick tea for the Russian market was the area where foreign technology made early inroads into Chinese production methods. The process, which involved compressing tea dust and poor-quality tea leaves, was done most profitably in the treaty ports—Foochow and Hongzhou—where the ingredients and coal were cheap and available. Russian investment in brick-tea factories took place in the 1860s. "The industry grew rapidly . . . and was one of the largest objects of foreign investment in nineteenth century China" (Gardella 1994, p. 188). However, Chinese producers could not maintain the quality of tea leaf, and by the 1920s China had lost the market to tea growers in Ceylon and India. Even before this happened, the bulk of foreign investment was moving into the production of cotton textiles, cigarettes, pressed oil, pig iron, and machinery (for the importance of the tobacco industry in Shanghai's manufacturing sector, see Perry 1993). After 1920 China's exports of tea, silk, and porcelain were overshadowed by exports of bean oil, leather, flour, eggs and egg products, ginned cotton, and hog bristles. The domestic market and the export sector also supported a large cotton textile industry concentrated in Shanghai (which boasted half of all spindles) and Tianjin.[9] By the third decade of the twentieth century the foreign share of urban industry was sizable, but Chinese ownership remained dominant. The types of manufacturing activities that attracted investment were such that a modern industrial system located in the large cities kept intact its linkages with input-supplying rural industries in a hinterland that was continuously being enlarged by the extension of railway lines, the improvement of existing roads, and the introduction of steamers.

Economic and Industrial Policy after 1949

For a 15-year period starting in the mid-1930s, wars in which national-ists fought communists and both fought the Japanese halted and in fact reversed industrial change in China. These pitiless conflicts impover-ished the country and inflicted great damage on China's nascent indus-trial sector. Soviet forces, which occupied parts of Manchuria in 1945, stripped factories of equipment, which they took back with them when they withdrew. Shanghai's capitalists transferred textile factories and many of their skilled technicians to Hong Kong, compounding such losses (see Wong 1988). This hemorrhage, which eroded the industrial base built over decades, finally ended with Mao's declaration, on Octo-ber 1, 1949, that "China has stood up." A period of consolidation and stocktaking followed, and industrial functioning, virtually stilled for several years, resumed. By 1952, with normalcy returning, Guangzhou, Shanghai, and Tianjin were once again in ascendance, accounting for 28 percent of China's industrial output. For the next several years, these cities, especially Shanghai and Tianjin, were in the vanguard of indus-trialization but in addition were harnessed by the planning system to promote industry in other parts of China.

After the mid-1950s, central planning began emphasizing economic self-reliance in order to make the inland regions more self-sufficient in industrial terms and also in the interests of national security. A belt of mountainous and dispersed locations within the inland region was tar-geted for industrial development—the Third Front. This policy trans-ferred industry, in Mao's words, to *shen* (remote areas), *shan* (mountains), and *dong* (caves and tunnels). New military production bases and test-ing stations were also built from scratch. Moreover, to aid military re-search and production, certain departments from major national uni-versities in Beijing were ordered to establish satellite campuses in the area. Much of the investment—one-third of the national total—was con-centrated in east Sichuan, west Hubei, south Gansu, and north Guizhou (see Naughton 1988; Zhao 1996).

Under the Third Front policy, Shanghai and Tianjin contributed skilled manpower to other regions of the country, from Sichuan to Xinjiang. Scores of factories and schools were moved to the interior of the coun-try. Following instructions from the central government, Shanghai transferred as many as 1 million skilled workers and technicians, not including rusticated youth with no industrial experience. The largely involuntary resettlement of youth and some professionals from urban to rural areas occurred during the Cultural Revolution, from 1967 to 1972 (see Bernstein 1977). Tianjin sent more than 10,000 skilled workers and technicians from the textile industry alone in order to foster the spread of that industry to other regions. Moreover, when the economy was faced with particular technological challenges, national planners sought solutions among enterprises and research institutes located in the coastal cities. For example, Shanghai enterprises aided in the recovery of Chinese industry after the withdrawal of Soviet assistance in 1960. They also developed the expertise to permit petroleum drilling to continue after access to Soviet technology was lost.

The most important channel for the transfer of technology from coastal cities to the remainder of China was the sale of investment goods, particularly machinery. Shanghai, Tianjin, and to a very limited extent Guangzhou were important sources of industrial machinery for the national economy. Shanghai firms supplied machinery to, among others, the electric power, building materials, shipping, and petroleum industries. Shanghai and Tianjin provided machinery to the textile and other light industrial sectors. In addition, they often served as intermediaries in the importation of advanced technology. Exemplars of advanced machinery were imported to Shanghai, which then had the task of replicating the technology and "exporting" it to the remainder of China. Examples include basic oxygen technology in the steel industry and the early development of petrochemicals. Thus, Shanghai and Tianjin, in particular, contributed vitally to the growth of the Chinese economy under conditions of near autarky between 1960 and 1978.

An even more important relation between coastal cities and the national economy came through the price and fiscal systems. The cities were manufacturing centers, importing raw materials from other parts of China in exchange for manufactured goods. These transactions were priced according to rules adopted from the U.S.S.R. during the 1950s. Manufactured goods had high relative prices, and agricultural and mining products were correspondingly underpriced. As a consequence, manufacturing was exceedingly profitable, and the three cities, which sold their products throughout the country, enjoyed large budgetary revenues. The national government then extracted most of these through the fiscal system. Although the industrialized coastal cities obtained substantially larger incomes than inland municipalities, their tax rates were also much higher.

In the mid-1970s development priorities began to favor the coastal regions again, and Shanghai and Tianjin enjoyed a burst of new investment. The shifting development policy during the mid-1970s prefigured the greater changes to come in the 1980s. China began to move away from the xenophobic isolation of the Cultural Revolution and prepared to increase its involvement with the world economy. Because Shanghai and Tianjin produced the highest-quality textiles in the country, they received investment funding and were required to increase exports. Port facilities were also expanded. Perhaps more crucially, the national government began to locate large new projects in coastal cities, particularly those that were technologically advanced. Petrochemical complexes were established in Shanghai and Tianjin, and the huge Baoshan Steel Mill was begun in Shanghai in 1978.

On balance, in the period through 1978, the central government neglected the infrastructure of the cities but recognized their superior endowment of human capital and industrial experience. As shown in table 2.2, about half of all higher education institutions were concentrated along the coast in the eastern region (512 out of 1,080 in 1994). The national government siphoned off resources but regularly turned to Shanghai to realize technological objectives or manufacture high-quality products. The government exploited the human capital and industrial experience accumulated by these large cities, while making inadequate and partial contributions to nurturing their long-run productivity. By 1978 the share of the three cities in national industrial output had shrunk considerably: Shanghai's to 12.1 percent and Tianjin's to 3.7 percent. Guangzhou marginally increased its share of national industrial output to 1.8 percent. This occurred in the context of a slight erosion in the weight of Guangdong Province in national output (from 4.9 to 4.7 percent). Thus, over the entire 1952–78 period, Guangdong's industrial output grew somewhat slower than the national average but became more concentrated in Guangzhou.

During the early stage of reform, starting in 1978, the central government recognized the necessity for balanced industrialization, which gave equal importance to consumer goods and eased the emphasis long given to heavy industry. The coastal cities responded to the signals from the center by expanding the output of light manufactures. Moreover, China's export surge during 1979–82 relied on the rapid growth of traditional manufactured consumer goods, primarily from the coastal cities. As the 1980s proceeded, the national government began giving greater economic priority to the coastal regions. The objective of equalizing industrial production throughout the nation was abandoned, and economic development was viewed as gradually spreading inland from coastal poles. Preferential policies were adopted for coastal regions to foster this process, and in 1984, 14 "open cities," including Guangzhou, Shanghai, and Tianjin, were given greater autonomy to manage foreign trade and investment as well as foreign exchange retention rights over the proceeds from their exports.

Transport development, which also favored the eastern region, further stimulated the economies of coastal cities (see table 2.3). By 1994 China's rail network measured close to 54,000 kilometers, following the completion of several strategic lines extending deep into the southwest (figure 2.1).[10] After the start of reforms, the increased demand for transport along the eastern corridor induced the government to invest in double tracking and electrification, to upgrade the rolling stock, and to add diesel and electric engines to a fleet composed largely of steam locomotives. These additions and technological improvements, although barely keeping pace with demand, permitted the coastal region to double if not treble its growth rates. Rail transport (and more recently road transport, see figure 2.2) made it possible for the eastern provinces, which have scarce energy and raw materials, to bring in much of the needed

Table 2.2   Higher Education Institutions in China, by Province, Selected Years, 1922–94

(numbers, unless otherwise noted)

Province	1922	1934	1949	1959	1965	1979	1985	1994
Eastern region								
Number in region	32	82	121	385	228	301	493	512
Percentage of country total	80.0	74.5	59.0	45.8	52.5	47.6	48.5	47.4
Beijing	7	17	15	50	53	48	62	67
Tianjin	2	—	—	—	—	14	21	22
Liaoning	0	0	8	55	26	34	62	61
Hebei	0	9	11	31	25	27	46	52
Shandong	1	3	7	35	16	34	49	49
Jiangsu	6	11	15	66	30	36	70	67
Shanghai	10	24	37	31	24	27	45	46
Zhejiang	1	4	5	28	13	19	35	37
Fujian	3	4	8	20	10	16	36	33
Guangdong	2	8	12	42	21	29	44	46
Guangxi	0	2	3	27	10	17	23	27
Hainan	0	0	0	0	0	0	0	5
Central region								
Number in region	7	20	34	307	126	197	328	354
Percentage of country total	17.5	18.2	16.6	36.5	29.0	31.1	32.3	32.8
Shanxi	0	5	1	29	11	16	22	26
Inner Mongolia	0	0	0	18	8	13	18	19
Jilin	0	0	6	35	17	25	44	43
Heilongjiang	0	0	6	39	19	27	40	43
Anhui	0	1	2	32	12	20	36	35
Jiangxi	1	3	5	32	12	17	26	31
Henan	0	3	2	42	12	24	43	50
Hubei	5	6	10	53	23	33	56	60
Hunan	1	2	2	27	12	22	43	47
Western region								
Number in region	1	8	50	149	80	135	195	214
Percentage of country total	2.5	7.3	24.4	17.7	18.4	21.3	19.2	19.8
Sichuan	1	4	36	55	30	42	56	63
Guizhou	0	0	3	16	6	14	22	22
Yunnan	0	1	3	9	6	15	26	26
Tibet	0	0	0	0	0	4	3	4
Shaanxi	0	1	3	30	21	28	44	47
Gansu	0	1	4	20	7	12	17	17
Qinghai	0	0	0	7	2	6	6	7
Ningxia	0	0	0	3	1	4	6	7
Xinjiang	0	1	1	9	7	10	15	21
Country total	40[a]	110	205	841	434	633	1,016	1,080

— Not available.

a. 40 campuses of 37 institutions.

Source: Ministry of Education 1984, 1986; Fairbank and Feuerwerker 1986; State Statistical Bureau, *Statistical Yearbook of China*, 1995.

Table 2.3 Transport Networks in China, by Province, 1994
(kilometers, unless otherwise noted)

	Railway		Inland	Road	
Region	Operating	Expanding	waterway	Total	Class 1
Eastern region					
Kilometers in region	15,882	23,286	58,536	394,843	164,143
Percentage of country total	29.4	32.9	57.0	35.3	46.5
Beijing	1,020	1,606	n.a.	11,532	8,081
Tianjin	502	896	90	4,156	3,624
Liaoning	3,557	4,953	508	42,763	17,155
Hebei	3,230	5,293	75	50,496	33,455
Shandong	2,048	3,060	1,891	50,225	34,781
Jiangsu	747	1,294	23,787	25,891	12,690
Shanghai	246	403	2,100	3,721	2,462
Zhejiang	937	1,355	10,592	33,170	11,602
Fujian	1,024	1,037	3,888	44,608	8,571
Guangdong	682	1,297	10,808	75,716	19,230
Guangxi	219	238	4,521	39,550	10,619
Hainan	1,670	1,854	276	13,015	1,873
Central region					
Kilometers in region	25,273	33,427	31,572	375,120	108,377
Percentage of country total	46.8	47.2	30.7	33.5	30.7
Shanxi	2,330	3,455	170	32,693	12,828
Inner Mongolia	5,072	5,836	602	44,202	7,223
Jilin	3,487	3,822	1,134	29,581	7,452
Heilongjiang	4,943	6,562	n.a.	48,356	6,453
Anhui	1,753	2,500	5,612	30,876	12,170
Jiangxi	1,581	2,204	4,937	34,556	6,964
Henan	2,133	3,945	1,104	47,704	27,940
Hubei	1,693	2,171	8,003	48,349	14,939
Hunan	2,281	2,932	10,010	58,803	12,408
Western region					
Kilometers in region	12,838	14,165	12,615	348,308	80,613
Percentage of country total	23.8	20.0	12.3	31.1	22.8
Sichuan	2,881	2,883	7,904	100,002	15,425
Guizhou	1,423	1,480	1,773	32,398	3,558
Yunnan	1,592	1,643	1,324	65,578	13,126
Tibet				21,842	868
Shaanxi	1,826	2,184	998	39,508	12,780
Gansu	2,219	2,940	219	34,984	11,304
Qinghai	1,095	1,098	n.a.	17,061	3,911
Ningxia	459	522	397	8,324	2,753
Xinjiang	1,343	1,415	n.a.	28,611	16,888
Nonprovincial			7,509		
Country total	53,993	70,878	102,723	1,118,271	353,133

n.a. Not applicable.
Note: Class 1 roads connect major cities and commercial centers. They carry large
volumes of traffic and are designed to higher standards. They have a minimum of two
traffic lanes of at least 3 meters width and shoulders of a prescribed size.
Source: State Statistical Bureau, *Statistical Yearbook of China*, 1995.

Figure 2.1 China's Railway System, 1994

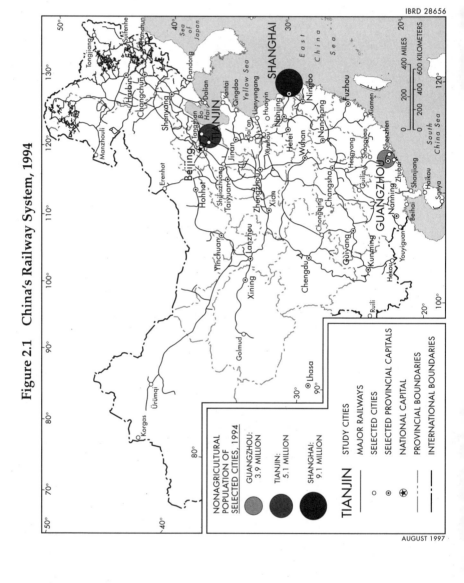

IBRD 28656

NONAGRICULTURAL
POPULATION OF
SELECTED CITIES, 1994

GUANGZHOU:
3.9 MILLION

TIANJIN:
5.1 MILLION

SHANGHAI:
9.1 MILLION

TIANJIN   STUDY CITIES

     MAJOR RAILWAYS

 °   SELECTED CITIES

 ⊙   SELECTED PROVINCIAL CAPITALS

⊛   NATIONAL CAPITAL

—·—· PROVINCIAL BOUNDARIES

—··— INTERNATIONAL BOUNDARIES

AUGUST 1997

34

Figure 2.2   China's Road System, 1994

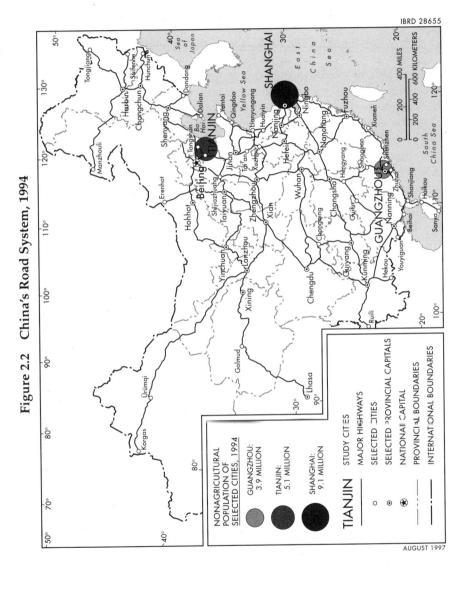

inputs and to service the demand for manufactures in the central and western regions of China.[11]

The shift in economic strategy spurred industrial development in the coastal provinces, but the large older centers did not immediately participate in this growth and prosperity for reasons that are related to the manner in which reforms were introduced. During the first half of the 1980s, although some provinces began to forge ahead, fast-growing provinces were scattered throughout the country, and no clear geographic pattern emerged. During the second half of the 1980s, growth did indeed become concentrated in coastal areas, but not in the traditional centers (this description excludes the province of Tibet). Shanghai and Tianjin were the two slowest-growing province-level units. Five coastal provinces emerged as superior performers (see table 2.4): ranked by annual industrial growth rates, these were Guangdong (17.4 percent during 1985–90), Fujian (15.8 percent), Shandong (14.4 percent), Jiangsu (13.0 percent), and Zhejiang (12.4 percent). The south coast became the most dynamic region of the country, with growth radiating northward through the middle coastal provinces. During the early 1990s, however, Shanghai and Tianjin's performance improved significantly and ranked in the midrange for all provincial units (table 2.5). The top five performers remained the same: Guangdong, Jiangsu, Zhejiang, Fujian, and Shandong.

Guangzhou, situated in the middle of the most rapidly growing region of all, maintained its growth at the national average during the 1980s. Despite Guangzhou's respectable overall growth rate, all three coastal cities failed to partake fully of the growth momentum in the 1980s. As a group their share of industrial output fell to 12 percent in 1990 and 10 percent in 1994 (compared with around 18 percent in 1978). To a certain extent, it was inevitable that these early developers would lose market share as China's industrialization spread nationwide. Nevertheless, the relative decline of at least Shanghai and Tianjin at a time when other coastal areas were forging ahead appears to have been overly rapid. It reflects the burden imposed by a large state sector and past neglect of infrastructure, as well as the central government's unwillingness to give these two cities sufficient latitude to pursue far-reaching reforms. It also reflects the slow pace at which municipal authorities used the measure of autonomy gained by way of decentralization to modernize their economies.

Urbanization and Urban Policy

Starting in the mid-nineteenth century, industrial and commercial development promoted urbanization, especially in the larger coastal cities. Among China's macro regions, only three had urbanization rates greater than 4 percent in the 1840s—the lower Yangtze, 5.8 percent; Lingnan, 5.3 percent; and southeast China, 4.2 percent, much of it in Canton, China's most populous city at the time. By the 1890s urbanization levels had increased substantially in the lower Yangtze and Lingnan

Table 2.4 Gross Value of Industrial Output in China, by Province, 1985 and 1990 (1980 Prices)

Province and rank by average annual growth rate	1985		1990		Average annual growth rate (percent)
	Billions of yuan	Share (percent)	Billions of yuan	Share (percent)	
1 Guangdong	46.1	5.6	102.7	7.9	17.4
2 Fujian	14.1	1.7	29.3	2.2	15.8
3 Shandong	54.0	6.5	105.7	8.1	14.4
4 Jiangsu	86.4	10.4	159.1	12.2	13.0
5 Zhejiang	44.4	5.4	79.5	6.1	12.4
6 Ningxia	2.2	0.3	3.7	0.3	11.0
7 Qinghai	1.9	0.2	3.1	0.2	10.3
8 Anhui	22.2	2.7	35.5	2.7	9.8
9 Shaanxi	16.9	2.0	26.5	2.0	9.4
10 Guangxi	12.4	1.5	19.4	1.5	9.4
11 Jiangxi	15.1	1.8	23.6	1.8	9.3
12 Hebei	33.3	4.0	50.2	3.9	8.6
13 Hunan	26.4	3.2	39.5	3.0	8.4
14 Inner Mongolia	9.5	1.1	14.1	1.1	8.2
15 Shanxi	19.0	2.3	27.8	2.1	7.9
16 Henan	32.1	3.9	46.9	3.6	7.9
17 Yunnan	12.1	1.5	17.6	1.4	7.8
18 Jilin	21.5	2.6	31.2	2.4	7.7
19 Gansu	11.4	1.4	16.5	1.3	7.7
20 Beijing	31.5	3.8	45.4	3.5	7.6
21 Guizhou	8.4	1.0	12.1	0.9	7.6
22 Hubei	42.3	5.1	60.9	4.7	7.6
23 Sichuan	45.4	5.5	64.9	5.0	7.4
24 Xinjiang	7.3	0.9	10.2	0.8	6.9
25 Liaoning	66.4	8.0	87.8	6.7	5.7
26 Tianjin	28.6	3.4	37.6	2.9	5.6
27 Heilongjiang	35.2	4.2	45.9	3.5	5.5
28 Shanghai	83.2	10.0	103.1	7.9	4.4
29 Tibet	0.12	0.0	0.14	0.0	3.1
Country total[a]	829.5	100.0	1,302.4	100.0	9.4

Note: Excludes village-run enterprises.
a. Excludes the new province of Hainan.
Source: State Statistical Bureau, *Statistical Yearbook of China*, 1986 and 1991.

regions, reaching 8.3 and 6.6 percent, respectively. Urbanization in northwest China had risen to 4 percent, mainly as a result of foreign investment in Manchuria, and the urban population of the southeastern macro region had increased marginally. Compared with Europe or Japan, China had fewer cities overall. This reflected not just the relative dearth of commerce but also the dispersed, rural, household-centered nature of industry.

Canton, Shanghai, Tianjin, and Wuhan were the main centers of population and of industry at the turn of the century, as they were in the 1920s (see table 2.1).[12] Thereafter, industrialization was concentrated along the east coast, the northeast, and the Yangtze River valley, mostly in large cities. When the nationalist government made Nanking the capital, the city acquired administrative functions and greater industrial significance (the capital was moved from Peking to Nanking by Yuan Shikai

Table 2.5 Gross Value of Industrial Output in China, by Province, 1990 and 1994 (1990 Prices)

Province and rank by average annual growth rate	1990 Billions of yuan	1990 Share (percent)	1994 Billions of yuan	1994 Share (percent)	Average annual growth rate (percent)
1 Guangdong	138.0	7.4	459.6	10.8	35.1
2 Jiangsu	206.1	11.0	629.5	14.8	32.2
3 Zhejiang	104.8	5.6	316.4	7.4	31.8
4 Fujian	39.4	2.1	108.6	2.6	28.8
5 Shandong	151.7	8.1	394.4	9.3	27.0
6 Guangxi	29.9	1.6	72.4	1.7	24.7
7 Anhui	52.9	2.8	122.5	2.9	23.4
8 Henan	71.3	3.8	158.3	3.7	22.1
9 Jiangxi	34.3	1.8	75.9	1.8	22.0
10 Sichuan	98.1	5.3	216.9	5.1	21.9
11 Hubei	81.6	4.4	174.9	4.1	21.0
12 Beijing	62.6	3.4	125.8	3.0	19.1
13 Shanghai	147.7	7.9	292.3	6.9	18.6
14 Hebei	75.5	4.0	149.2	3.5	18.6
15 Tianjin	52.5	2.8	103.4	2.4	18.5
16 Xinjiang	17.4	0.9	33.9	0.8	18.1
17 Ningxia	5.7	0.3	10.4	0.2	16.2
18 Hunan	58.7	3.1	105.2	2.5	15.7
19 Shaanxi	36.0	1.9	63.3	1.5	15.2
20 Liaoning	130.2	7.0	226.1	5.3	14.8
21 Yunnan	30.8	1.7	53.2	1.2	14.6
22 Inner Mongolia	23.1	1.2	38.7	0.9	13.8
23 Guizhou	18.8	1.0	31.1	0.7	13.4
24 Jilin	47.8	2.6	79.0	1.9	13.4
25 Shanxi	42.4	2.3	68.4	1.6	12.7
26 Gansu	24.8	1.3	39.9	0.9	12.6
27 Qinghai	5.1	0.3	7.9	0.2	11.6
28 Tibet	0.26	0.0	0.34	0.0	6.9
29 Heilongjiang	77.9	4.2	99.9	2.3	6.4
Country total[a]	1,865.4	100.0	4,257.4	100.0	22.9

Note: Excludes village-run enterprises.
a. Excludes the new province of Hainan.
Source: State Statistical Bureau, *Statistical Yearbook of China,* 1991 and 1995.

in 1928; see Gray 1990). In 1937, under pressure from invading Japanese forces, the nationalists were forced to move the capital to Hankow and then, in 1938, to Chongqing. This also triggered the relocation of many coastal manufacturing establishments to the interior. Industry continued to be concentrated in a relatively few major cities, but now the mid–Yangtze valley area acquired an industrial status closer to that of Shanghai and Tianjin. By 1953 the census placed Chongqing fifth and Nanjing ninth in the city hierarchy.

When the communist government took over in 1949, about 39.5 million Chinese constituted the urban population, more than two-thirds of whom were living in the eastern region. This region also contained close to half of all cities, including most of the largest ones (see table 2.6). The densely populated central region was predominantly rural, with some

Table 2.6 Urban Development in China, by Region, Selected Years, 1949–94

Indicator and region	1949	1958	1970	1980	1985	1991	1994[a]
Number of cities							
Eastern region	69	72	68	78	113	191	278
Central region	50	73	75	100	133	194	231
Western region	13	39	34	45	78	94	113
Total	132	184	177	223	324	479	622
Distribution of cities (percent)[b]							
Eastern region	52.3	39.1	38.4	35.0	34.9	39.9	44.7
Central region	37.9	39.7	42.4	44.8	41.1	40.5	37.1
Western region	9.9	21.2	19.2	20.3	24.1	19.6	18.2
Total	100.1	100.0	100.0	100.1	100.1	100.0	100.0
Urban population (millions)							
Eastern region	26.8	51.7	47.8	65.2	99.8	170.3	96.9
Central region	7.9	23.3	30.2	44.0	70.5	121.6	66.2
Western region	4.8	17.2	15.2	24.9	42.1	54.1	28.7
Total	39.5	92.2	93.2	134.1	212.4	346.0	191.8
Distribution of urban population (percent)[b]							
Eastern region	67.9	56.1	51.3	48.60	47.0	49.2	50.5
Central region	20.0	25.3	32.4	32.8	33.2	35.1	34.5
Western region	12.1	18.6	16.3	18.6	19.8	15.6	14.9
Total	100.0	100.0	100.0	100.0	100.0	99.9	100.0
Average city size (thousands of persons)							
Eastern region	390	720	700	840	880	890	350
Central region	160	320	400	440	530	630	290
Western region	370	440	450	550	540	580	250
Total	300	500	530	600	660	720	310

a. Estimated urban nonagricultural population.
b. Percentages may not sum to 100 because of rounding.
Source: State Statistical Bureau 1990; *China: Urban Statistical Yearbook,* 1992; *Statistical Yearbook of China,* 1995.

7.9 million urbanites living in 50 small cities. The western region, though it had a handful of medium cities, was almost wholly rural. Once normalcy returned, there was an immediate resurgence in the growth of cities. In the course of a decade, the urban population of the eastern region doubled, with large centers such as Shanghai leading the way. The urban populace of central China increased threefold, although from a small base, but the number of cities also rose from 50 to 73, so that the average city size did not climb as much as it did in the coastal zone.

Urban policy changed soon after, following a distinctive antiurban, anticoast bias. Urbanization and urban policy since the mid-1950s and before the reforms can be characterized as discouraging the growth of large cities and promoting medium and small cities, as developing industrial and urban centers away from coastal areas, and as using a variety of administrative measures to control the general growth and distribution of cities (Pannell and Ma 1983; Yeh and Xu 1990), including the recruitment of city dwellers to work in rural areas, strict controls on rural-urban migration through food rationing and household registration, and the dispersion of millions of young people to work in inland

and frontier provinces.[13] Despite these controls, urban population continued to grow in China, albeit slowly. The government policy of containing very large cities appeared to have some effect, and rural-urban migration was far below levels observed in other countries. Between 1953 and 1978 China's rate of urbanization fluctuated between 13 and 16 percent. It reached 20.6 percent in 1982 (see Zhao and Zhang 1995).

Unlike many other developing countries, China has never had a full-blown primate city structure dominated by a single large city (Parish 1990). Data for 1953 and 1970 indicate that China's urban system had a very smooth profile and that cities were quite evenly distributed across various size classes (Pannell and Ma 1983). This can be attributed largely to the rapid growth of medium and small cities (figure 2.3). The very largest city, Shanghai, and the very smallest towns lagged behind, although the populations of Beijing, Tianjin, and some other large cities were less successfully contained. All the large cities were growing at a steady but unspectacular pace, whereas medium cities witnessed the fastest rate of population growth. The story with the small towns was peculiar. As the economic and administrative functions of small market towns declined, their numbers shrank, and many ceased to qualify as urban places. This was also intended to centralize fiscal control. The net results were a rapid decline in the number and function of cities at the lowest end and a break in the traditional link between city and countryside. On the whole, the state policy of deemphasizing the production of consumer goods and services affected small towns adversely (Chang 1994; Parish 1990).

The redistribution policy stimulated the growth and development of interior centers, including Lanzhou, Wuhan, Xian, and Zhengzhou (table 2.1).[14] All cities on the coast, particularly treaty ports, had to demonstrate their contribution to the national economy as industrial producer cities. The underlying rationale was that the treaty ports still suffered from ideological and political "pollution" as a result of their former commercial status, foreign participation, scale of service activities, and persistent consumer attitudes (Pannell and Ma 1983). The impact of this inland-oriented urban policy was very large. From 1958 to 1970 government efforts to contain and even reverse urbanization in the eastern region were fairly successful in dampening population growth in cities along the coastal belt. From 1966 until the early 1970s this policy was reinforced by the Third Front policy. In 1949 about two-thirds of the urban population was concentrated in the eastern region, but by 1980 this proportion had fallen to half (table 2.6). The central region experienced the most rapid growth of urban population and represented a third of China's urban population in 1980. Much of the industrial investment that took place during these years was in capital goods industries tucked away in small towns and medium cities in Gansu, Hubei, Hunan, Sichuan, and elsewhere. Growth in the absolute numbers of the urban population slowed dramatically. The only growth was in the cen-

Figure 2.3 China's Urban Population by City Size, Selected Years, 1950–90

Percentage of
urban population

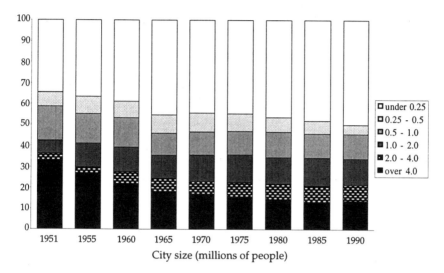

City size (millions of people)

Note: This figure shows that, for example, the share of the largest cities (city size over 4 million) population in national urban population declined from about 33 percent in 1951 to about 15 percent in 1990.
Source: Asian Population and Development Association 1991.

tral region, where the populace rose by a fifth. This was also the one region in which the number of cities multiplied.

Under the system of planning, cities were assigned quite narrow roles. Although they provided industrial technology and served as revenue collection points, they ceased to be financial, trade, and business centers or the foci of regional economies. Financial and information functions were transferred to Beijing. Central planners and financial officials took over much of the economic coordination that had previously been performed in the coastal cities. They ceased to orchestrate the commercial activities of a region by anchoring a nested hierarchy of markets. Furthermore, the vertical integration of urbanized state industry and the insulated nature of communal manufacturing activities severed the long-standing organic links between cities and their hinterlands. China's great cities were forcibly cut adrift from the nourishing rural economy. Most damaging, they also lost their role as traders and contacts with the international economy. A planned economy that sought self-sufficiency had no use for outward-looking commercial centers.

With the start of the reform era in the late 1970s, urban policy changed substantially. First of all, the measures to control urban growth by restricting migration began to lose a great deal of their sharpness, largely as a result of rising rural prosperity and the increasing problems of enforcement (Kirkby 1985). Second, the government again recognized the advantages of the coastal region and designated various types of growth centers, including five Special Economic Zones and 14 coastal open cities (see Howell 1993). Third, the downward trends among small towns began to reverse as many old market centers sprang back to life. The relaxation of criteria for classifying towns in 1984 also led to a spurt in the level of urbanization (Lee 1989). Last, and most important of all, there was a greater willingness to allow cities and towns to respond to market forces free from government intervention (Yeh and Xu 1990). This can also be attributed to the recognition that the growth of inland cities in the period before reform was achieved at high cost and worked against the economies of scale available to large existing coastal centers.

The two-decade transition from central planning has had profound consequences at many levels that are only slowly becoming apparent. The macroeconomic effects are well known and basically positive. China's rate of inflation in the mid-1990s was moderate; the trickle-down effects of high growth on poverty have been weaker than expected since the mid-1980s, and predictably, income equality has declined both within and between sectors. Perhaps more significant for the longer term is the ground swell affecting the urban and industrial geography. An almost 50-year hiatus in the urbanization of China began to come to an end in the 1980s. The push to urbanize, restrained intermittently for decades, began in earnest and promises to move China toward a "normal level" of urbanization in the years ahead. In 1993 the level of urbanization rose to 28 percent, which is close to the average for all low-income developing countries. Attempts to channel urban development toward the central region and away from the large cities have also slackened. As shown in table 2.6, the share of the eastern region in the number of both cities and urban nonagricultural population has been growing again since the 1980s. It is now up to the cities themselves to contain and manage the migrant streams (see Wong 1994).

Summary

Starting in the mid-nineteenth century and continuing for 100 years, China entered an early stage of urbanization, drawn at first by increasing commercial development and, around the turn of the century, by the emergence of modern industry in regions that had long been hospitable to proto-manufacturing. Urbanizing tendencies were strongest in the eastern region and pulled China down a path other countries had trod before. People and industry gravitated toward strategically located agglomerations along the coast and major waterways. A few cities that stood at the intersection of domestic and international markets took the lead. By exploiting the advantages conferred by their hinterlands and the economies associated with size, these cities established themselves at the top of the urban hierarchy. The central government exercised relatively little direction or control. Regional dynamics were decisive. Growing cities mobilized and effectively employed resources, both domestic and external.

This first stage had run its course by the middle of the twentieth century. The communist victory completely altered the economic as well as the political parameters of urban development. Foreign influence on China's urbanization was at an end. The new government did not view urbanization as either inevitable or necessarily desirable. Cities were seen not as autonomous players but as counters in a larger socialist plan of modernization that emphasized regional self-sufficiency, rural development, and limited mobility of the populace. China's premier cities were harnessed to the plan—cast in the role of handmaidens in the development of China's interior as users of resources obtained from the rest of the economy and transformed into industrial products using the special advantages conferred by agglomeration. This strategy, implemented with varying degrees of conviction, reached its high-water mark in the early 1970s, but the rules employed were not seriously undermined for almost another 15 years, by which time China was beginning to dismantle the administrative and fiscal checks imposed on its big cities and to give them the capacity to shape their own economic destinies. In the reform era, a new urban policy aimed at using large cities as the loci of regional growth began to take effect. Cities are now expected to serve as growth centers for the surrounding countryside, benefiting the entire region through economies of scale, externalities, and spillover effects (Kuo 1989).

The large Chinese cities have come full circle. The decade of the 1980s was a period of profound reorientation, with the economy changing gears and planning being superseded by market autonomy within a few years. First Guangzhou and later Shanghai and Tianjin were challenged by vast new opportunities. An expanding menu of choices replaced the confines of the planned system, in which the city was assigned a delimited role. Starting in 1978, reform began transferring responsibility from the center to provinces and municipalities. Cities were given a mandate to modernize and the powers to fulfill it. There was no body of rules on how to proceed, and the changed thinking was assimilated quite slowly, with Guangzhou, as one of the earliest modernizers, leading the way. Its reform initiatives have embraced a wide range of functions, such as building infrastructure and institutions and reviving trade and commercial networks. Dominated by large state sectors, Shanghai and Tianjin were much slower to reform. Shanghai's strategic industrial and fiscal position in the national economy constrained the options permitted by the central government. But after the success of reforms in south China, Shanghai was finally set free in the late 1980s, and it has embarked on a path of rapid industrial restructuring. Tianjin, the latecomer among the three in reforms, was still inching its way forward, and significant efforts did not commence until the early 1990s.

3

Shanghai: Renaissance City

Shanghai is competing aggressively for the mantle of China's premier metropolis. Already the leading industrial center, it is attempting to increase its edge over China's other major cities by augmenting its technological capability in a range of subsectors. By modernizing its port facilities and communications infrastructure, Shanghai is restoring a source of economic dynamism that contributes directly to its industrial strength. Three-quarters of a century ago, modern banking and other producer services began taking root in Shanghai, alongside the growth of manufacturing activities and the expansion of trade. Virtually eliminated after 1949, these are being revived once again. Last but not least, early in the century, Shanghai was the crucible in which the cultural activities associated with a modern industrial society made their appearance. By all accounts, the city was the cultural capital of China in the 1920s and 1930s. Together with Beijing, Shanghai was where institutions of higher learning were first established, starting a tradition that has endured and flourished since. Shanghai is again gaining a lead over other cities, drawing on the largest and most diverse pool of talent in China and reserves of cosmopolitanism that survived three decades of cultural drought.

These efforts to position Shanghai in the forefront of China's major industrial centers are the result of radical changes in the outlook of urban elites, who are finding a voice after years of enforced passivity that extended into the mid-1980s. Shanghai's renaissance also stems from a new equation with the central government that permits Shanghai to tap into the full range of reform possibilities and to embark on a municipal development strategy that departs markedly from the strategy of the past three decades.

Between 1979 and 1993 Shanghai averaged a GDP growth rate of 7.9 percent a year, well below the 11.3 percent achieved by Guangzhou (see table 3.1). As a result, Shanghai's industrial ranking among China's provinces—second place in 1952—fell to fifth place. Since then, growth of municipal GDP has accelerated significantly and has averaged somewhat more than 14 percent a year during 1993–96, raising Shanghai's performance above the national average, approximately on a par with that of Guangzhou, but well ahead of the performance of Tianjin.[1] Underlying this recent growth is a series of reform measures and developmental initiatives launched after 1988 that, if sustained, should substantially improve Shanghai's fortunes.

This chapter first examines the principal defining characteristics of Shanghai's development strategy through the mid-1980s. It then explores how these have been altered by a series of reforms beginning in the early 1980s but achieving a critical mass only in the 1990s. These reforms have enabled Shanghai to loosen some of the inherited constraints, to begin harnessing more fully resources within as well as outside the municipal economy, to exploit externalities inherent in the diversified municipal economy, and to remedy some of the inadequacies of the economy, es-

Table 3.1 Macro Indicators for Shanghai, Tianjin, and Guangzhou, Selected Years, 1952–93

Indicator	Shanghai	Tianjin	Guangzhou	China
GDP index				
1952	100.0	100.0	100.0	—
1978	888.6	619.3	1,065.5	100.0
1991	2,255.4	1,599.7	4,977.5	295.0
1993	—	2,003.0	5,314.6	379.0
Annual growth rate of GDP index (percent)				
1952–78	8.8	7.3	9.5	—
1978–91	7.4	7.6	12.6	8.7
1978–93	7.9ᵃ	8.1	11.3	9.3
GVIO index				
1952	100.0	100.0	100.0	100.0
1978	1,216.6	913.6	1,849.9	1,659.0
1991	3,104.1	3,276.2	9,410.5	7,419.4
1993	—	5,098.6	16,486.3	12,112.3
Annual growth rate of GVIO index (percent)				
1952–78	10.1	8.9	11.9	11.4
1978–91	7.5	10.3	13.3	12.2
1978–93	9.1ᵃ	12.1	15.7	14.2

— Not available.
Note: GDP, gross domestic product; GVIO, gross value of industrial output.
a. Annual average rate between 1979 and 1993.
Source: State Statistical Bureau, *Statistical Yearbook of Shanghai*, 1992 and 1994; *Statistical Yearbook of Tianjin*, 1994; *Statistical Yearbook of Guangzhou*, 1992 and 1994; *Statistical Yearbook of China*, 1994.

pecially in the sphere of producer services and infrastructure (on producer services, see Healey and Ilbery 1990).

Shanghai's size and the complex, multifaceted nature of its modernization allow us to examine its development from the angles indicated in chapter 1, including industrial development, producer services, external trading and investment links, fiscal relations, and R&D capabilities. When we turn to Tianjin and Guangzhou in later chapters, we take a more selective approach that highlights the role of critical sectors and industries.

Industrial Transition: From the 1940s to the 1960s

In most respects, Shanghai in the late 1940s was typical of large industrial cities in a developing country. Textiles, food processing, and a handful of other light industries dominated the manufacturing sector and, by way of backward linkages, supported small-scale engineering and metalworking subsectors. Service industries provided the bulk of employment, whether in formal activities such as banking or in informal ones such as petty retailing (Howe 1981; Sung 1991). Because Shanghai was China's main port, trade was a vital component of the economy. Local merchants managed the city's own commerce and served as intermediaries for the external trade of the lower Yangtze region, which was funneled largely through Shanghai. The interactions between hinterland and city, production linkages, and trading ties were numerous and strong. Even when warfare compromised market functioning, interfered with the flow of goods, and caused Shanghai's industrialists to flee to Hong Kong with as much of their equipment as they could ship, Shanghai's basic economic configuration and its role in the regional economy changed very little (Howe 1981). But after 1949, the turn toward centralized planning and the placement of increasing emphasis on heavy industry, regional self-sufficiency, and minimal reliance on foreign trade began to transform the character of China's large coastal cities, in particular, Shanghai.

One major tenet of Maoist socialism was that cities must be cast in the mold of producers rather than of consumers living off the surplus of the rural economy.[2] The practical implications of this were far-reaching and involved a large increase in the share of manufacturing relative to services. Industry was expanded because it was viewed as productive, whereas services, which in the Marxist scheme contributed little to the economy, were reduced in scale. Furthermore, heavy industries were targeted for expansion because overriding importance was attached to metallurgical products, machinery, and petrochemicals. Heavy industry was viewed as the touchstone of economic strength and consequently received the largest allocations of capital through the state plan (see Donnithorne 1967; Riskin 1987). Starting in the mid-1950s, Shanghai's industrial center of gravity began to shift away from light manufacturing and toward machine building, a process that continued for the next two decades.

The stress on heavy industry was combined with an equally strong impetus toward self-sufficiency in which the widest possible range of subsectors was developed so that the maximum number of input-output relationships could be contained within Shanghai. In fact, an enormous range of industries, spanning 140 of the 146 listed subsectors, was established in order to attain the highest measure of industrial independence. Almost all of the growth took place in the state sector, and the central government rather than the municipality controlled state enterprises. Shanghai not only acquired a strong base of heavy industry and a highly diversified industrial structure but also surrendered much of the industrial autonomy it once enjoyed, becoming a creature of the planned economy dedicated to achieving narrow production goals to the virtual exclusion of all else. The pronounced strain of autarky in national policy also meant that earlier trading ties with the international community were largely severed, and the focus of the city turned inward toward the domestic economy. Each of these trends calls for further elucidation.

Socialism's Industrial Pillar

Shanghai was one among a handful of Chinese cities in the early 1950s that had a functioning modern industrial sector, the supporting infrastructure, and the necessary fund of skills. These cities were the natural candidates to spearhead China's industrialization along socialist lines. Hence the first goal of the central government was to build state-owned heavy industries in Shanghai and to use their production of capital equipment as well as intermediate products to initiate industrial growth in other parts of the country. Because machinery alone was insufficient to induce development, thousands of Shanghainese found themselves transferred to exceedingly remote parts of the country, sometimes to train the locals in manufacturing techniques and frequently to run the newly built factories. The accumulation of human capital from Shanghai's universities and numerous production establishments was China's key to higher technology, which became all the more valuable when the Soviets withdrew their technicians in 1960 and halted scientific exchanges. Forced to rely on its own relatively meager fund of manufacturing skills and modest scientific base, China began cultivating Shanghai's research potential and using it to advance a number of major industrial projects. Likewise, Shanghai's laboratories were entrusted with the task of building some of China's ballistic missiles and transport aircraft. In the process, Shanghai added a military wing to its industrial complex, which also contributed to the production of satellite launchers and the development of aircraft (Norris 1994; *Aviation Week and Space Technology*, March 24, 1997).

Planned economies committed to maximizing growth using heavy industry as the leading sector have an insatiable hunger for resources. China was no exception. The industrial engine constantly demanded capital, but raising such a large volume of resources in a poor and predominantly rural economy was administratively problematic. The Chinese government solved this by using the pricing of industrial products (and also agricultural staples) as the main vehicle for extracting revenue. State and collective enterprises manufacturing capital equipment but also consumer durables earned sizable profits by selling their goods at high prices that were fixed by the state, while receiving raw materials at prices that were kept deliberately low. Central authorities then appropriated these profits, which constituted three-quarters or more of central government revenue. Shanghai, with its concentration of industrial products, became the largest single source of revenue for the state, providing about 25 percent in an average year during the latter part of the 1970s. In fact, nine-tenths of Shanghai's enterprise earnings were not controlled by the municipality, which remained perennially cash-poor and dependent on earmarked funds that central ministries supplied for industrial units or research facilities. For example, over the 25-year period from 1953 to 1978, the city devoted Y18.73 billion to capital construction, but central ministries provided more than 70 percent of this for selected state enterprises.

For the central authorities, Shanghai served as a pillar of the planned economy. Its manufacturing facilities, among China's most advanced, were crucial for meeting production targets. Shanghai's human resources were instrumental in igniting industrialization elsewhere in China and in making possible a modicum of technical progress. In fulfilling output goals, the city also acted as the state's revenue collector; the pricing system ensured the profitability of Shanghai's state-owned enterprises, and the central government then exercised its rights to siphon the funds into the budget.

Preparing the Ground for Reform

Prior to liberation, Shanghai was China's foremost trading city and the largest recipient of foreign investment. Trade and foreign capital introduced Chinese entrepreneurs to the industrial technology and producer services essential to a modern economy. The coming of socialism pulled Shanghai into a lower orbit. It ceased to be a "world city" with diverse functions and became instead an industrial workhorse for a plan-bound economy. Its growth rate was constrained first by the limitations on investment in light industry and the supposedly "unproductive" services and next by restraints on migration to the city, as well as the transfer of thousands of engineers and technicians to other parts of China. With industry soaking up the lion's share of capital, little was left for urban infrastructure, and the austere official attitude toward the development of large cities provided little scope for investment in housing, transport, and other urban amenities. Tightly laced socialism turned Shanghai into a somber and congested city, frugally supplied with services and forced to subsist on infrastructure inherited from the early decades of the century.

These lean years were helpful in at least four respects. First, in the industrial sphere, Shanghai acquired industrial diversity and production experience to an extent that has no parallels in China and few anywhere in the world. This was excellent preparation for the reform era and beyond. Second, the embedding of defense-related activities within the municipal industrial system stimulated entry into high-technology activities such as electronics, precision machining, computers, and other relatively advanced subsectors. As was the case with Los Angeles, São Paulo, and the western suburbs of London, defense industries provided substantial direct production benefits and knowledge-related externalities.[3] Moreover, the manufacture of weaponry and aircraft called for research, and this brought into existence a handful of well-equipped laboratories with pilot production facilities and state-of-the-art testing equipment. In a limited but meaningful way, it also established links between research centers and state enterprises along the lines that have proved so fruitful in the United States. Third, the importance of Shanghai as an industrial center and one of the bulwarks of military research sheltered the city from the turbulence and dislocation that plagued the country during the Cultural Revolution.

Fourth, the years of high socialism significantly added to the fund of production, technical, and scientific skills. Undoubtedly Shanghai was taxed each time the central government sought to disperse industry and set up new industrial centers. But the multiplication of industrial enterprises, and tertiary-level educational institutions and research establishments, suggests that the state partially compensated Shanghai for the drain. The city responded sluggishly to the opportunities presented by reforms—and we deal with the reasons for this later—but the speed of diversification in the 1990s and the surge in industrial growth are irrefutable indicators of pent-up economic energy somewhat belatedly released by a well-timed succession of reform policies.

The Scale of Agglomeration

Whether experienced firsthand or perceived through myriad statistics, the size and sheer density of Shanghai's population are impressive. The scale is economic rather than geographic. The city core covers just 300 square kilometers out of a municipal total of 6,341 square kilometers. In 1980 the metropolis had a population of 11.5 million. This had risen to almost 13 million in 1993, 8.9 million of whom resided in the city proper, where the density exceeded 43,000 persons per square kilometer (see table 3.2). None of the other crowded cities in the developing world,

Table 3.2   Major Indicators for Shanghai, Tianjin, and Guangzhou, 1993

Indicator	Shanghai Number	Shanghai Percent	Tianjin Number	Tianjin Percent	Guangzhou Number	Guangzhou Percent
Land						
Land area	6,341	n.a.	11,305	n.a.	7,434	n.a.
(square kilometers)						
Built-up area	300	n.a.	339	n.a.	207	n.a.
Population						
Population (millions)	12.95	n.a.	8.86	n.a.	6.20	n.a.
Nonagricultural population	8.93	n.a.	5.00	n.a.	3.75	n.a.
Workforce						
Total workforce (millions)	7.85	100.0	5.03	100.0	3.85	100.0
Staff and workers[a]	4.90	62.4	2.93	58.3	2.11	54.7
State employees	3.52	44.9	2.07	41.0	1.39	36.0
Primary sector	0.75	9.6	0.89	17.7	0.95	24.8
Secondary sector	4.55	58.0	2.45	48.7	1.46	38.0
Tertiary sector	2.55	32.4	1.69	33.6	1.43	37.2
Average wage (yuan)	5,650	n.a.	4,003	n.a.	6,342	n.a.
Economic indicators						
GDP (billions of yuan)	151.16	100.0	53.61	100.0	74.08	100.0
Primary sector	3.82	2.5	3.54	6.6	4.76	6.4
Secondary sector	90.03	59.6	30.25	56.4	35.17	47.5
Tertiary sector	57.31	37.9	19.82	37.0	34.15	46.1
GDP per capita (yuan)	11,699	n.a.	6,075	n.a.	11,989	n.a.
GVIAO (billions of yuan)	341.63	n.a.	147.25	n.a.	121.96	n.a.
GVIO (billions of yuan)						
1993	286.10	100.0	106.58	100.0	100.25	100.0
State-owned enterprises	155.95	54.5	62.80	58.9	46.53	46.4
Collective-owned						
enterprises	35.89	12.5	24.13	22.6	16.22	16.2
Others	94.26	32.9	19.66	18.4	37.50	37.4
1994	375.80	100.0	129.38	100.0	—	—
State-owned enterprises	180.29	48.0	64.81	50.1	—	—
Collective-owned						
enterprises	48.39	12.9	23.01	17.8	—	—
Others	147.13	39.2	41.56	32.1	—	—

n.a. Not applicable.
— Not available.
Note: GDP, gross domestic product; GVIAO, gross value of industrial and agricultural output; GVIO, gross value of industrial output.
a. Excludes workforce employed in rural establishments.
Source: State Statistical Bureau, *Statistical Yearbook of Tianjin*, 1994; *Statistical Yearbook of Guangzhou*, 1994; *Statistical Yearbook of China*, 1995.

such as Calcutta, Dhaka, and São Paulo, conveys the extraordinary sense of teeming humanity as does downtown Shanghai during peak hours. Industry has been and remains the lifeblood of the municipality. Shanghai accounted for 11.6 percent of the national industrial output in 1980. This declined to a still impressive 6.9 percent in 1994, with the bulk of manufacturing facilities crowded into roughly a quarter of the city's built-up area.

Table 3.3 Gross Value of Industrial Output in Shanghai, Selected Years, 1985–93

Indicator	1985 Billions of yuan[a]	Percent	1991 Billions of yuan[b]	Percent	1993 Billions of yuan[b]	Percent	Enterprises in 1993 Number	Percent
City total	82.96	100.0	179.61	100.0	298.98	100.0	13,688	100.0
Light industry	46.15	55.6	89.16	49.6	122.25	40.9	7,937	58.0
Heavy industry	36.81	44.4	90.45	50.4	176.73	59.1	5,762	42.1
State-owned enterprises	64.29	77.5	126.31	70.3	162.97	54.5	4,270	31.2
Collective-owned enterprises	16.01	19.3	25.21	14.0	38.47	12.9	6,762	49.4
Others	2.65	3.2	28.10	15.6	97.55	32.6	2,656	19.4
Top subsectors in 1993	64.31	77.5	136.92	76.2	232.85	77.9	9,228	67.4
Metallurgy[c]	8.81	10.6	27.36	15.2	61.35	20.5	290	2.1
Machine building[d]	16.12	19.4	30.74	17.1	48.56	16.2	3,066	22.4
Transport equipment	2.80	3.4	11.24	6.3	28.07	9.4	638	4.7
Textiles	14.65	17.7	22.19	12.4	25.29	8.5	1,119	8.2
Chemicals	5.74	7.0	12.91	7.2	17.20	5.8	700	5.1
Electronics	4.58	5.5	8.39	4.7	12.69	4.2	436	3.2
Food[e]	2.61	3.2	6.37	3.5	10.66	3.6	789	5.8
Metal products	3.02	3.6	6.21	3.5	10.38	3.5	1,205	8.8
Synthetic fiber	3.21	3.9	5.99	3.3	9.42	3.2	51	0.4
Clothing	2.76	3.3	5.53	3.1	9.24	3.1	934	6.8
Herfindahl index		0.077		0.067		0.071		

Note: All numbers exclude village-run enterprises.
a. 1980 prices.
b. Current prices.
c. Includes smelting and pressing of ferrous and nonferrous metals.
d. Includes machine building and electrical machinery.
e. Includes food processing.
Source: State Statistical Bureau, *Statistical Yearbook of Shanghai,* 1992, 1994.

Metallurgy, machine building, and transport equipment are Shanghai's biggest subsectors. Together they were responsible for 46 percent of the gross value of industrial output (GVIO) in 1993 (see table 3.3). Behind them, in order of importance, are textiles, chemicals, and electronics. But as noted above, Shanghai's industrial reach is quite extraordinary and extends into virtually all subsectors of any consequence. Compared with the situation in 1985, two changes in the structure of production are noteworthy: textiles had lost ground and were being overtaken by metallurgy and machine building, and transport equipment had almost tripled its share (see figure 3.1). In addition, the degree of concentration of industrial subsectors had decreased somewhat since 1978, as demonstrated by the shrinking Herfindahl index measured in output value (from 0.077 to 0.071). Light and heavy industry were evenly balanced in the late 1970s—each accounting for half of GVIO—and remained so for

Figure 3.1   Industrial Structure of Shanghai, 1985 and 1993

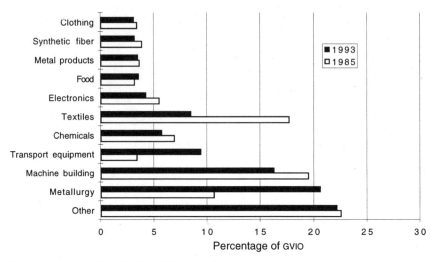

Note: GVIO, gross value of industrial output.
Source: Table 3.3.

13 years, until 1991. However, state-owned enterprises that had claimed more than 90 percent of industrial output saw their share fall to 55 percent in 1993 (and 44 in 1995), with the remainder being equally divided between collectives and others, principally joint ventures, which have mushroomed since the mid-1980s.

On closer examination, the dynamics of industrial change in Shanghai reveal the working of significant agglomeration effects and the emergence of noteworthy trends. By Chinese standards, Shanghai's state-owned enterprises were among the best equipped and most efficient producers in the country. As reform transformed the economic milieu, they found it relatively easy to introduce new product lines, upgrade their output, and restructure production. Once foreign investors began to explore seriously the possibilities of manufacturing in China, those interested in the assembly of light manufactures concentrated on the southeastern provinces, while large multinationals were more attracted to Shanghai. The wealth of skills is just one factor. Equally important, especially for the production of items such as automobiles and computers, is that a joint venture which is prepared to subcontract, breaking from the long-standing practice of vertical integration, can, with some experimentation and training, source a wide range of components from within the municipality. This took on considerable significance as the government required multinational corporations to aim for a high level of local content. Such diversity would be a plus under any circumstances, but it had special merit in a country where transport and communications facilities were backward in the 1980s and, in spite of feverish investment, remain inadequate in the late 1990s.

Industrial depth has been a huge asset for Shanghai, generating externalities and also inducing foreign investment in electronics, chemicals, and transport equipment industries. The entry of foreign companies and the subsequent focus on growth, increased industrial competition from other parts of China, growing exposure to the international economy, and greater scope for nonstate enterprises to expand their operations and compete with state-owned enterprises for market share gradually induced a spiral of growth feeding off positive agglomeration effects that had not yet been fully tapped. The lagged nature of the response is related to the pace of reforms, but once change began, it covered a broad spectrum, drew on Shanghai's advantages, and attempted to cope with its serious handicaps.

Automobiles and Fashion Garments: Externalities at Work

Over time Shanghai will find it expedient to narrow the compass of its industrial activities and concentrate on fewer leading sectors that will provide the sources of growth well into the next century. Undoubtedly, Shanghai will also diversify into services and in all probability will be the foremost financial center in China. However, the experience of New York suggests that prosperity built on producer services alone is precarious and distributionally lopsided (see chapter 6). A broad economic base including advanced manufacturing and services is the most dynamic. Among possible industrial leading sectors, Shanghai has the luxury of choosing from among a range of candidates because it is currently well positioned in so many subsectors. Autos, quality apparel, office equipment, telecommunications, pharmaceuticals, and medical equipment are growth industries that have taken root in the municipality. They are all skill- and research-intensive activities peculiarly suited to Shanghai's multifaceted resource endowment. But they by no means exhaust the range of options, which also include heavy machinery, machine tools, and metallurgical industries. If Shanghai perseveres with the development of the auto industry, as is highly probable, metallurgical and machine tool subsectors will be encouraged to invest and to refine their technology. The apparel subsector will build on a textile industry with long experience. Likewise, a robust pharmaceutical industry will promote fine chemicals, and the manufacture of advanced medical equipment will have backward linkages to other chemical industries, optoelectronics, as well as precision engineering. A brief review of the auto sector and the garment industry offers a taste of how two leading sectors are faring and of the factors that will influence their future.

Automobiles

At the start of the 1980s, fewer than 2 million autos were on China's roads (output of cars and trucks in 1979 was about 120,000; see Harwit 1995). As a ratio to the population, the number of automobiles was among the lowest in the world. The number rose to 4.3 million in 1988 and to more than 10 million in 1995, with passenger cars accounting for close to 3 million of the total. In spite of this steep increase, the number of passenger cars per 1,000 persons was little more than 2.0, compared with 86.2 in Brazil (Maxton 1994; *New York Times,* March 28, 1995). As long as the economy maintains a healthy rate of expansion, the scope for continued growth is substantial. Even if the number of registered cars rises to the projected 4.5 million by 2000, China will have only 3.4 cars per 1,000 persons. China stands on the threshold of automobility. The potential demand, looking a decade and more into the future, is huge, and the current scale of the auto sector is small by comparison. Moreover, many of the forward linkages to auto-related services have barely been tapped, suggesting that future direct and indirect employment effects will dwarf the number of jobs created in core manufacturing activities.

Although there are more than 160 auto assembly facilities in China, the three front-runners for passenger cars are Changchun (First Auto Works–Audi), Shanghai (Shanghai-Volkswagen), and Wuhan (Magic Dragon–Citroën). In addition, there are three lesser production centers in Beijing (Beijing-Cherokee Co.), Tianjin (Tianjin-Daihatsu Corp.), and Guangzhou (Guangzhou-Peugeot). Total production reached 1.3 million vehicles in 1994, of which about 250,000 were passenger cars. Shanghai has a commanding lead in sedans, with 52 percent of the national output of 385,000 sedans in 1996.[4]

Volkswagen entered into a 50-50 joint venture with Shanghai Auto and the China Auto Industry Corporation in 1984 with the intention of producing its Brazilian-designed Santana. After a trial assembly from knockdown kits, production commenced in 1985 and built up to 18,000 units in 1990, when 50 percent of the value of the vehicle was being sourced domestically. Production rose to 200,000 in 1996, when 90 percent of the value of the Santana was domestically sourced. This considerable achievement highlights Shanghai Auto's success in solving a variety of teething problems and serves to identify where the performance of the local manufacturing system falls below international standards.

Whenever the leading international automakers are making a fresh start, they prefer a greenfield site and a youthful, well-educated labor force with no experience in auto manufacturing. This ensures that facilities incorporate the latest knowledge of plant layout and process technology. An educated but inexperienced supply of workers combines learning skills with the absence of ingrained, possibly dysfunctional habits and internalized organizational routines. In short, the best employees are easily trained and flexible in what they do as well as how they do it. When Volkswagen commenced operations in Shanghai, it had neither of these advantages. Existing facilities had to be adapted or rebuilt, and a sizable part of the workforce was composed of the tenured employees of Shanghai Auto Industry Corp., a state enterprise founded in 1958.[5]

Volkswagen acquired two assets of great significance in China's urban industrial environment. First, it was linked to a partner with the right bureaucratic and industrial connections. These connections brought access to officialdom, won favors, and greased the wheels of business. They also served as an entry into long-term relations with future suppliers. The automobile business depends on efficient coordination between a few assemblers and many suppliers. Ten years ago, most major assemblers were served by hundreds of suppliers, but experience has shown that the ideal is to have 300 or fewer principal suppliers. Assemblers are now seeking to establish broadly cooperative relations with suppliers but at the same time are anxious to sustain a measure of competition among component manufacturers to keep prices down and maintain quality. Striking a balance between these goals calls for delicate footwork. The link with Shanghai Auto made it possible for Volkswagen to begin creating a local network of suppliers, starting with the 107 enterprises related to Shanghai Auto. The Shanghai Santana Commonwealth now embraces not just input suppliers but also universities and research institutes that, with encouragement from municipal authorities, are committed to the progressive deepening of the auto industry in the city.

Second, Shanghai Auto gave the joint venture access to a pool of engineering skills, which are invaluable for undertaking a complex manufacturing operation and for transferring process technology in a short space of time. Volkswagen augmented these skills by sending more than 1,000 Chinese engineers overseas (through 1993) for training. Beyond that, association with a major state-owned enterprise loosened the constraints on credit from local banking channels and, in the late 1980s, made it easier to bid for foreign exchange.

Ten years ago it was difficult to predict how the marriage between an old-line state-owned enterprise and one of the world's premier auto companies would evolve. Urban reform had barely started, and Shanghai had yet to loosen the state's tight grip on industry. Socialism as practiced by China's state-owned enterprises was far removed from the world of Volkswagen. To fuse such dissimilar cultures and systems into a workable hybrid posed a challenge for the partners and also for the municipal government. If the experiment failed, Shanghai stood to lose the investment of the more tentative multinationals waiting in the wings, and Volkswagen would not gain a prized foothold in one of the largest markets of the next century. The municipality's desire to reach a high level of domestic content within a handful of years complicated Volkswagen's task and made it imperative to concentrate from the outset on the manufacture of components, the bedrock of the auto industry. By dint of trying, the joint venture succeeded in a remarkably short span of time and in so doing underscored the roles of the government, the economy of Shanghai, and the approach of the foreign partner.

By assigning a high priority to the auto industry, the government made it a focus of ministerial interest and municipal commitment. It also provided tariff protection along with a guaranteed market for the vehicles produced during the initial years of operation.[6] The combination of bureaucratic support, investment funds, and large profits lowered the odds to acceptable levels. Shanghai could not offer a greenfield site, but in the Chinese context it was the ideal place to set up a network of suppliers within a short trucking distance of the assembly plant. Volkswagen discovered that there were enterprises in the metropolitan region with the skills to produce almost any item in small lots. With sustained coaching and technical assistance, these firms could learn the design and process skills they needed to participate effectively in a modern automobile production network. Building such a network with some infusion of foreign capital into the parts industry took several years, and it is still incomplete.[7] It was a hard slog to win adherence to acceptable standards in the virtual absence of competition, but the industrial strength of the city helped. By 1995, 180 suppliers, many of them joint ventures, were able to produce all but the most technically demanding components for the Santana.[8] Many are still unable to meet Volkswagen's specifications to the fullest extent, but progress has been steady.

Shanghai-Volkswagen was not empowered to recruit an all new workforce, but the city's labor force had the highest level of education and skills in China. These advantages partially offset other drawbacks. Moreover, the auto industry had a plentiful supply of engineers with whom to augment the quality of the assembly-line workforce, troubleshoot, control quality, and repair equipment. The ratio of engineers to the total workforce is viewed as an indicator of efficiency, and in this regard Shanghai-Volkswagen was operating in one of the best labor markets in China. Such skills are not just an asset on the assembly line; they also underpin R&D capability throughout the supplier network.

An early start and a wise selection of product have maximized the gains for Volkswagen. Because it dominates the market for sedans, Shanghai Auto Industries achieved annual sales of $4 billion in 1993, giving it a financial lead over rivals and putting it ahead of other giants such as Daqing Petroleum and Anshan Steel ($3.8 billion and $2.5 billion, respectively). Selecting a mature design—the Santana—that had been thoroughly debugged and customized for a developing-country market smoothed away innumerable problems at the stage of assembly, eased the task of manufacturing components, and simplified the setting up of engine manufacturing in Shanghai (Shaiken 1991). As other producers struggle to launch a first generation of cars, Volkswagen is ready to move into the next generation, having invested $300 million and spent the past decade accumulating hard-won experience with manufacturing in China's state sector.[9] This firm will face competition on its home turf from General Motors, which in 1997 entered into a $1.57 billion contract with Shanghai Auto Industry Corp., to produce Buick sedans.

Fashion Garments

The car industry is one of Shanghai's new leading sectors that are making good use of the agglomeration economies at hand. At the other end of the industrial spectrum is a subsector that still has plenty of life but must take some strong medicine if it is to remain competitive. Shanghai once was China's largest textiles producer. With almost 500 mills employing close to 500,000 workers and $2.4 billion in exports in 1992, it is second only to Guangdong.[10] But to survive, Shanghai must move upscale and into high-quality apparel.

Modern high-technology production of apparel is research- and information-intensive, requiring, if not proximity to markets, then continuous feedback on demand and shifting tastes. It puts great store in design, type of material, quality, and finish. Sophistication in design has special importance, and the application of computer techniques has raised the technological stakes. Improvements in design must go hand in hand with careful choice of material and access to modern dyeing and finishing facilities if clothing is to appeal to exacting customers in exceedingly competitive markets. Competition is also responsible for the increasing specialization of apparel producers and suppliers of equipment. The continuous need to change weave, texture, and appearance calls for an interaction between designers and marketers, makers of clothing, and manufacturers of equipment.[11] The business relies on the ability to respond quickly to shifts in the market and to deliver lots of the desired scale with a lead time of a few months.

The trend is toward greater capital intensity at virtually every stage, including design and cutting. Expensive, highly specialized machinery is essential for finish, and mechanization also serves to hold down labor costs, although these costs are of less consequence in China, where wages are relatively low. The information system that links retailer to producer is tied to new communications technology. Warehousing and distribution are becoming inseparable from computer networks, and tight inventory control is one of the main determinants of competitiveness.[12]

Recognizing that survival depends on raising value added, Shanghai's producers are shifting to apparel, which now constitutes 80 percent of exports. Local designers have appeared and established themselves through regular fashion shows and advertising.[13] The large metropolitan market, China's most sophisticated, is a definite advantage, as is the vertically integrated production system, rich in skills of every sort. Nevertheless, only the most efficient and innovative producers will survive. Old facilities, an aging workforce, weak marketing skills, and a fledgling infrastructure to cope with design and marketing are all trouble-

Table 3.4 Foreign Trade in Shanghai, Selected Years, 1978–93

	1978		1980		1985		1990		1991		1993	
Indicator	Millions of U.S. dollars	Percent	Millions of U.S. dollars	Percent	Millions of U.S. dollars	Percent	Millions of U.S. dollars	Percent	Millions of U.S. dollars	Percent	Millions of U.S. dollars	Percent
Total exports	2,892.6	100.0	4,266.4	100.0	3,360.7	100.0	5,317.3	100.0	5,739.8	100.0	7,381.8	100.0
Light industry	1,636.0	56.6	2,325.0	54.5	1,966.0	58.5	3,388.0	63.7	3,451.0	60.1	—	—
Heavy industry	355.0	12.3	813.0	19.1	628.0	18.7	1,268.0	23.9	1,561.0	27.2	—	—
Agriculture	902.0	31.2	1,128.0	26.4	767.0	22.8	661.0	12.4	728.0	12.7	—	—
Export destinations												
Asia	1,363.4	47.1	1,914.5	44.9	1,475.4	43.9	2,557.2	48.1	2,955.1	51.5	4,175.4	56.6
Africa	289.6	10.0	326.8	7.7	151.8	4.5	138.2	2.6	163.3	2.8	204.8	2.8
Europe	915.2	31.6	1,361.8	31.9	850.7	25.3	1,142.7	21.5	1,108.7	19.3	1,072.8	14.5
United States	233.5	7.7	481.0	11.3	614.0	18.3	957.1	18.0	1,059.6	18.5	1,542.9	20.9
Others	101.0	3.5	182.2	4.3	268.8	8.0	522.1	9.8	453.2	7.9	386.0	5.2
Total imports[a]	132.8	100.0	239.9	100.0	1,812.9	100.0	2,110.5	100.0	2,303.8	100.0	5,349.9	n.a.
For production	111.8	84.2	156.9	65.4	1,620.8	89.4	2,027.9	96.1	2,130.0	92.5	—	n.a.
For consumption	21.0	15.8	83.0	34.6	192.1	10.6	82.6	3.9	173.7	7.5	—	n.a.
Commodity trade balance	2,759.9	n.a.	4,026.5	n.a.	1,547.8	n.a.	3,206.9	n.a.	3,436.1	n.a.	2,031.9	n.a.

n.a. Not applicable.
— Not available.
a. Includes only imports purchased with municipal foreign exchanges.
Source: State Statistical Bureau, *Statistical Yearbook of Shanghai,* 1992, 1994.

some handicaps. Parts of the industry will not be able to muster the needed capital and skills and will be squeezed out, although the silk industry, for instance, could consolidate its position as a leading sector. China commands 70 percent of the world market for silk and has few competitors in a wide range of products.

Diseconomies: State-Owned Enterprises and Infrastructure

Even though Shanghai grasped reforms by slow degrees, the city provides rich soil for fresh entrepreneurship. Collective enterprises have enlarged their share of output and provided the local state-owned enterprises with their first dose of serious competition. Skills and industrial traditions, not to mention the pull of a vibrant commercial history, are the basis for the spread of producer services—banking, finance, consulting, and information—that are contributing to industrial efficiency and providing an additional impetus to growth of the metropolitan economy. Clearly, agglomeration effects, once released by reforms, can powerfully reinforce the conventional sources of growth, although in Shanghai's case the disabilities of a sprawling state sector and the poverty and attendant congestion of the transport infrastructure undermine the advantages of agglomeration.

Shanghai's state-owned enterprises include some of the most dynamic industrial entities in the country. Through their own efforts and with the help of imported technology, these enterprises are gradually drawing abreast of their competitors in East Asia in terms of productive efficiency and quality. Shanghai's exports nearly tripled between 1978 and 1993, and much of the $7.4 billion in goods exported in 1993 was produced by the state sector (see table 3.4).[14]

But the average state enterprise is in poor health and struggles with serious disabilities (in 1996, about 30 percent were losing money). Many enterprises have been in existence for two or three decades, their cramped facilities in the central city are frequently run-down, and their equipment is technologically obsolescent. The practice of providing the workforce with tenured employment, guaranteed pensions, and health, housing, and other benefits saddles each state-owned enterprise with overheads that are difficult to sustain as the shift to market-based pricing, rising interest costs, and the press of competition narrow their profit margins. Overstaffing, which inflates labor costs, and social security for an ever-growing pool of pensioners would be a serious drag on firms in any country, but in China, they compound the problems inherent in outdated management practices, excessive vertical integration,[15] the organization of the manufacturing process, work ethics, and relations with supervisory municipal industry bureaus. Such systemic disabilities are responsible for the financial losses of state-owned enterprises, which amounted to over half of total industrial losses in 1991 (see table 3.5).

Many state-owned enterprises have managed to revamp their operations and achieve financial health, but the persistence of soft budget constraints discourages initiatives, the tax system inhibits enterprises from striving for profitability, and the political economy of labor relations induces firms to honor their tenurial commitments to workers (Rawski 1992; Jefferson and Rawski 1994). The social consequences of large layoffs also dissuade municipal authorities, which own most of the state-owned enterprises, from pressing hard for a reduction of the enterprise workforce.

The actual and potential benefits of a many-layered industrial sector are manifold, but they are undermined by the continued preponderance of state-owned enterprises that have been slow to respond to the challenge of modernization and have imposed a heavy fiscal burden on the municipality. Enterprise reform, by changing the incentive regime, is forcing state-owned enterprises to become competitive, but it will be many years before the legacy of state-owned enterprise problems will be whittled down to insignificance.[16] A partial solution may be found in an experiment launched in 1995 that created a mergers-and-acquisitions market in which assets from state-owned enterprises can be sold to the highest bidder. It is likely that contracts will constrain buyers from shut-

Table 3.5   Loss-Making Industrial Enterprises in Shanghai and Tianjin, 1987–94

| City and year | Loss-making enterprises | | Total losses | | Losses of state-owned enterprises | |
	Number	Percentage of total enterprises	Billions of yuan	Percentage of net value of industrial output	Billions of yuan	Percentage of total losses
Shanghai						
1987	674	7.4	0.12	0.4	0.03	25.9
1988	660	6.8	0.23	0.7	0.12	53.1
1989	1,127	11.0	0.57	1.5	0.37	64.5
1990	1,793	17.7	1.47	3.8	1.01	68.3
1991	1,594	15.6	1.35	3.0	0.75	55.6
1992	1,632	19.2	1.15	2.1	—	—
1993	2,029	20.1	1.69	—	0.65	38.5
1994	2,818	19.6	3.76	—	1.88	50.0
Tianjin						
1987	600	12.3	0.13	1.3	0.08	64.3
1988	551	10.8	0.19	1.6	0.11	57.8
1989	776	14.5	0.69	5.6	0.57	82.0
1990	1,032	19.0	1.11	8.5	0.86	78.0
1991	999	18.0	1.20	8.8	0.85	71.0
1992	1,131	19.1	1.50	9.8	—	—
1993	1,990	10.4	2.08	—	1.48	71.2
1994	2,579	22.9	1.79	—	0.88	49.2

— Not available.
Source: State Statistical Bureau, *Yearbook of Industrial Statistics,* various years; *Statistical Yearbook of China,* various years.

tering factories and laying off workers. At this stage, the exchange is not open to foreigners, but there are plans to include them in the future. Reinforcing this experience, a program introduced in 1996 aims to convert 80 percent of all state-owned enterprises into limited-liability companies over a five-year period (*Business Week*, March 13, 1995; "Shanghai," Oxford Analytica, June 4, 1996).

The state of urban infrastructure, which was starved of capital throughout the Maoist era, makes it hard to realize the full extent of agglomeration economies.[17] As table 3.6 indicates, per capita paved roads and living space in Shanghai were lower than the national urban average in 1990. Shanghai was ahead of Tianjin on all but one count, Tianjin having more than twice the area of paved roads as Shanghai and two-thirds more than Guangzhou by 1994. Shanghai also compares favorably with Guangzhou in the availability of public transport. But Guangzhou is better endowed than Shanghai and Tianjin in many respects, particularly per capita living space and consumption of water and electricity. While the comparative perspective shows Shanghai in one light, the absolute numbers are much more telling. Living conditions in China's cities are spartan, and both transport and communications facilities fall far short of standards reached by other East Asian countries (see table 3.7). The housing shortage reflects the steady growth of population, which has outpaced the expansion of urban areas and the determined effort to renovate older living quarters, mainly row houses and bungalows, and to construct apartment buildings on the outskirts of the city.[18]

A significant housing reform plan was launched in 1991, introducing a new mechanism of housing finance. It stipulated that the city, employers, and employees would all contribute to a compulsory fund. Other elements of the housing reform scheme included increase in rent, use of housing coupons, discounts for buyers of housing units, and establishment of a housing commission. Shanghai's plan was much more comprehensive than plans in other cities, and it has attracted attention across China (Wang and Murie 1996). There has been some further progress since the start of housing reform during the early 1990s. For instance, a Y3.4 billion savings fund had been raised to finance new housing construction, the rebuilding of old endangered housing, and mortgage loans for commercially produced units.[19]

Shanghai's graceful tree-lined boulevards were designed for an age when the ricksha was the linchpin of urban transport. The system coped when bicycles displaced rickshas after 1949, but problems surfaced when the number of automobiles began increasing after the mid-1980s. In the early 1990s, the tempo of automobility quickened appreciably, and mixed traffic conditions gave rise to severe congestion along the major arteries virtually throughout the day. For instance, it can take up to two hours to cover the short distance from Pudong to the Bund. Currently much of the traffic is composed of bicycles and public transport. The continued

Table 3.6 Urban Infrastructure of Shanghai, Tianjin, and Guangzhou, 1990 and 1994

	Shanghai		Tianjin		Guangzhou		National urban
Indicator	1990	1994	1990	1994	1990	1994	average, 1990
Per capita living space (square meters)	6.6	7.5	6.7	7.1	8.0	8.4	6.9
Per capita paved road (square meters)	2.3	3.5	4.9	7.1	3.0	4.7	2.7
Public transportation per 100 residents	8.5	13.8	3.2	5.6	4.1	10.2	1.8
Telephone installation per 100 residents	9.0	—	4.9	—	9.2	—	2.7
Per capita electricity consumption (1,000 volts per hour)	144.1	—	98.0	—	169.0	—	80.1
Access to faucet water (percent)	100.0a	100.0	77.8a	100.0	87.8a	98.1	81.0b
Per capita water consumption (tons)	81.9	—	42.9	—	173.5	—	63.7
Natural gas usage (percent)	46.1	80.8	48.0	90.8	2.3	85.2	8.1
As a percentage of the national urban average in 1990							
Per capita living space	95.9		97.2		116.6		
Per capita paved road	85.2		181.5		111.1		
Public transportation	472.2		177.8		227.8		
Telephone installation	332.0		179.4		338.6		
Per capita electricity consumption	179.9		122.3		211.0		
Access to faucet water, 1987	123.5		96.0		108.4		
Per capita water consumption	128.6		67.3		272.4		
Natural gas usage	569.1		592.6		28.4		

— Not available.

a. 1987 data.

b. 1985 data.

Source: State Statistical Bureau, *China: Urban Statistical Yearbook*, 1988, 1991; *Statistical Yearbook of China*, 1995.

Table 3.7 Indicators for Infrastructure in Selected Countries, Various Years

Indicator	Brazil	China	Hong Kong (China)	Indonesia	Japan	Rep. of Korea	Mexico	Singapore	Thailand
Telephone installation per 100 residents, 1990	6.3	2.0[a]	43.4	0.6	44.1	31.0	6.6	38.5	2.4
Access to safe water, urban (percent), 1990	95.0	89.2	99.0	65.0	—	100.0	89.0	100.0	85.0
Households with electricity (percent), 1984	79.4	—	—	14.2	—	100.0	74.6	98.3	43.0
Paved road (kilometers per 1 million persons), 1988	703.6	640.0[b]	—	159.7	6,007.4	236.1	820.2	—	513.4
Roads in good condition (percent), 1988	30.0	—	—	29.9	—	69.9	84.9	—	50.0
Fixed investment, housing (percent of GDP), 1985	—	—	6.2	—	3.4	4.6	4.4	13.5	3.6
Fixed investment, transport (percent of GDP), 1985	—	1.3	1.3	—	3.0	3.2	3.0	4.9	1.9

— Not available.
Note: GDP, gross domestic product.
a. 1993 figure.
b. 1990 figure for cities.
Source: World Bank, World Development Report, various years; Social Indicators of Development, various years; State Statistical Bureau, Statistical Yearbook of China, 1994.

Figure 3.2   Shanghai and Its Environs

64

inadequacy of bus transport and the limited use of mass rail transit systems mean that bicycles and walking are still the principal means of transport in China's cities, including the three covered in this study (see Kubuta and Kidokoro 1994). Nevertheless, the number of private vehicles is rising steadily, further straining the antiquated road system.

Somewhat belatedly, both central and municipal authorities have begun attempting to alleviate Shanghai's transport bottlenecks. During 1990 and 1993, Y20 billion was invested in large infrastructure projects, while new investment is running at the same level each year. Projects include two completed bridges across the Huangpu River and a tunnel underneath, an overhead inner-ring road, an outer-ring road, a six-lane north-south expressway along Chengdu Road, a new airport (to the east of Pudong), and new power plants. Shanghai's port is being upgraded so as to accommodate a much larger traffic in containers, and procedures are being streamlined to expedite the flow of freight. Under construction at great speed is a subway system, which is supported by foreign capital and technology. This will take some of the pressure off Shanghai's choked streets once sections of it become operational. The first phase of the subway system, which is a single 10-mile-long track with 13 stations, was completed in April 1995. The $680 million project took just five years to complete, a feat unrivaled by other countries. A second 18-mile segment that is expected to become operational by 2000 will connect East Pudong with western Shanghai.

Shanghai's future economic prospects rest in part on the successful completion of industrial and infrastructure projects in the old city. They also depend in part on the development of Pudong (see figure 3.2), a zone akin in certain respects to the Shenzhen Special Economic Zone and five-sixths the size of Singapore, and in part on a closer integration of the municipal economy with that of the lower Yangtze region. Constructed after 1990, Pudong is in fact a new city (see Jacobs and Hong 1994). It has an industrial area of about 18 square kilometers, out of a total area of 500 square kilometers, and encompasses six special zones: Jinqiao (export processing of high-technology products in large-scale operations), Huamu (residential, commercial, financial, and cultural facilities), Liuli (metallurgical and construction industries), Lujazui (finance and trade zone across from the Bund that will be a center of producer services), Waigaoqiao (export processing and petrochemicals and energy), and Zhangjiang (scientific, research, and educational facilities). The development of Pudong, divided into three phases and with $36 billion of government investment, is designed to relieve spatial pressures on old Shanghai (the Puxi area) and to provide a framework for infrastructure planning and development, with concessionary policies for foreign investors.[20] Perhaps even more ambitious, work commenced on a second international airport south of Pudong in 1995. With both sea and air transport capacity, Pudong can further enhance the city's trading capacity. In fact, the airport, which will be the biggest in Asia, and Waigaoqiao port are crucial to the emergence of Shanghai as a center of international commerce.

If the expectations are fully realized, Pudong will become the axis of the city's industry and commerce, particularly high-technology industrial and trading activities. By 1994 Pudong's GDP accounted for 15 percent of the total for Shanghai's, compared with a mere 8 percent in 1990 (Yeung 1996). Some major industrial and property developments have already taken shape in Pudong. China's biggest steel conglomerate, Baoshan Steel Corporation, has leased 82 acres of land for a giant steel plant to expand its production (*East Asian Executive Reports*, August 15, 1994). Japan's Yaohan Group, in partnership with Shanghai's No. 1 Yaohan Department Store, has built a $100 million shopping complex, one of the largest in Asia.[21] Meanwhile, Carrefour, the French hypermarket chain, is planning a major outlet, having opened one in Beijing. Pudong will also provide space for new industries such as packaging, and, in fact, the China National Packaging Corporation is going to construct a modern packaging zone. Since 1995 the Shanghai Securities Exchange and some other financial institutions have occupied new premises in Pudong, and starting in 1996 foreign banks could open branches there. Pudong's growth rate during 1994–95 averaged more than 26 percent a year, and by mid-1996 contracted foreign direct investment (FDI) in 3,900 enterprises had reached $10.3 billion (see Oxford Analytica, February 4, 1997).

But caution is needed, because even Pudong's success cannot solve the problems facing the metropolis; it can only assist and, in essence, be a catalyst for the city's modernization. Moreover, the price of industrial land is steep, and the quality of services provided needs to be improved.[22] Many manufacturers prefer other special districts in the city, such as the Minhang District, in the southwest of Shanghai, which is adjacent to the airport and an expatriate community housing estate. As a consequence, much of the industrial and office space in Pudong's Waigaoqiao Free Trade Zone remained unoccupied in mid-1997.

Neighborhood Effects

Shanghai has the most prosperous economic hinterland of any city in China (Jacobs and Hong 1994). In the pre-1949 period, linkages with the hinterland and the spillover benefits from proto-industrialization in the neighboring provinces, along with the buoyancy of regional commerce, contributed significantly to Shanghai's prosperity. However, in the years following liberation, Shanghai's ties with its hinterland weakened. A number of factors were responsible for this growing isolation. The deliberate effort to cast Shanghai in the role of "producer" city has already been noted. Shanghai imported industrial materials from across China and in turn provided the country with manufactures and capital equipment. Each province, including the two immediately adjacent to Shanghai (Jiangsu and Zheijiang), attempted to create a relatively self-contained industrial economy and buttressed their attempts to achieve industrial autonomy by minimizing cross-provincial linkages and instituting administrative controls on the flow of trade. Rigidly enforced greenbelt regulations restricted rural industrialization in the immediate environs of Shanghai in an effort to contain the spread of the city into the adjacent farmland. Urbanization in the areas of Jiangsu close to Shanghai was also restricted so that the closest urban settlements, such as Changzhou, Jiaxing, and Suzhou, were arrayed 100 kilometers away.

Once reform commenced and the advantages of closer regional integration became apparent, central and municipal governments cobbled together the lower Yangtze economic region in 1982 to coordinate development and begin dismantling trade barriers between Shanghai and the neighboring provinces. This effort soon foundered, but linkages nevertheless multiplied as mutual interests began overriding bureaucratic obstacles and growth-creating effects became manifest. For Jiangsu's flourishing agricultural economy, Shanghai was the preferred source of consumer goods and a range of household durables. Township and village enterprises that proliferated in southern Jiangsu and nearby Zheijiang turned to Shanghai for skills, equipment, and markets. Many of these were established by workers who were transferred from Shanghai in the 1970s and not permitted to return because of population controls. Retirees from Shanghai's state-owned enterprises returning to home villages in Jiangsu or emigrating from the city because of enticing salaries provided much-needed technical skills for setting up factories and supervising production.[23] Thus former Shanghainese made it easier for rural-based producers in southern Jiangsu to obtain equipment and technical support from Shanghai.

Enterprises in Shanghai quickly discovered the advantages of moving some production facilities out of the city and entering into subcontracting arrangements with manufacturers in the hinterland. Such subcontracting allowed enterprises to rationalize production and cut the expenses of extreme vertical integration. Through much of the 1980s, enterprises wanting to relocate facilities had to leapfrog the protected belt of farmland girding Shanghai and to transplant production in Jiangsu or Zheijiang. But after 1988, the ban on rural industry within the municipal precincts was relaxed, and the immediate hinterland became part of an industrial continuum extending from the city into the lower Yangtze region. Shanghai's economic neighborhood now embraces 45 of the 100 richest small towns in China, all of which lie in the Sunan area (*China Focus*, October 1, 1994). Its interconnectedness derives additional force from the multimodal transport network that is being rapidly improved by investment in road, rail, and canal infrastructure.

Neighborhood effects have taken close to a decade to flower and are beginning to reshape the regional economy to the advantage of all par-

Table 3.8   Education of the Labor Force in Selected Sectors in Shanghai, 1990

Indicator	Industry		Transport		Research and development		Government	
	Thousands of employees	Percent	Thousands of employees	Percent	Thousands of employees	Percent	Thousands of employees	Percent
Total	4,252.3		344.2		98.5		291.4	
Level of education								
University	84.5	2.0	8.5	2.5	32.6	33.1	18.9	6.5
Community college	167.6	3.9	13.5	3.9	16.5	16.7	42.0	14.4
Vocational school	169.0	4.0	19.2	5.6	10.2	10.4	30.3	10.4
Senior high school	1,041.6	24.5	88.1	25.6	18.2	18.5	74.7	25.6
Junior high school	1,997.1	47.0	155.0	45.0	17.8	18.1	92.0	31.6
Elementary school	646.1	15.2	49.4	14.4	2.8	2.8	28.9	9.9
None	146.4	3.4	10.3	3.0	0.5	0.5	4.4	1.5
Nature of work								
Technical	378.9	8.9	38.5	11.2	53.8	54.6	67.8	23.3
Administration	125.6	3.0	10.3	3.0	6.0	6.1	58.9	20.2
Staff	185.2	4.4	38.2	11.1	8.5	8.6	109.4	37.5
Sales	123.7	2.9	6.4	1.9	1.6	1.6	8.2	2.8
Services	291.3	6.9	30.5	8.9	4.4	4.5	16.0	5.5
Production	3,141.8	73.9	219.3	63.7	23.8	24.1	29.4	10.1
Other	5.8	0.1	0.9	0.3	0.5	0.5	1.6	0.5

Note: Numbers may not sum to totals because of rounding.
Source: State Statistical Bureau 1992b.

ticipants. Under the planning system, urban centers pursued industrial diversification. This approach is giving way to a pattern of greater specialization and increased trade. To the extent that exit barriers to state-owned enterprises permit, Shanghai is gaining the freedom to expand high-technology and human capital–intensive industries in which it has a comparative advantage. It has also begun concentrating on producer services that supply sophisticated industries with capital, information, and skills. If the trend persists—and the resurgence in growth during the first half of the 1990s suggests that it should—Shanghai and its hinterland will come to resemble other large industrial regions such as the Kanto plain in Japan and the belt connecting São Paulo with Rio de Janeiro in Brazil (see Becker and Egler 1992; Park and Markusen 1995). By 1995 the Yangtze delta region accounted for one-third of China's total industrial output, compared with 10 percent for Guangdong.

Human Capital and Technology

Human, financial, and fiscal resources provide industrial leverage. Until recently, restraints on migration (especially of skilled labor), the virtual absence of capital mobility, and the modest extent of fiscal redistribution meant that local effort at mobilizing resources was essential for growth to become self-sustaining. Although barriers to the movement of resources remain, they are not as constrictive and will become progressively less meaningful in the second half of the 1990s. Nevertheless, municipal efforts to build skills, raise capital, and attract foreign investment remain profoundly important. Shanghai entered the 1980s with a handsome endowment of human capital and a solid tax base, albeit largely in the grip of the central government. Initial attempts to mobilize local resources were diffuse and yielded limited dividends. Since 1988 increased support from the central government and a more determined reform drive have brightened the picture.

Compared with those of other industrial cities in China, Shanghai's workforce commands an impressive range of educational skills. Most workers have an elementary education or better, and the vast majority have at least graduated from junior high school. For instance, in industry, 85 percent of workers have completed a minimum of eight grades and 6 percent have some college education. The shares are much higher in transport, government, and, of course, R&D (see table 3.8). The state sector employs close to 900,000 technical personnel and more than 40,000 scientific and technological professionals working in state-owned enterprises, research institutes, and universities. The city hosts at least 266 independent research institutes. In addition, there are nearly 50 universities and colleges, 28 of which are under the jurisdiction of central ministries or commissions.[24] With 37 postdoctorate research centers, these universities have become the cradle for young research scientists and produce several hundred research findings every year, but so far a shortage of funds has prevented the commercial development of many promising ideas.[25]

Research institutes are scattered across many different university, ministerial, agency, and even enterprise jurisdictions. In the majority of cases, they tend to concentrate on their own narrow fields and lack multiple contacts with researchers in neighboring disciplines. Until recently, commercial orientation was weak, and neither the mix of staff nor the incentives in many institutes were conducive to high-quality research, its patenting, or its application. This appears to be changing as stringent budgets force institutes to compete for contracts from the enterprise sector.

Although China's economy has grown at double-digit rates since 1993, the demands of infrastructure have absorbed a large volume of investment and constrained the availability of public resources for scientific research. China spent $7.5 billion in 1993 on science and technology, about a third of which went to R&D. Of this, less than 40 percent was devoted to research. China's senior leaders recognize this stagnation and intend to triple the funding to reach 1.5 percent of GDP by 2000. In 1994 the central government spent $275 million on research, a 13 percent increase over 1993 ("Leaders Pledge More for a Shrinking Pool," *Science* 268, June 9, 1995; "The Long March to Topnotch Science," *Science* 270, November 17, 1995). Nevertheless, the strain on funds means that university science departments and research institutes must generate part of their own revenue. Shanghai's leaders have enthusiastically endorsed the new policies and are providing a small pot of money that local scientists can use to attract larger sums from other sources.[26] But the financing of research is likely to remain a problem, even as the research imperative acquires greater force.

The Infrastructure of Finance

Human resources can be used fruitfully only if a sufficient supply of financial capital is generated and industrial initiatives are adequately backstopped by producer services. After a lengthy period of gestation in the 1980s, the city is finding its stride, and financial development is proceeding apace, albeit not without difficulties. Indigenous banking activities commenced in the mid-nineteenth century, and by the end of the century foreign banks had also arrived on the scene. By 1947 there were 128 government- and privately owned banks, 14 foreign banks, 13 trust companies, and 79 money exchanges, whose activities spanned the entire country (Fung, Yan, and Ning 1992).

Following a period of dormancy, financial reforms, introduced in small doses throughout the 1980s, promoted the institutional elaboration of the banking industry and of capital markets. This was inevitably a halting process because banks were inexperienced, financial skills were lacking, and three decades of socialism had engendered a high degree of caution. Early attempts to create an interbank market to permit a regional pooling of financial resources and to provide both households as well as enterprises with a wider range of instruments had just begun to achieve momentum when these innovations were put on hold. Stabilization measures and direct controls were first applied tentatively in late 1988 to arrest inflationary pressures and were then exerted with redoubled force following the Tiananmen incident in mid-1989 (see World Bank 1990 for an account of China's macropolicies during 1988–90). After 1988 interprovincial credit flows through the banking system slowed to a trickle, and financial development resumed only in 1991.

Until the very start of the 1990s financial resource mobilization was treated with utmost passivity. By and large, banks and urban credit cooperatives collected household savings and allocated these in accordance with guidelines handed down by the People's Bank of China or municipal supervisory agencies. There was little attempt to stimulate savings, which were admittedly high, by offering attractive rates on a variety of instruments. Nor was allocative efficiency, using market channels, pursued systematically and with reference to clear goals. Many ad hoc experiments were launched, and these only began to coalesce and acquire the semblance of a coherent program in the early 1990s. The financial initiative with the greatest promise for Shanghai was the setting up of a stock market in December 1990.[27] The initial significance of this market has little to do with the mobilization of resources or the effective disposition of capital. Rather its importance lies in its symbolic value and the inducement it gives to institution building.[28] An active and growing stock market is tangible evidence of successful transition. It also pushes the enterprise sector to improve its financial performance, pay greater attention to auditing and accounting practices, accept the need for legal discipline, and be willing to abide by the letter of the rules.

With each passing month the Shanghai Stock Exchange is adding to its fund of financial experience, engendering investor confidence, and staking Shanghai's claim to becoming a world-class player. It is also attracting funds that local businesses urgently need to modernize industry. By the end of 1995, the Shanghai Stock Exchange had about 7 million registered investors (IFC 1996). The combined capitalization of the Shanghai and Shenzhen markets is expected to reach $168 billion by the end of 1997 (*Financial Times*, July 28, 1997). Although government agencies still hold a high proportion of the market's capitalized value, individuals and other entities have already demonstrated their willingness to invest. As its listings expand in the future, the stock exchange will pull in many more investors from outside the municipality, initially from other locales in the lower Yangtze region.[29] Starting in January 1992, the issue of shares in corporatized state-owned enterprises to overseas investors was a significant step toward broadening the market.

Financial reform and the attempt to raise the technological tenor of industrial activity have created a market for a broad range of producer services. Shanghai has designated six service industries as the top priorities of development. These include finance and insurance, commerce and trade, telecommunications and transportation, real estate, tourism, and information. The first three subsectors have already become the driving force behind Shanghai's service industry, contributing about 73 percent of the sector's value added in 1993. The service sector as a whole accounted for 38 percent of the city's GDP, and employment exceeded 170,000 in 1994 (FBIS-CHI-94167, August 29, 1994, p. 69).[30] Since 1990 the city has opened exchanges for securities, metals, coal, farm production materials and equipment, chemicals, grains and edible oils, motor vehicles, building materials, and technology. In the coming years, there are plans to expand the money market (already China's largest), as well as the markets for securities, foreign exchange, and insurance (FBIS-CHI-94107, June 3, 1994, p. 43). In the Huangpu, Jingan, and Zhabei districts, clusters of private and cooperative consulting firms provide a wide range of services. The Shanghai Academy of Social Sciences set up a consultancy center as early as 1979 to provide economic, legal, and public opinion services. This network, and the approximately 1,000 computer science graduates from local tertiary institutions, made possible the export of computer software services (primarily to Japan) during the 1980s. It reflects Shanghai's superior human skills and points toward a type of activity in which Shanghai may have a real comparative advantage. A rich stock of technical manpower has given life to small businesses offering consulting services and undertaking research contracts.[31]

Financial services are perhaps the largest and fastest-growing subsector, gradually opening a variety of activities. More than 2,200 banking organizations have branches and offices in the city, including 117 branches of foreign banks at the end of 1995 (in all, 137 foreign financial institutions were in Shanghai by the close of 1995, with assets of $18 billion; FBIS-CHI-94103, May 27, 1994, p. 57; "Renminbi Business," Oxford Analytica, April 5, 1996). The British Standard Chartered Bank, which dates back to 1858 and retained its presence throughout the post-1949 period, leads the way. Citibank has shifted the headquarters of its Chinese business from Hong Kong to Shanghai, and many others are expected to follow suit. So far, foreign banks have mainly concentrated their activity in the lucrative area of trade finance and cash settlement of B share issues, but eight foreign banks were allowed to engage in Chinese currency business as an experiment in late 1996 (Oxford Analytica, February 4, 1997). Loans to Chinese enterprises are still largely arranged in Hong Kong.

At the beginning of 1993, the country's first batch of 31 professional brokers to be licensed by the state government for forward trading of treasury bonds started working at the Shanghai Stock Exchange. In November a technology brokerage office was opened to attract domestic and overseas brokers and promote technological exchanges (FBIS-CHI-93225, November 24, 1993, p. 46). By July 1994 Tullet & Tokyo Forex

International Ltd., the world's largest transnational currency brokerage company, had set up its first representative office in Shanghai and planned to set up a branch company in the near future to connect with its other four branches in Australia, Hong Kong, Singapore, and Tokyo (see FBIS-CHI-94134, July 13, 1994, p. 39). It was the first overseas currency brokerage institution to receive government approval. The municipal government has also begun rebuilding the Bund, the famous area along the Huangpu River, which housed 113 bank buildings before 1949, as China's Wall Street. Housing management units have established a special institute to help relocate government departments in the former buildings lining the street. Quite a few buildings have already been vacated and have changed ownership (FBIS-CHI-94016, January 25, 1994, p. 81).

The number of persons employed in the securities market has grown rapidly. Shanghai International Securities, the country's largest stockbroker, employed a staff of 120 in 1991; this had grown to 1,500 in 1994. Arthur Anderson, a big transnational accountancy firm, has 120 employees in Shanghai, compared with a mere handful in the early 1990s. Bear Stearns, Goldman Sachs, Merrill Lynch, Morgan Stanley, and Nikko are among the many financial firms now present in the city. However, the local stock market remains too restricted for much foreign investment. Many foreign investors also prefer those Chinese companies listed in Hong Kong and New York. Shares of Chinese firms in Hong Kong are four times more liquid than B shares in Shanghai when measured by turnover per share.[32]

Since 1992 some drastic reform measures have been introduced in the financial sector. For instance, the Shanghai Foreign Exchange Swap Market, founded in 1986, has removed the ceiling for exchange quotation and position to allow individuals to trade foreign currency freely. Another major step in 1994 nudges various state-owned specialized banks into becoming commercial banks through the pursuit of "risk-related management." Credit cooperatives in both urban and rural areas are also being turned into cooperative banks to help spur the growth of the local economy (FBIS-CHI-94004, January 6, 1994, p. 58). To involve local banks in the foreign exchange business, the People's Bank of China set up an unusual U.S. dollar clearing center in Shanghai; this is the first not only in the country but also in the world. In April 1994 China's first interbank currency market opened in Shanghai, replacing the fragmented system of currency swap centers. In August the Shanghai Securities Exchange was already doing on-line business linked with 15 other securities exchange centers throughout the country. Moreover, the People's Bank of China and the Ministry of Finance selected the exchange as the base on which to establish the issuing, trading, and clearing of treasury bonds.

Aside from the producer services that are fairly closely associated with industry, Shanghai's agglomeration economies are a stepping-stone to other services that sustain the economies of cities such as New York. These are advertising, book publishing, fashion design, and media conglomerates active in television, magazines, and newspapers. Although the ease of transferring information by electronic means has lessened the importance of propinquity and hence the need for firms to locate their offices in a central business district, the media industry still thrives on face-to-face encounters and draws its lifeblood from the meetings, lunches, informal encounters, and frequent exchanges of gossip that are most easily conducted within a large, densely populated city. Getting information at the earliest possible stage, maintaining social relations, and making deals require personal interaction and not merely an exchange of information by way of computers, which nevertheless also greatly facilitate media-related and publishing activities. Many of the industries that once buttressed New York's prosperity, such as textiles and meat packing, have long since deserted the city, which has ceased to be a regional transport hub. But all those activities whose consummation depends on propinquity, such as finance, publishing, and fashion garments, have remained because New York is the ideal urban arena in spite of the drawbacks posed by congestion, crime, and public services of uneven quality (Sassen 1991).

The services that now sustain New York's economy are at an embryonic stage in Shanghai. But they are bound to grow exponentially, and Shanghai more than any other city in China can, with some effort, achieve a commanding lead over other aspirants. It certainly has the advantages of scale, the pool of talent, the industrial diversity, and the supportive traditions from an earlier era. However, the city must enhance its physical and cultural attributes if it is to attract service activities with a high income elasticity. This will require investment, of which much will have to be found locally, but some might be sought abroad.

Capital Flows and Industry

When China cautiously opened the door to foreign investment in 1978, the trickle of capital first flowed into the Special Economic Zones and the open cities in Guangdong and Fujian. In fact, the pattern of FDI through the first half of the 1980s favored the southeast region (see chapter 5). The overwhelming majority of investors were businessmen from Hong Kong and Macao wanting to move some of their assembly-line operations to a familiar part of China. Moreover, other "open cities" such as Tianjin and Shanghai were much less aggressive in bidding for FDI and, to a degree, were constrained by the reform mandates assigned to them by the central government.

Until 1985 the cumulative investment utilized in Shanghai amounted to $232 million. A quickening of the efforts of Shanghai authorities to induce FDI in 1987–88 produced a temporary surge in 1987–89, but investor interest waned in 1990–91 as a result of Tiananmen. Deng

Xiaoping's visit to Guangdong in January 1992 and his strong endorsement of the reform drive galvanized all provincial players, in particular Shanghai, to seek foreign capital. Shanghai's own determined initiatives and a rapid rekindling of interest on the part of overseas investors brought a rush of funds, and utilized foreign investment increased almost tenfold, reaching $3.2 billion in 1993 (see table 3.9). Contracts with foreigners continued rising over the next two years so that total contractual investment exceeded $50 billion by the end of 1996, with Japan emerging as the leading investor, having committed $5 billion (*Financial Times*, April 9, 1997). In the second half of the 1980s, much of the FDI was in advanced manufacturing activities, the hotel industry, and affiliated travel services: for example, Volkswagen in automobiles, McDonnell Douglas in aircraft assembly, Pilkington in glass, and Foxboro, IBM, Xerox, and Wang in computers, copiers, and electronic equipment (U.S. Congress, Office of Technology Assessment, 1987). Between 1979 and 1993, about half of foreign investment was from Hong Kong, about a fifth from Japan, 12 percent from the United States, and the balance mostly from Europe (roughly two-thirds of all FDI in China originated in Hong Kong and Macao; see Jacobs and Hong 1994). Japanese money went into retailing, and other funds were drawn into real estate, hotels, infrastructure, power, and, of course, manufacturing.

The volume of FDI in Shanghai has not been large, although it is now assuming sizable proportions. During 1987–89 it was just about 8 percent of annual capital construction outlay. However, it played a catalytic role in several strategic sectors. Foreign capital and expertise were instrumental in equipping Shanghai with the hotel and other facilities of a caliber to attract long-distance tourists in large numbers. These facilities have also enhanced Shanghai's attractiveness for conventions and conferences. FDI helped initiate the modernization of commercial real estate, and Hong Kong financiers are responsible for a good proportion of the office buildings that are reshaping Shanghai's skyline. German investment rejuvenated the auto industry and has made Shanghai the most important producer of midsize sedans in China. The aircraft industry has derived much benefit from the local assembly of U.S. MD-82 passenger planes and the setting up of repair facilities in collaboration with Swissair. The electronics industry has begun obtaining badly needed capital and technology by way of joint ventures with major international corporations seeking entry into China's market. For instance, Intel is building a $50 million facility to assemble and test flash memory chips and micro controller devices. NEC decided in 1997 to build a $1 billion plant to manufacture state-of-the-art dynamic random access memory chips (DRAMs). And in mid-1997 Bell Labs entered into a multimillion-dollar venture with Chinese universities to develop telecommunications products for the Chinese market.

Real estate developers, the major hotel chains, and the multinationals have come to Shanghai because it has the potential to join the ranks of

Table 3.9 Foreign Investment in Shanghai, 1986–93
(millions of U.S. dollars, unless otherwise noted)

Indicator	1986	1987	1988	1989	1990	1991	1992	1993	1979–93
Utilized foreign investment	281.16	575.63	440.47	466.49	321.04	330.25	899.29	3,175.00	10,751.69
Loans	132.26	361.62	207.30	44.37	147.03	185.06	405.68	853.18	5,097.48
Direct investment	148.90	213.66	233.17	422.12	174.01	145.19	493.61	2,317.62	5,132.44
Other	—	0.35	—	—	—	—	—	4.20	521.77
Contracted foreign direct investment, by source	—	338.31	333.28	359.75	374.63	450.01	3,357.25	7,016.14	13,705.29
Hong Kong (China)	—	217.89	104.91	113.29	110.91	128.35	—	4,337.76	7,001.96
Percentage of Shanghai's total	—	64.4	31.5	31.5	29.6	28.5	—	61.8	51.1
Percentage of Hong Kong's total	—	11.7	2.9	3.4	2.7	1.8	—	—	—
Japan	—	4.60	22.10	27.71	23.93	131.69	—	370.15	1,190.06
Percentage of Shanghai's total	—	1.4	6.6	7.7	6.4	29.3	—	5.3	8.7
Percentage of Japan's total	—	2.1	7.4	7.8	11.1	18.3	—	—	—
United States	—	55.95	58.21	42.01	88.41	50.07	—	598.58	1,665.52
Percentage of Shanghai's total	—	16.5	17.5	11.7	23.6	11.1	—	8.5	12.2
Percentage of U.S. total	—	16.5	18.8	8.3	26.4	10.4	—	—	—
Taiwan (China)	—	—	—	7.52	101.81	31.44	—	540.00	916.89
Percentage of Shanghai's total	—	—	—	2.1	27.2	7.0	—	7.6	6.7
Percentage of Taiwan's total	—	—	—	1.7	10.3	2.6	—	—	—
Others	—	59.87	148.06	169.22	49.57	108.46	—	1,179.65	2,930.86
Percentage of Shanghai's total	—	17.7	44.4	47.0	13.2	24.1	—	16.8	21.4

— Not available.

Source: State Statistical Bureau, *Statistical Yearbook of China,* 1987, 1988, 1990, 1992, 1993; data by source for 1987–91, State Statistical Bureau 1992a; 1993 data from State Statistical Bureau, *Statistical Yearbook of Shanghai.*

world-class cities. A hundred years ago under quite different geopolitical circumstances, foreign capital and technology pushed Shanghai over the threshold into industrial modernity. Capital flowed to the city because its location was a great asset. A deepwater port and proximity to Japan conferred advantages not easily overlooked. Now foreigners are involved in a second industrial transformation for these reasons and fresh ones as well. In this round Shanghai is far better equipped to absorb capital and technology—it is after all China's foremost industrial city—and in sheer scale of manufacturing capability Shanghai has no rival in the developing world. The enemies of promise in Shanghai's case are the congestion-related diseconomies of great size and the problems associated with having invested too much in technology that is now outdated and in plant better suited to an earlier industrial era, in embracing organizational practices that are now seen to hobble competitiveness, and in adopting workplace rules that severely compromise enterprise flexibility even as reforms steadily enlarge the autonomy of industrial entities. A century ago, FDI helped Shanghai to sink new industrial roots. Now it is helping to stiffen the city's resolve to push ahead with systemic change and has contributed $1.83 billion during 1985–92 toward the renewal of production facilities. More important, it has insinuated new skills, new ideas, and new work habits into every major sphere of the municipal economy. Over the long term, that counts for much more. It is influencing grassroots receptivity to changes and preparing people in all domains of industry to meet the challenge posed by other cities in China and beyond.

Fiscal Relations and Revenue Generation

The story of resource mobilization would be incomplete without a further look at fiscal sources and potential. Under planning and well into the first decade of reform, Shanghai was the single most important element in the revenue system established by the central government, contributing nearly 83 percent of central revenues in 1981 (Jacobs and Hong 1994). However, Beijing controlled and reallocated much of this revenue. A succession of adjustments in tax arrangements between central and city governments have altered the municipality's fiscal circumstances.

Between 1949 and 1980, roughly 86 percent of Shanghai's revenue was remitted to the central government. This slowed urban development and placed industrial expansion largely in the hands of the central government.[33] The only discretionary income under the control of municipal authorities was derived from user fees on public services and surcharges, among which the one levied on the industrial and commercial tax was the most significant. With the start of reforms in 1978, the central authorities introduced a new decentralizing fiscal regime that visualized each provincial entity as a "separate kitchen." Under this arrangement, participating provinces were allowed a fixed and an adjustable share of revenues. They retained all income collected in excess of these ratios. In exchange for receiving a bigger slice of revenue, provinces were also required to accept responsibility for most expenditures.

Because of its strategic role as an industrial center and its revenue-gathering function, Shanghai was largely bypassed during this round of reforms, which conferred most of the advantages on the southeastern provinces. However, the central government did ease its tight grip on expenditure decisions, with the result that municipal spending rose moderately between 1980 and 1983 and tripled over the 1983–86 period. Increased expenditures were not matched by an upward shift in retained income. In fact, Shanghai's overall revenue situation deteriorated as reforms whittled away at price controls and cut centrally mandated resource allocation. In 1980 the average profit ratio for Shanghai's enterprises was 75 percent as against 24 percent for the whole country (Lin 1994). Four years later, the national average had fallen a percentage point, but the profit ratio for Shanghai's state-owned enterprises dropped to 63 percent. Both the central government and Shanghai municipality suffered an erosion in tax revenues, with the municipality's earnings decreasing almost 5 percent between 1980 and 1984.

Although Shanghai was allowed to keep 30 percent of the revenues collected above the planned targets and received an additional Y150 million in grants, these were inadequate. In 1980 the city received a further Y200 million and double this amount in the following year. These ad hoc contributions proved insufficient because growth of industry remained sluggish throughout the first half of the 1980s. As Shanghai's fiscal condition worsened, its political assertiveness mounted. It began lobbying intensively for easier treatment. Pressure from Party Secretary Jiang Zemin and Mayor Rui Xingwen, who came to power in 1983, finally carried the day. In 1984 the State Council approved a decree giving Shanghai Y1.5 billion over and above actual expenditures of Y2.26 billion in 1983. This translated into a retention ratio from municipal revenues of just under one-quarter (Lin 1994).

The fiscal injection permitted the city to take the first few steps toward improving urban infrastructure and housing. But with the profitability of state-owned enterprises continuing to sink (to 32 percent in 1988), and municipally controlled enterprises being especially hard-hit, Shanghai was compelled to approach the center in 1987, well before the six-year term of the fiscal contract had ended. What forced the municipality's hand was the steep rise in subsidies for enterprises and basic food items. By the mid-1980s Shanghai's industry was losing its lead over other provinces that had been quicker to exploit the opportunities posed by reform. Aging industrial plant and an excessive reliance on state-owned enterprises were beginning to tell. Once again Shanghai sought to renegotiate its fiscal contract with Beijing using its political ties with central leaders and citing its crucial significance for China's

Table 3.10   Fiscal Relations in Shanghai, 1980 and 1984–91
(billions of yuan, unless otherwise noted)

Indicator	1980	1984	1985	1986	1987	1988	1989	1990	1991
Revenue									
Total revenue	16.92	16.40	18.42	17.95	16.90	16.16	16.69	17.00	17.52
Budgetary income	16.68	—	18.16	—	—	—	—	16.27	16.51
Nonbudgetary income	0.24	—	0.26	—	—	—	—	0.73	1.01
Transport and energy funds	—	—	—	—	—	—	—	0.30	0.33
Self-financing income	0.24	—	0.26	—	—	—	—	0.43	0.68
Revenue sharing									
Total revenue	16.92	16.40	18.42	17.95	16.90	16.16	16.69	17.00	17.52
Remittances to the central government									
Amount	—	13.69	13.53	14.41	11.99	10.50	—	—	—
Percentage of revenue	—	83.5	73.4	80.3	71.0	65.0	—	65.0	—
Percentage of GDP	—	35.0	29.0	29.5	22.0	16.2	—	—	—
Local spending	1.92	3.03	4.61	5.91	5.39	6.59	7.33	7.56	8.61
Central subsidies									
Total fiscal subsidies	—	—	0.67	0.77	1.19	2.46	—	—	—
As a percentage of local expenditures	—	—	14.6	13.0	22.1	37.3	—	—	—

— Not available.
Note: GDP, gross domestic product.
Source: State Statistical Bureau, *Statistical Yearbook of Shanghai,* 1992; Lin 1994; Ho and Tsui 1996.

industrial future. The effort paid off, and in 1988 the city entered into a revised arrangement that gave Shanghai terms broadly similar to those enjoyed by Guangdong since the early 1980s. These entailed remitting a fixed annual sum of Y10.5 billion to Beijing during 1988–90 (see table 3.10). In 1991 and 1992 Shanghai was required to remit the base amount and half of all revenues collected in excess of Y10.5 billion. Along with the tax contract, Shanghai was allowed greater leeway in defining fiscal relations with county governments. Notionally, the municipality gained Y11.4 billion in supplementary revenues in 1988 and 1989. In reality, special payments to the central government of Y400 million in 1990 and Y570 million in the next two years ate into Shanghai's enlarged share. The net gain was modest, and it forced the municipal authorities to widen the ambit of resource mobilization.

Urged on by the central government, Shanghai launched a wide-ranging program of resource mobilization and expenditure management starting in 1990 using the full discretion allowed under the latest contract. First, the municipal authorities enlarged their take from user charges, which were raised in steps for a host of services. Second, fiscal extrabudgetary revenue was increased through fees and other levies on municipally controlled enterprises along the lines of other coastal provinces. Third, Shanghai began using the lucrative fiscal window opened by urban land reform to raise funds from the leasing of land. This is potentially of the highest significance.[34] Shanghai's population density, its relative prosperity, and the nature of commercial development now under way mean that real estate throughout the municipality is extremely valuable and likely to become even more so a few decades hence. In the foreseeable future, Shanghai's land market will rival those of Bombay, London, Seoul, and Tokyo.[35] More than 450 plots of land have been leased to foreigners in old central Shanghai on leases that vary from 50 to 80 years ("Shanghai's Amazing Property Boom," *Asiamoney*, October 1994, pp. 22–25). Although still small, this figure is bound to swell as land use in the central city is rationalized and made more intensive. Factories in the core city are being relocated or closed, and the land is being put to commercial use. More than 2,000 factories producing textiles, machine tools, and aerospace equipment are being relocated from the city center to rural counties to facilitate commercial development in the downtown area ("Factories Forced Out of Shanghai," *Wall Street Journal*, June 28, 1995), but much investment is needed before the city acquires a modern face.

Fourth, the attempt to enhance local property values and draw in capital from the outside is being spearheaded by the building of infrastructure. This is an avenue to resource mobilization in the medium run because it will stimulate local industry and attract funds to Shanghai. Over the long run, these trends will push up land values and, thereby, the tax base of the municipality. Fifth, Shanghai has initiated its own county-level fiscal decentralization so as to generate additional revenue and transfer some of the expenditure responsibilities to lower-level governments. Typically the formula used allows county finance bureaus to retain the right to a fixed proportion of revenues collected above a base value. This encourages greater tax effort, some of which contributes to the municipality's budget, while the assignment of expenditures improves the allocation of resources. By 1990 the net transfer from local governments to the municipality was on the order of Y80 million. Sixth, the development of Pudong described earlier brought Y6 billion in grants from the center. This was augmented by the flow of FDI into new businesses and infrastructure for the industrial district.

The fiscal picture for Shanghai has brightened considerably since 1990. The agreement reached with Beijing in 1988 was a good beginning, and it was usefully buttressed by subsequent actions, direct and indirect, to mobilize funds. Success at accelerating industrial growth beginning in 1992 strengthened revenue performance. It also demonstrated to skeptics that there is life yet in the old city. Shanghai's recent economic performance has allayed some of the fears of outsiders, whose interest was aroused by heightened municipal desire for FDI, by the money being poured into infrastructure, and by the promise of the Pudong project.

Fiscal experimentation is bound to continue. The tax package and intergovernmental sharing arrangements put into effect in January 1994, as they evolve, will affect Shanghai's finances, but the precise implications are far from clear. The new system is supposed to levy a universal tax rate on all provinces and cities directly under the central government. The trends regarding revenues are beginning to crystallize. It is likely that the importance of direct taxes and the value added tax will grow at the expense of extrabudgetary sources of revenue. User fees and real estate taxes will also bulk very large as Shanghai modernizes and in the course of doing so adopts the fiscal lineaments of a world-class city. Even the sharing arrangements with Beijing are not immutable. It is probable that some increment in Shanghai's revenues will have to be transferred to meet the central government's needs. But there is no likelihood of a reversal of decentralization, except on the margin. Municipalities such as Shanghai will continue to be responsible for most local expenditures and be assigned the revenues from local sources to pay for them. The extra revenue effort and expenditure efficiency, differentiating the dynamic cities from others, will depend on local initiative rather than central prompting.

Expenditure management is the other half of the fiscal equation. Fiscal health depends not just on raising revenue but also on keeping a close watch on expenditures. This has been problematic in a city such as Shanghai, with its armada of state enterprises and large tenured labor force. As reform has exposed the state sector to competition, many state-owned enterprises that have been unable to upgrade equipment, skills, and organization are running losses (for the country as a whole, 44 percent of state-owned enterprises were running losses in 1995, and more than two-thirds ran losses in 1996; United Press International, February 4, 1997). Municipal authorities are unwilling to countenance widespread closure because of the sociopolitical costs of unemployment in the absence of an adequate safety net. Even if unemployment compensation were available, many workers would consider that shutting down the large number of enterprises in distress would constitute breaking a social compact. The Shanghai municipality has shied away from mass closure and preferred to pay the fiscal penalty. A sizable part of the city's limited resources has gone into shoring up weak state enterprises. Additional funds have been swallowed up by subsidies for food and basic services. These fiscal burdens divert resources away from projects critical for Shanghai's modernization. Clearly, the significance of the state sector has been a handicap in the reform era. Some of the characteristics that made Shanghai an outstanding industrial player in the Maoist years have proved a handicap as liberalization has rapidly diminished the odds favoring state-owned enterprises.

Price reform in the early 1990s cut consumer subsidies and decreased fiscal pressure. Enterprise reform and the piecing together of a municipal social safety net have restored the health of some enterprises and increased the government's readiness to allow bankruptcy. For Shanghai and other cities, this administering of market medicine has extraordinary significance: it allows the municipality to gauge the social acceptability of market-based solutions, it adds to the weight of precedence, and it eases fiscal constraints. The gradual introduction of rational pricing schemes for municipal services beginning in the early 1990s reduced subsidies. Meanwhile, decentralization of spending decisions to the county level provided a useful check on the growth of expenditures and enhanced efficiency. Resources have been freed for uses that are more likely to yield the desired economic results.

Summary: Reform and Urban Development

Looking back over Shanghai's performance in the past 15 years, it is quite evident that nationwide reforms were responsible for creating an environment in which progress was feasible but that municipal policy actions were required to grasp the possibilities. There were externalities to be realized from industrial depth and neighborhood effects to be exploited, there was increasing scope for domestic resource mobilization, and there were inefficiencies of the state sector that could be remedied. But all these tasks demanded activism on the part of municipal and central authorities. By sketching the reform context and the unfolding of policy in Shanghai, it is possible to show how policy promoted urban modernization in a transition economy.

Six reform events serve to frame the experience of Shanghai. The first brought into existence the household responsibility system in the rural areas and, in stages, curtailed production quotas, state procurement at fixed prices, and constraints on the marketing of agricultural output. The result was a vast increase in agricultural productivity, which raised incomes and widened the markets for industrial products of cities such as Shanghai. Rural counties and townships used their newly gained freedom to expand industry, which generated employment, catered to rural demand, and gradually branched into a wide range of production activities. Reform induced rural development in Jiangsu and Zheijiang and enormously increased the prosperity of Shanghai's hinterland. Market linkages, greatly attenuated by socialist planning and control for more than three decades, resurfaced and provided stimulus and competition for Shanghai's industry, breathing new life into a regional economy that had been marking time throughout the 1970s.

A second change, instituted piecemeal, is the reversal of past emphasis on attaining self-sufficiency and on subdividing the country into a matrix of weakly connected provincial markets (Shue 1988). At first cautiously but then more openly, Beijing supported the formation of regional markets and their eventual coalescence into a national market.

Although initially painful for enterprises accustomed to being sheltered from competition, market integration has been crucial for realizing industrial scale economies (World Bank 1994a).

Third, the full benefits of market integration and a rich hinterland have been predicated on the successful implementing of enterprise reform. One of the reasons why China's urban industry has registered such a dismal record of productivity is its excessive vertical integration. Most large enterprises attempted to produce three-fourths or more of all essential intermediate inputs to minimize reliance on outside suppliers. Since the mid-1980s many enterprises have been encouraged to rationalize production and have made full use of a more open environment to subcontract components, specialize, and establish networking arrangements through which to exchange information and share overheads such as marketing or research. Thus enterprise reform, in conjunction with market integration, is critical to fully realizing agglomeration economies.

Fourth, one kind of neighborhood effect arises from the immediate hinterland. A second set is associated with FDI and international trade. The former is an important conduit for technology transfer at many levels; the latter enlarges market possibilities and provides the spur of competition. Starting with the joint venture law in 1979, which permitted foreign investment in four Special Economic Zones in Fujian and Guangdong, the Chinese government then opened another 14 coastal cities to overseas investors in 1984. Thereafter, a series of decrees elaborated the legal framework governing foreign investment and widened provincial discretion in dealing with investors. Apart from affording foreigners the right to invest in China, the government slowly loosened its monopoly over trade, decentralized the trading system, and allowed partial retention of foreign exchange earnings and, eventually, the trading of foreign exchange through special trading centers. Guangdong was the first to obtain these trade privileges, which were extended to Shanghai and Tianjin in 1983. For a variety of reasons, which are discussed in chapter 5, Guangzhou was the quickest to introduce reforms for the purposes of local development. The others followed with a lag.

The fifth reform initiative of far-reaching consequence was fiscal decentralization and the incentives for financial widening touched on above. Decentralization set the stage for intensive resource mobilization. It also enabled cities to start a virtuous spiral through investments that raised growth directly and via larger agglomeration economies. Higher growth improved revenue prospects and generated more capital, which fed the impulse to grow. The earliest reforms, other than those with a rural focus, were aimed at the southeastern coastal provinces. Other coastal cities began to benefit from the enabling environment first tested in Guangdong only about the middle of the 1980s.

Last, although Shanghai began asserting at least its fiscal rights after 1983, the city initially showed little determination to define and implement the policies necessary to modernize the economy. Even though Shanghai was an "open city," and foreign investors were clearly interested, the authorities did little to reduce red tape and use the incentive mechanisms at their disposal to bid for overseas capital. When, under prodding from the center and in response to the sluggishness of the municipal economy, the local government began trying in earnest, FDI increased sharply. Similarly, the urgency in dealing with the problems of municipally controlled state enterprises was slow to register. Reforming state enterprises posed formidable difficulties, political as well as economic. Tinkering on the margins was clearly insufficient, and a more determined assault would challenge powerful vested interests. It was easier to let matters drift.

Only the insistent pressure of fiscal need and the central government's unwillingness to bail out the city induced Shanghai from about the late 1980s to pursue a multipronged restructuring strategy with the assistance of international agencies. One prong encompassed vertical disintegration, subcontracting with township and village enterprises, and the shifting of production facilities to neighboring provinces, where land and labor are cheaper. Slow to gather momentum, these tendencies are accelerating with amazing speed now that the commitment of the local government is unequivocal. A second prong is the creation of "internal markets" for restructuring. Industrial bureaus are helping to set up industrial corporations, which bring together affiliated producers under a single organizational umbrella so as to precipitate the necessary rationalizing of production and trimming of overhead.

The building of a social security system independent of the enterprise—the third prong—frees firms of onerous obligations, weakens the iron bonds of tenure, and introduces flexibility into the labor market. Fourth, there is bankruptcy, which Shanghai was chary about using so long as its growth performance was weak and employment generation modest. As the economy has gathered speed and job prospects have multiplied in the service sector, resistance to closure of insolvent enterprise is less troublesome. Shanghai has begun translating the central government's broad mandate for enterprise reform. In many respects this is the most difficult hurdle on the road to modernization, but it is not an obstacle to be sidestepped. Enterprise reform has to be pursued to an industrially and fiscally acceptable conclusion through an incremental application of policy.

Shanghai's efforts to raise fiscal revenues, the remaining prong, have already been discussed. However, the city's initiatives in mobilizing financial resources deserve further attention. The central government's financial reforms selectively allowed certain provincial entities the right to issue construction bonds domestically, to raise money in international capital markets, and to permit enterprises to acquire funds by issuing shares to workers or others.

Borrowing from the international market commenced on a modest scale in 1986, but Shanghai began lobbying the central authorities for greater access to funds from international agencies toward the very end of the 1980s. Once permission had been granted, Shanghai was able to raise $4.4 billion by 1991. The issuing of construction bonds has grown steadily as the city acquires experience and markets gain in maturity. Less has been done to tap local savings to augment enterprise resources. County-level firms in neighboring provinces are far ahead of the game. However, Shanghai's industrial structure is shifting toward collective and private enterprises, again with support from the authorities. These types of enterprises are far readier to explore a variety of avenues, and the use of new financial instruments sanctioned by the authorities is sure to increase.

Shanghai's many advantages are clear: an industrial tradition, a broad manufacturing base, human capital, and a strategic location. It must use these assets, the benefits conferred by agglomeration and by spillovers from surrounding economies, and its ability to mobilize resources to sustain its standing as China's premier industrial metropolis. Through farsighted policies and judicious investments, Shanghai can become a world-class center for producer services. But it must make haste to remedy its infrastructure shortcomings, to give sustained attention to the weaker parts of its industrial system, and to meet its social security obligations to an aging workforce in a manner that is socially just while being financially sustainable. Any one of these tasks is well within Shanghai's capabilities. To accomplish all three simultaneously—because that is what the situation demands—calls for creative solutions that squeeze the utmost from each yuan of outlay.

4

Tianjin: A Port, Its Neighborhood, and Its Ambition

The first impression many have on arriving in Tianjin from Shanghai is a sense of spaciousness, a slow pace of life tied to the rhythms of the bicycle, and a quiet. The quiet is deceptive. Tianjin's industrial reach is almost as great as Shanghai's. Smokestacks with their ubiquitous plumes are everywhere feeding the brown smog that drapes the city. What life remains in the Haihe River fights a losing battle against the ferocious effluent from industries of every stripe: petrochemicals, electronics, metallurgy, dyeing, and textiles. Tianjin lies near the core of China's old industrial heartland. It is a city where state-owned enterprises still dominate industrial activity and their influence pervades all economic institutions. Tianjin's story reveals another side of urban development in China. Although its recent economic history closely parallels Shanghai's own experience and Tianjin has many of the same industrial attributes, the difference in economic geography has influenced the dynamics of agglomeration, the pattern of change, and the readiness to challenge socialist practices with the weapons of reform. Because of its location, resource endowment, and proximity to Beijing, Tianjin's options are narrower and its feasible development strategy is better delineated.

Tianjin's experience can broaden our understanding of urban development in a transition economy in four respects. First, it indicates how the expansion of transport facilities can increase the fruitfulness of interaction with the hinterland and enable a city to derive additional impetus from entrepôt trade. Thus transport can offset the industrial and agricultural weaknesses of the immediate hinterland, promoting trade and the flow of goods from farther afield. Second, Tianjin's deepwater harbor, the presence of mineral resources in neighboring counties, and their availability for industrial purposes have sharpened the choice of manufactures. Third, Tianjin's accumulated industrial skills and possibility of pooling its human capital with that of Beijing open possibilities in the realm of high-technology industry. Fourth, the large share of state industry within the municipality and the absence of rapidly growing town and village enterprises in the vicinity of the city have slowed the restructuring of the municipal economy. Existing institutions, which affect the allocation of labor, cannot be challenged so long as alternative employment prospects are few and industrial workers are the dominant political force.

Resource Endowment and Growth

The Tianjin municipality covers an area of 11,305 square kilometers, and the city proper stands on 222 square kilometers, some 16 percent less than Shanghai. The urban population in 1993 was 5 million, three-fourths of the population of its sister metropolis to the south. The total population of metropolitan Tianjin was a little under 9 million, compared with 2.69 million in 1953 (table 3.2). Aside from a lower population density, living space per capita is larger than in Shanghai. In the period before liberation, Tianjin was a jumble of unplanned, poorly articulated neighborhoods, a legacy of the largely self-contained foreign concessions that appeared after 1860. Piecemeal investment in urban infrastructure gradually imposed a new topography on the city. But the city's urban infrastructure and layout improved significantly when the central government mounted a drive to repair the damage caused by the Tangshan earthquake of 1976 (which caused extensive damage to structures and killed 25,000 people in Tianjin alone; see Chang, Hu, and Sun 1992). Starting in the late 1970s, Tianjin constructed 14 new residential areas, a major sewage treatment plant, a complete-ring road system, and freeway connections to Tanggu and Beijing. The highway network now integrates intracity routes with intercity trunk lines. Road space per capita, which was well above the level for the two other cities and greater than the national average in 1990, grew from 4.9 square meters to 7.1 square meters by 1994 (table 3.6).

Eight hundred years ago under the Yuan dynasty, the town was known as Haijinzhen, or Sea Ford Town. Famous among sailors, the port of Tianjin flourished in spite of problems caused by siltation, the obstacle posed by the Taku Bar at the mouth of the Haihe, and ice buildup in the Bohai Sea during winter. Divided into three parts—Tanggu, Tianjin, and Xingang—Tianjin harbor is the largest in north China. Railway links with Beijing and Shanghai to the west and south and to Harbin in the north enable the harbor to service a number of key economic regions, such as the northeast and northwest. A railway line connecting Tianjin to its satellite port of Tanggu was built in 1888. Later construction established lines to Qinhuangdao and Tangshan. By 1912 railway connections ex-

Table 4.1   Education of the Labor Force in Selected Sectors in Tianjin, 1990

Level of education and type of work	Industry		Transport		Research and development		Government	
	Thousands of employees	Percent	Thousands of employees	Percent	Thousands of employees	Percent	Thousands of employees	Percent
Total	1,927.9		207.8		47.3		198.1	
Level of education								
University	31.1	1.6	2.6	1.3	14.2	30.1	12.6	6.4
Community college	69.6	3.6	5.6	2.7	8.2	17.2	31.4	15.9
Vocational school	95.2	4.9	11.1	5.4	5.8	12.3	26.8	13.5
Senior high school	458.4	23.8	46.1	22.2	7.8	16.4	52.2	26.3
Junior high school	914.3	47.4	103.2	49.7	9.3	19.6	53.0	26.7
Elementary school	330.7	17.2	36.6	17.6	1.9	4.0	18.5	9.4
None	28.6	1.5	2.5	1.2	0.1	0.3	3.6	1.8
Type of work								
Technical	181.3	9.4	20.1	9.7	25.1	53.0	49.1	24.8
Administration	74.4	3.9	5.5	2.7	3.8	7.9	47.4	23.9
Staff	66.7	3.5	14.7	7.1	2.9	6.2	61.2	30.9
Sales	62.7	3.3	4.8	2.3	0.9	1.9	5.6	2.8
Services	124.5	6.5	15.9	7.7	2.1	4.5	12.2	6.2
Production	1,414.2	73.4	146.2	70.4	12.3	26.1	21.6	10.9
Other	4.2	0.2	0.4	0.2	0.2	0.4	0.9	0.5

Note: Numbers may not sum to totals because of rounding.
Source: State Statistical Bureau 1992b.

isted with Shanghai and Wuhan. By the 1930s, 10 to 12 percent of China's trade passed through Tianjin, amounting to cargo throughput of more than 2 million tons. Among the principal exports were wool and raw cotton, while imports serviced the demand for oil, timber, and manufactures (Todd 1994).

In contrast to Guangzhou and Shanghai, Tianjin has a substantial endowment of natural resources. The Dagang oil field 60 kilometers away yields 4 million tons of low-sulfur crude a year. Another 1 million tons is produced from nearby offshore fields. Under the suburban counties of Baodi and Jixian, 500 million tons of coal have been verified but so far remain untouched. Salterns in Hangu and Tanggu are the source of Changlu salt for the chemicals industry. And abundant geothermal energy sources are located in the vicinity of the municipality. Whereas scarcity of land for industrial purposes severely constrains the two other cities, plenty of underused land around Tianjin is available for industrial purposes. However, unlike Shanghai, Tianjin lacks a rich agricultural hinterland comparable to the lower Yangtze basin and is not linked to a powerful, rural-based manufacturing system such as that of southern Jiangsu and Zhejiang. However, its proximity to Beijing provides a degree of industrial reinforcement. In the past, Beijing's presence was a mixed blessing, on occasion diverting resources and attention away from Tianjin. More recently, complementarity between the two cities and the scope both for collaborative ventures and for efficient specialization have opened promising vistas in technology.

To exploit these, Tianjin will rely on its reserves of human capital as the building blocks for a research network. There are 29 universities and colleges, more than 140 research institutes, and 200 technical schools. Most workers have a junior high school education or better, and roughly 300,000 employees have some technical qualifications (see table 4.1). At the same time, costs per worker, after factoring in the entire suite of benefits, are 10 percent less than the costs for an equivalent employee in Beijing, 35 percent less than in Shanghai, and a full two-thirds less than in Guangzhou ("Heavenly Investment," *Business China*, July 12, 1993, pp. 8–9).

Its resource position notwithstanding, Tianjin lagged behind Guangzhou and Shanghai between 1952 and 1978 in terms of GDP growth (see table 3.1). GVIO also rose more slowly and, in addition, was below the national average. Throughout the period, Tianjin was overshadowed by Beijing, where industrial growth averaged 14.5 percent annually. GDP growth was only marginally better during 1978–93, with much of the improvement taking place in the early 1990s. In this period, the trend in Tianjin's GVIO was superior to that in Shanghai, but only three-fourths the rate in Guangzhou. The sluggish performance relative to the national average through the 1980s draws attention to structural impediments and the cautious implementation of reform, although the spurt in growth since 1991 suggests that progress on both fronts is being made.

Industrial Development and Services

Tianjin, much like Shanghai, started its industrial life as a producer of textiles and light manufactures for the north China economy. In turn, these industries spawned affiliated engineering and metallurgical activities. That was where matters stood till the mid-1950s, when the central government promoted a steady widening of the industrial base with emphasis on machine building, chemicals, metals, and manufacturing. By 1985 heavy industry accounted for 49 percent of industrial output, although textiles, together with garments, retained 16 percent of industrial production (see table 4.2). During the mid-1980s the 10 largest subsectors were responsible for more than 70 percent of GVIO valued at current prices. In several respects, this industrial structure hampered growth and was disadvantageous for Tianjin. Continued dependence on textiles and garments was a significant handicap. Rising wages and the backwardness of manufacturing, dyeing, and design facilities eroded Tianjin's competitiveness. Furthermore, the weight of these industries in the total was a constraint on productivity. Tianjin's considerable industrial breadth was achieved at some cost. Not only did the city lack a few economic foci to orchestrate development, but its national industries, unlike many of Shanghai's producers, were rarely leaders in their fields (on the comparative advantage of selected subsectors, see chapter 6). Tianjin attained a well-deserved reputation in bicycle manufacturing and was one of the foremost suppliers of television sets, but even in these industries, it was not a force for technological change. In machine tools and metalworking, it was in the front ranks but never dominated either subsector.

The metallurgical industry is Tianjin's largest manufacturing subsector. Private sector firms constructed steel rolling mills with two Martin furnaces in 1937. Output in 1952 was 62,000 tons. It rose to 130,000 tons in 1957 and increased further in the early 1960s following the installation of eight Bessemer converters (Etienne 1990). An alloy steel unit began operating in 1969, and there commenced a major expansion in capacity based on imported equipment. After three years of expansion, Tianjin became one of the seven major production bases for iron and steel in China. In 1993 it produced more than 2.2 million tons of steel and 1.5 million tons of pig iron, adequately meeting current local demand. Tianjin is an established medium-size steel production center, and in 1993 its output ranked eighth in the country. It has developed a complete chain of production, embracing iron foundries, steelmaking, rolling mills, and final products. Steelmaking and other metallurgical industries dovetail effectively with downstream producers of machinery and transport equipment, creating a vertically integrated system of considerable competitive potency. Much like similar industrial cities in Japan and Korea, Tianjin can be a key player in several strata of heavy industry.

Table 4.2   Gross Value of Industrial Output in Tianjin, Selected Years, 1985–93

Indicator	1985 Billions of yuan[a]	Percent	1991 Billions of yuan[a]	Percent	1993 Billions of yuan[a]	Percent	Enterprises in 1993 Number	Percent
City total	29.10	100.0	59.93	100.0	106.81	100.0	12,454	100.0
Light industry	14.79	50.8	27.47	45.8	35.48	33.2	6,813	54.7
Heavy industry	14.31	49.2	32.47	54.2	71.33	66.8	5,641	45.3
State-owned enterprises	23.23	79.8	43.64	72.8	62.88	58.9	2,548	20.5
Collective-owned enterprises	5.34	18.4	10.94	18.3	24.28	22.7	7,874	63.2
Others	0.53	1.8	5.35	8.9	19.66	18.4	2,032	16.3
Top subsectors in 1993	20.50	70.4	41.76	69.7	81.92	76.7	—	—
Metallurgy[b]	3.02	10.4	7.60	12.7	17.73	16.6	—	—
Machine building[c]	4.97	17.1	8.38	14.0	15.13	14.2	—	—
Transport equipment	1.11	3.8	3.49	5.8	12.38	11.6	—	—
Chemicals	2.51	8.6	6.46	10.8	8.81	8.3	—	—
Textiles	3.77	12.9	5.44	9.1	6.56	6.1	—	—
Metal products	1.44	4.9	2.86	4.8	6.37	6.0	—	—
Electronics	1.31	4.5	2.91	4.8	5.34	5.0	—	—
Petroleum processing	0.87	3.0	1.36	2.3	4.38	4.1	—	—
Clothing	0.76	2.6	1.84	3.1	2.74	2.6	—	—
Building materials	0.75	2.6	1.42	2.4	2.50	2.3	—	—
Herfindahl index		0.062		0.057		0.064		

— Not available.

Note: All numbers exclude village-run enterprises.

a. Current prices.

b. Includes smelting and processing of ferrous and nonferrous metals.

c. Includes machine building and electrical machinery.

Source: State Statistical Bureau, *Statistical Yearbook of Tianjin*, 1991, 1992, 1994.

Tianjin was the first city in China to establish a production line for black and white television sets (in 1959), and over the years it capitalized on this base of research and manufacturing to maintain its role as one of China's leading producers (Hussain, Lanjouw, and Li 1990). Research was fed by defense considerations, as in Western countries, and the city acquired a complex of research institutes and factories that steadily added to scientific knowledge as well as production skills in the field of electronics. Once government policies began favoring consumer goods in the early 1980s, Tianjin quickly expanded the output of consumer electronics, especially television sets. To achieve this, the city imported assembly lines and technology from overseas and assimilated these within the existing industrial structure. By 1990 production of items such as black-and-white televisions, color televisions, and radios had risen manifold. Tianjin's Great Wall Television Company sold 70 percent of its black-and-white televisions in northern China, but it also exported to Europe, the United States, and the Middle East, mainly for industrial use.

Tianjin was also developing backward linkages into the high value added components that are at the core not just of televisions but of telecommunications equipment, industrial robots, and modern automobiles. Motorola's decision in 1992 to set up a plant to manufacture pagers was a breakthrough. It is introducing advanced, large-scale production methods and giving incentives for the expansion of research. Because the electronics industry is intrinsic to progress in so many other subsectors, its development has large spillover effects.

Starting in the second half of the 1980s, Tianjin embarked on a program of restructuring and specialization: textiles production was reduced in scale; some facilities were transferred to Handan, Shijiazhuang, and Xingtai; others moved to Xinjiang in the northwest; and large resources were devoted to upgrading the textiles sector.[1] After reappraising its competitive standing in other areas, the municipality narrowed its sights and opted for greater specialization in a more limited group of industries: metallurgy, machine building, transport equipment, electronics, and chemicals. To finance this strategy, the city redirected its own considerable resources and, in addition, requested funding from the central government, from international agencies such as the World Bank, and from foreign investors, who are also the principal suppliers of technology.

By the early 1990s the strategy had begun to yield results, albeit sparingly. Industrial growth accelerated after 1991. The broad sectoral aggregates had shifted, with the share of light industry falling to just over a third as Tianjin scaled down production in those subsectors where rural industry in other parts of China had gained a decisive lead. At the level of subsectors, much greater concentration was evident. The top four subsectors now accounted for 50 percent of output, and the share of textiles had fallen from close to 13 percent to a shade over 6 percent (see figure 4.1). In a handful of years, Tianjin had restricted the compass of its activities and carved out areas of core competence in certain choice heavy industries. In the face of a continuing integration of the national market and increasing competition from producers in other cities, the strategy is clearly a rational one. But the full benefits of agglomeration have yet to be exploited for the purposes of maximizing productivity and reforming enterprises.

Like all other Chinese cities, Tianjin was lightly equipped with producer services. State-owned banks provided financial services, foreign trade corporations and other government organs handled all forms of commerce, and research centers embedded within the domain of an industrial bureau supplied consulting services. To the extent possible, enterprises struggled to be self-sufficient, doing in-house what firms in market economies have been subcontracting for decades. Without the adequate availability of producer services, industrial change is seriously hobbled.

Figure 4.1   Industrial Structure of Tianjin, 1985 and 1993

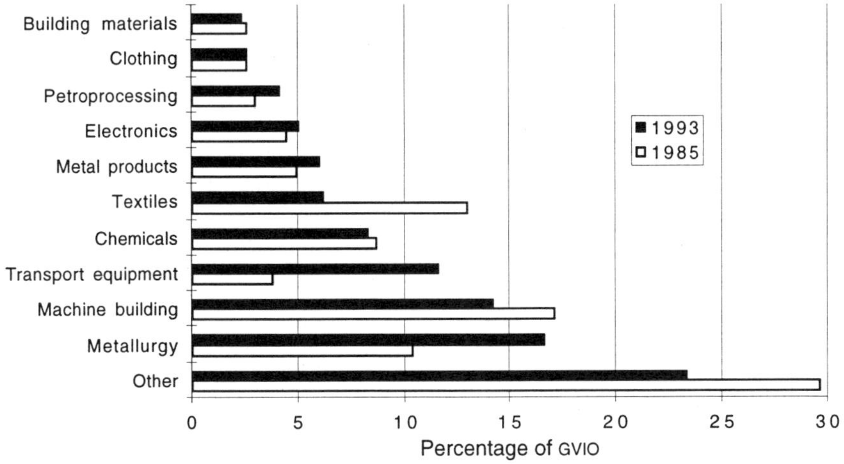

Note: GVIO, gross value of industrial output.
Source: Table 4.2.

Early in the 1990s Tianjin finally began taking steps to deepen service activities. This was almost a decade behind Guangzhou and several years after Shanghai. As a consequence, industrial strategy was guided far more closely by bureau directives, with less support and feedback from the market. Tianjin's enterprises had to grope their way forward in an environment that is still quite poorly furnished with institutions and service providers relative to Shanghai and Guangzhou. Thus the pace of industrial reorganization has been more tentative, and the outcomes have been uneven. Nevertheless, Tianjin has been remarkably effective in lessening the preponderance of state-owned enterprises. In 1985 state-owned enterprises accounted for 80 percent of GVIO and joint ventures for a bare 2 percent. By 1993 the share of state-owned enterprises had declined to 59 percent. Collective-owned enterprises had increased their share by 3 percentage points to about 23 percent, but the output of joint ventures exceeded 18 percent (see table 4.2).[2] Hence the proportion of more innovative enterprises, free from some of the constraints binding state-owned enterprises, was starting to leaven the industrial environment, weakening the resistance to new technology and to changes in labor relations, flexible work practices, and new managerial techniques. However, compared with those of both Shanghai and Guangzhou, Tianjin's state sector remains dominant. The market power of state enterprises can still deter the entrance of small private firms and put pressure on the ones already operating.

Tianjin's large, vertically integrated firms have been under less pressure to restructure and to subcontract than their counterparts in Shanghai. One reason is that they are still relatively insulated by transport costs from aggressive competitors in the coastal provinces to the south and are not sufficiently challenged by producers from the old industrial heartland of Manchuria. Another reason is the sparseness of rural industry, which has been the source of economic buoyancy in other coastal provinces. Rural enterprises in the counties encircling Shanghai and Guangzhou have profoundly influenced the transformation of industry in the cities through production and market linkages. Production linkages are composed of subcontracting deals that permit urban state-owned enterprises to focus on the principal operations and allow affiliated town and village enterprises to supply components. Market linkages are a combination of product competition and market demand. Although the effects of these on urban firms are difficult to quantify, casual empiricism suggests that the interaction between a city and its surrounding rural industry is of vital significance.

Such symbiosis has yet to materialize in Tianjin.[3] Possibly because the agricultural economy lying beyond the city is poor and the commercial tradition of Guangdong or Zhejiang is absent, rural industry of comparable vigor has not emerged. Tianjin's enterprises have therefore not yet managed to arrive at a mutually fruitful division of labor with enterprises in the hinterland.[4] Moreover, Tianjin's policymakers do not have a large enough nonstate sector to absorb the pain of industrial restructuring by sustaining growth momentum and absorbing displaced workers. For this reason, the political and social costs of enterprise reform have rendered change a perilous venture. If failing enterprises are allowed to go under, it is harder to place the unemployed, and the city is not sufficiently prosperous to absorb the cost of extensive layoffs. The voice of labor in Tianjin is far stronger than in Guangzhou and stronger, perhaps, than in Shanghai, where exit is less problematic and a limited social security system is easier to finance. The full benefits of agglomeration are beginning to accrue, but slowly, because reformers must balance political and economic concerns much more finely.

Neighborhood Effects and Transport-Induced Development

The neighborhood effects on which Tianjin is attempting to capitalize are different from those that are central to the strategies of Shanghai and Guangzhou. Exploring Tianjin's approach unveils the workings of geography along different pathways. The two prime determinants of spillover benefits for Tianjin are its potential as a transport hub and its nearness to Beijing. A glance along China's northeastern coast and across the northern one-third of the country reveals, first, that, besides Dalian, no other sheltered, deepwater port is a match for Tianjin.[5] Much of the developing trade of this highly industrialized region is being funneled through Tianjin harbor. Once China's northeastern provinces become more outward-oriented and jointly develop the region's surface transport network, the significance of Tianjin as an entrepôt can only increase. Second, the city is near the eastern apex of the triangular north China plain, where it intersects with the northeast region and Inner Mongolia. The shape of the Bohai peninsula is such that Tianjin lies closer to the inland provinces of northwestern China—as well as Mongolia—than any other port. In fact, an expansive delineation of Tianjin port's hinterland covers 1 million square kilometers embracing the municipalities of Beijing and Tianjin, five contiguous provinces (Gansu, Hebei, Shaanxi, Shanxi, and Qinghai), and three autonomous regions (Inner Mongolia, Ningxia, and Xinjiang).

The current configuration of Tianjin port dates back to the early 1890s, when the Japanese colonial administration shifted the main port from the head of the river closer to the sea. Through the 1950s and 1960s traffic was divided between the upriver Tianjin port and the outpost at Tanggu Xingang. Gradually the former was relegated to the status of a river port, being finally eclipsed by the destruction wrought by the 1976 earthquake. From the early 1970s, container handling facilities were built at Tanggu Xingang, and Tianjin became part of the containerized traffic network that tied together several of China's coastal cities. By 1990 the port was equipped to handle 400,000 TEUs (twenty-foot equivalent units), although actual throughput was 287,000 TEUs. In 1993 the port had a throughput of 37 million tons and functioned both as a seaport (Tanggu Xingang) and as a riverport (Tianjin proper). By 1996 handling capacity had risen to 700,000 TEUs, which exceeds that of the major nearby ports such as Dalian, Lianyungang, and Ningbo; by early in the next century, Tianjin port expects to have a handling capacity of 100 million tons as against 60 million in 1997 ("China: The Bohai Sea Rim," Oxford Analytica, May 29, 1997; *Ports and Harbors*, July–August 1992, p. 32).

The role of a busy entrepôt serving multiple, rapidly developing regions can be exceedingly advantageous, as the experience of Singapore clearly underscores. By expanding its port facilities, systematizing and computerizing information requirements, and mechanizing all cargo handling, Singapore has made itself the busiest transport hub in Asia.[6] Port operations and associated warehousing, trade-related services, and repair facilities have become a major source of income for the island republic and a pillar of Singapore's future prosperity. Tianjin is proceeding down a similar path, although some elements of its strategy are less well specified than in the case of Singapore: there is a strong emphasis on port development, which is under the control of the municipal authorities, whereas plans for pursuing transport projects that would speed the flow of cargo to and from the hinterland are much less certain.

In 1992 the city began a major effort to turn the existing, largely commercial harbor with its 31 cargo and 4 passenger berths into an international port with multiple functions and modern facilities. It began constructing new wharves and berths, improving container transportation, and laying special railway lines to allow easier access. The port now has the country's first 10,000-ton, three-sided freight berth. An expanded wharf is capable of handling 3.5 million tons of grain. In the southern

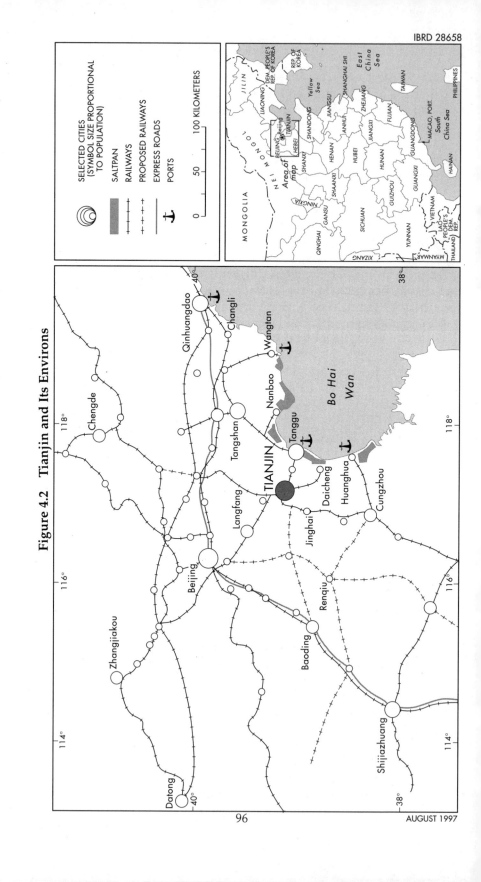

Figure 4.2   Tianjin and Its Environs

part of the port, berths have been developed for crude oil, coal, timber, and chemicals. The neighboring Qinhuangdao port ranks as the largest coal-export terminal in China. About $4.6 million has been invested in Tianjin to build China's largest unloading facility for liquid chemicals. The port is the first in China to have autonomy over collecting funds and expanding cooperation with overseas companies. It has a bonded free trade zone of 5 square kilometers, which is the only free trade zone in China for international transit trade (to Mongolia and the Central Asian Republics) and is similar to Hong Kong (FBIS-CHI-92045, March 6, 1992, p. 68). By the end of 1993 more than 2,300 enterprises had been established in the free trade zone, with total investment of $1.76 billion; goods valued at $1.3 billion were shipped into and out of the zone during 1991–93. However, the difficult fluvial environment of the port imposes some constraints. Although Tanggu Xingang can accommodate container ships with 3,000 TEU capacity, it cannot yet berth the newer 4,000 TEU vessels, unlike its competitor, Dalian (Todd 1994).

The attractiveness of port facilities depends also on their accessibility to users in the surrounding regions. Around Tianjin, the road system is of good quality and is bolstered by the network of waterways that permit delivery by barge. Before the advent of railways, the five rivers linked to the Haihe River—Beiyun, Daqung, Nanyun, Yongding, and Ziya— provided the avenues for distributing goods entering through Tianjin widely across the hinterland. Railway connections to the coastal areas and principal cities are also adequate. Tianjin is connected to the major industrial city of Lining and to provinces to the north: Jilin and Heilongjiang. It is also connected via Beijing to Shanghai and points south. Construction of highways, which will become increasingly important for the flow of containerized cargo, is a priority of the government. Seven highways of national standard link Tianjin with neighboring cities, and there is a 142-kilometer expressway to Beijing (see figure 4.2). The city spent Y800 million on transport development in 1994 and has earmarked sizable funds for this purpose in the coming years. Tianjin airport has been upgraded to handle international flights. Currently it accommodates flights diverted from Beijing, but the expansion program initiated in 1994–95, once completed, will make it the mainland's largest airport.[7]

In spite of all this investment, the intermodal infrastructure that would permit Tianjin to serve its hinterland, especially the interior areas, remains inadequate. Neither road nor rail facilities leading to the western provinces are developed sufficiently, and containerized cargo still cannot penetrate much beyond Beijing and the neighboring parts of Hebei Province. Thus the advantages of the capabilities built up at Tanggu Xingang and at Tianjin airport have yet to be exploited. Building this infrastructure, initially to accommodate freight but later to facilitate high-speed multimodal passenger traffic, requires a cross-provincial effort spearheaded by the central government and involving, possibly, the infusion of foreign capital.

By modeling itself as a regional transport hub, Tianjin has opened the door to growth of a variety of commercial services and transport-intensive industries. Warehousing is but one of the services linked with port and airport development. Of equal significance are storage, trucking, forwarding, brokerage, insurance, and trade financing services. Together these generate thousands of well-paid jobs, some of which are open to workers displaced by the restructuring of state-owned enterprises. Relative to openings in many other service occupations, such jobs call for a higher level of skills, and there is more scope for increments in productivity. The building of warehousing, container handling, and refrigerated storage facilities around the airport, together with the scheduling of air cargo services, could catalyze a response across several industries. It would reinforce the transport-led strategy and allow Tianjin to use neighborhood effects to a much greater extent.

Industrial Prospects

Tianjin's broad industrial base and the presence of an international airport open up possibilities of a radically different kind. Over the past two decades there have appeared on the international stage light manufacturing industries and some horticultural activities that depend on close interaction with their final markets and the ability to airship goods to destinations in high-income countries. Two products that loom large in this trade are of special interest for Tianjin: designer clothing and fashion watches.[8] Each one of these could build on the success of existing production, and their export would involve acquiring and combining many new skills. Sophisticated air transport facilities would bring in foreign expertise and encourage Tianjin's most dynamic enterprises to view the world as their oyster.

Garments and textiles have been a mainstay of Tianjin's industrial sector since early in the century. Now, as rising costs diminish the city's competitiveness in these fields, Tianjin is being forced to close some factories, move upscale, modernize dyeing and finishing facilities, and search for niches, which the remnants of its industry can occupy. As in the case of Shanghai, fashion garments made in small lots for select Western markets are an obvious choice. But to establish itself, Tianjin's producers must forge connections with retailers and distributors overseas. Beyond this, there is a need to improve design standards, quality control, and capacity to manufacture small lots on quite short cycles and to ship the clothing on schedule, usually by air, to their destinations. Many of the ingredients of such restructuring are coming together as the city confronts a market environment in which survival demands competitiveness. In some subsectors—including textiles—marketing, design, and a reputation for reliability as a supplier are being recognized as critical. But weaknesses in quality standards, flexibility of response, and speed of delivery will be overcome only through a concerted effort of industry as well as government. This will entail radical changes in managerial practices and attitudes of the workforce and parallel changes in technology as well as work organization. These changes will be slow to materialize without a credible hardening of the budget constraint signaled by closure of several major money-losing enterprises.[9]

Tianjin's mechanical watch industry is among China's largest industries. It offers the prospects of entering the lower end of the automatic (and mechanical windup) watch market and, in conjunction with the electronics subsector, the mass market for quartz fashion watches. Here again (as the success of the Indian company Titan has shown), the keys to success are innovative design, marketing, production technology, and the ability to supply retailers across the world with efficiency and speed. The hurdles are higher in this area than in garments. Neither municipal enterprises nor private entrepreneurs have moved rapidly to develop producer services or to seek foreign partners who could provide capital together with skills. This is a serious drawback. The possibilities exist, but firms have not actively sought spillover effects to reorient and modernize this industry.

Shipping facilities of a high order make possible a class of industries, some already in existence and others that can be established. Among the industries that are present and could be expanded are petrochemicals, oil refining, and metallurgy. The first two use feedstocks from Dagang and salt from counties within the municipality. In the early 1970s three petrochemical plants and an oil refinery with a throughput of 2.5 million tons were built in the suburbs. Recently more petroleum and marine chemical projects have been completed, including a 140,000-ton ethylene project, a 200,000-ton polyester plant, and a 2.5-million-ton refinery. Tianjin's efforts to build its petrochemicals subsector are being aided by the desire of European producers to shift capacity to China, which could constitute a $100 billion market by 2000.[10] The Bohai Chemical Group, the country's largest salt-chemical industrial group, was listed in 1994 on the Hong Kong Stock Exchange in an effort to raise additional capital. It is embarking on joint ventures with Rhone-Poulenc to manufacture methionine, with Showa Denko of Japan to produce epoxy resins, and with Lucky Chemicals of Korea to establish a plant for polyvinyl chloride. Fine chemicals are also a priority. The combined share of chemicals and petroleum refining in the municipal economy was more than 12 percent in 1993, making it the third largest subsector.

Transport development is crystallizing neighborhood effects that are setting the stage for industrial progress in another area. The proximity to Beijing has had its drawbacks. In the distant past, Beijing's importance as the administrative capital greatly enhanced Tianjin's role as a port and transshipment point. More recently, Beijing has competed against Tianjin for resources and industry. This might explain the slow pace of urban modernization from 1949 through the 1970s. Competition between the two cities has continued during the reform era. But as the spirit of industrial rationalization has taken hold, each city has begun to pursue a measure of specialization and to seek cross-metropolitan synergy. The expressway connecting Tianjin with the capital is a first step, but a long one, toward building an industrial corridor that might eventually mimic Route 128 outside Boston. Whether or not such an industrial axis eventually exists will depend on the future of several industries, with microelectronics as a leading candidate. In fact, the electronics sector can serve as a useful prism for understanding how Tianjin's industry might neutralize some of its constraints and join forces with industry around Beijing so as to create a concentration of high-technology manufacturing in north China.

The Rise of a High-Technology Corridor: Electronics

Industrial expansion in Beijing and trends in applied research have, to some extent, paralleled those occurring in Tianjin. In 1986 Beijing municipality designated a 100-square-kilometer zone surrounding Zhongguancun in Haidian District as a high-technology industry development zone offering tax holidays and 45 percent tax rebates on profits equivalent to those given by Special Economic Zones. An enterprise seeking certification to produce in the zone must ensure that a third of its employees have university-level education and that 3 percent of all revenue from sales is plowed into research.[11] Within eight years, the zone attracted more than 2,000 enterprises and became the most successful of the country's 51 economic and technological development zones (Seki 1994).

Some of the most advanced segments of Beijing's manufacturing establishment are producing electronic equipment of all kinds but have staked out a position in personal computers, peripherals, components, and software. Suppliers of aeronautical equipment and other defense products have used their expertise to acquire a foothold in medical electronics, an immense and fast-growing field. A major new electronics product that looms on the horizon is the wireless personal communication system for short-distance use. Such devices, which are being perfected in Japan, are ideal for China's geographically compact and densely populated cities, where a small number of cells can cover a large number of people. Production of phones and cell stations could generate lucrative manufacturing opportunities far into the future.[12]

China's market for computers grew 65 percent annually during 1990–94, and this trend is likely to persist through the balance of the decade, with annual sales of personal computers projected to reach 6 million by

2000. Local and foreign producers are competing aggressively for a share of sales, which reached 1.15 million in 1995, with foreign producers such as AST, Compaq, Digital, and IBM accounting for 80 percent.[13] Among Chinese producers, Legend had the largest slice of the market in 1995, followed by Great Wall, Long Chao, and several small producers. Both Great Wall and Legend have capitalized on the pool of skills in the Beijing area. In the case of Legend, scientists from Academia Sinica teamed up with a Hong Kong firm to produce their own products and serve as intermediaries for Apple, AST, IBM, and Sun Microsystems. This strategy has adroitly brought together Chinese talent, foreign technology, and Hong Kong capital. There is considerable scope for more collaboration along these lines and for the development of indigenous research capacity and technology. Compaq has invested $1 million in a research center in Beijing, and other multinational corporations will find it advantageous to invest in China, as they have in India and Israel. Many small start-ups are engaged in the specialist software and applications business. In particular, "hanzification" has opened new avenues, as software engineers refine the ability of computers to read and write Chinese characters.[14] With many other foreign manufacturers such as NEC, DEC, and Casio prepared to license technology or set up facilities in China, the Beijing-Tianjin Silicon Axis is moving from a vision to a stirring of action in the two cities and finally to actual agglomeration of industry that could one day create a long industrial bridge.

In both Tianjin and Beijing, the rise of electronics is being supported by backward linkages with engineering, transport, and telecommunications industries, whose own advance is keyed to the successful incorporation of microchip technology. Another linkage that has begun acquiring significance as China integrates with the international economy is the flow of contracts for software and data processing from abroad. This is creating openings for businesses that are the handmaidens of a successful, full-service electronics sector. Thus at the two ends of the new expressway, many "Silicon Shoots" are in evidence, as the two cities begin mobilizing their reserves of human capital and nudging industry along new pathways. Whether a "Silicon Corridor" will emerge and whether Tianjin will be able to contribute to its building will depend on whether policies are woven to minimize constraints on high-technology industries that are rich in spillovers.

The semiconductor industry, which constitutes the axis of the electronics subsector, illustrates both the nature of the constraints and the policies to deal with them. Semiconductor production is one of the pillars of the industry and a technology driver.[15] It is also the entry point for countries seeking to establish a strong electronics complex. The technology is relatively accessible, and competitiveness is a function of production scale, clean room practices, and process skills. However, as Korea's experience shows, entry costs are high because a plant of optimal size for producing a mass-produced item such as DRAMs or SRAMs involves a large outlay of capital; several years of learning are needed to produce defect-free chips that are on a par with industry standards; and innovation or the manufacture of higher value added items, such as ASICs, requires heavy expenditure on R&D. A bimodal industrial structure seems to have several advantages. Frequently, small new entrants introduce new technology, experimental products, and fresh ideas; produce customized chips; and design application-specific software. However, only large firms with deep pockets can undertake mass production, which greatly reduces unit costs but is exceedingly capital-intensive.

Role of State-Owned Enterprises

Tianjin has an abundance of big state enterprises that are controlled by both the central government and the municipality. The municipal authorities have adopted policies that accommodate collectives and joint ventures and have increased the number of entrants, so the emerging industrial structure is achieving a good balance between state and nonstate enterprises. But problems remain. First, the established state-owned enterprises, while long on experience, are short on process skills of the sophistication needed to produce advanced electronics. Quality control, clean room practices, and in-plant research capability are particularly backward. Second, red tape still hampers the entry of new firms and the product diversification of existing large state-owned enterprises. The planning and control mentality, although in retreat, continues to interfere with industrial functioning. Third, specialization among firms and networking are crucial in the field of electronics. Without such interaction, firms cannot internalize spillovers, shorten the product cycles, or keep costs in check. Spillovers also depend on labor mobility between firms, which acts as a transmission belt for ideas and production practices.

Since the late 1980s, Tianjin municipality, together with the central government, has accelerated the tempo of industrial restructuring, which includes networking and loose conglomerate arrangements. It has pushed labor contracting so as to introduce flexibility into the job market. Both initiatives have begun to influence behavior, but ingrained habits and beliefs do not change overnight. Much like other Chinese cities that are implementing reforms, such as Shanghai, Shenyang, and Wuhan, the first few steps are the hardest. Once some momentum is attained, progress can be much more swift.

A "Silicon Corridor" will emerge and flourish over the long term if technological advancement is a prime and consistently pursued goal across an interrelated range of fields encompassing components and production equipment.[16] Such simultaneous effort in several areas lessens the dependence of firms on outside suppliers and eventually reinforces technological momentum. To achieve minor but cumulatively significant innovations necessarily calls for networking among many small niche-targeting companies and involving large firms capable of developing and mass producing a promising innovation. Networking principally means the sharing of technology, joint product development, and subcontracting, which allows for specialization, the pooling of skills, and the internalizing of many links in the production chain.

Technical Manpower and Foreign Direct Investment

Tianjin and Beijing together have the largest slice of research manpower in China and several of the most prestigious universities. There are many government-owned research laboratories in the area, some of which are well equipped. In any case, acquiring equipment is not a vast expense. Furthermore, the government—through state-owned enterprises—is a reliable source of contracts, especially for R&D on electronics, which offers growth prospects for large state-owned enterprises and smaller nonstate enterprises alike. The Tianjin municipal authorities, taking their cue from other open cities and neighboring East Asian economies, have created an economic and technology development zone (ETDZ). Covering an area of 24.8 square kilometers, it is Tianjin's equivalent of the technology development zone in Beijing.

By the end of 1996, 2,800 foreign-funded enterprises had been established, with foreign investment amounting to $8.0 billion, as had a small number of local start-up and joint ventures ("China: Bohai Sea Rim," Oxford Analytica, May 29, 1997). Some of these enterprises produced high-technology products. With a GVIO of 1.45 billion yuan, the Tianjin ETDZ was the largest and most profitable in China. Among investors in the Tianjin area were a number of multinational corporations, from Japan, the United States, and Korea, whose willingness to remain in Tianjin and expand their operations will certainly boost the prospects of a technology corridor. Mention has already been made of Motorola's investment. The company's $300 million state-of-the-art factory produced $1.5 billion worth of pagers and cellular telephones in 1994. Even though the venture has yet to achieve profitability, Motorola is planning to invest another $1 billion in production facilities, which includes a $500 million semiconductor wafer plant, also in Tianjin. Others include Otis from the United States, NEC from Japan, Henkel from Germany, Zanussi from Italy, and Karry from Hong Kong.

More FDI targeted toward selected areas of the electronics industry could provide a much needed spillover for local producers, linkages for input suppliers, and a demonstration effect to stimulate the entry of home-grown producers. Tianjin can learn from China's southeastern provinces how to entice FDI in sufficient volume into the desired industries (see table 4.3). Two other policies thus far neglected have the potential to stimulate the growth of electronics. One is the provision of

Table 4.3 Foreign Investment in Tianjin, 1986–93
(millions of U.S. dollars, unless otherwise noted)

Indicator	1986	1987	1988	1989	1990	1991	1992	1993	1979–93
Utilized foreign investment	134.8	223.4	242.7	167.8	98.6	260.9	831.2	935.0	4,016.5
Loans	83.4	90.3	181.5	136.3	61.6	128.3	599.2	391.1	2,739.8
Direct investment	51.4	127.4	31.9	28.0	34.9	132.2	231.4	541.2	1,218.0
Other	—	5.7	29.3	3.4	2.0	0.5	0.6	2.7	58.8
Contracted foreign direct investment, by source	—	14.4	91.7	84.6	163.7	196.6	1,219.3	2,255.7	4,270.2
Hong Kong (China)	—	6.7	28.2	42.3	87.0	92.8	629.2	996.5	2,002.7
Percentage of Tianjin's total	—	46.8	30.8	50.0	53.2	47.2	51.6	44.2	46.9
Percentage of Hong Kong's total	—	0.4	0.8	1.3	2.1	1.3	1.6	—	—
Japan	—	2.1	18.6	25.1	16.3	6.6	90.1	113.2	307.2
Percentage of Tianjin's total	—	14.9	20.3	29.7	10.0	3.4	7.4	5.0	7.2
Percentage of Japan's total	—	1.0	6.2	7.1	7.6	0.9	4.2	—	—
United States	—	0.9	4.9	4.7	19.5	32.2	237.8	337.9	687.8
Percentage of Tianjin's total	—	6.1	5.3	5.6	11.9	16.4	19.5	15.0	16.1
Percentage of U.S. total	—	0.3	1.6	0.9	5.8	6.7	7.6	—	—
Taiwan (China)	—	—	—	4.8	13.7	18.6	90.9	288.1	411.7
Percentage of Tianjin's total	—	—	—	5.7	8.4	9.5	7.5	12.8	9.6
Percentage of Taiwan's total	—	—	—	1.1	1.4	1.5	1.6	—	—
Korea, Rep. of	—	—	—	—	—	—	19.9	172.0	211.4
Percentage of Tianjin's total	—	—	—	—	—	—	1.6	7.6	5.0
Percentage of Korea's total	—	—	—	—	—	—	4.8	—	—
Others	—	4.6	40.0	7.7	27.2	46.4	151.5	348.0	649.3
Percentage of Tianjin's total	—	32.2	43.7	9.1	16.6	23.6	12.4	15.4	15.2

— Not available.
Source: State Statistical Bureau, *Statistical Yearbook of China*, 1987; 1988; 1990; 1992; and 1993; data by source for 1987–91, State Statistical Bureau 1992a; 1992 and 1993 data and cumulative figures from State Statistical Bureau, *Statistical Yearbook of Tianjin*, 1994.

venture capital to launch products developed jointly by Tianjin's universities and entrepreneurial researchers or other sponsors. State-owned enterprises are prepared to sponsor initiatives, and county authorities are ready to put up risk capital. At this juncture, institutional arrangements that enable the research establishments of Tianjin and also Beijing to make commercial use of research results could truncate what might otherwise be a slow maturation of university-business partnerships. The Massachusetts Institute of Technology has shown that the use of venture capital can be unusually fruitful in pushing university-based research down the path of commercial realization (Saxenian 1994; Kargon and Leslie 1994). Harvard has taken similar steps to commercialize research. In 1988 it created Medical Science Partners Inc., a $36 million venture capital fund managed by Harvard Medical School to back marketable medical discoveries.[17]

Research

Acquiring effective R&D skills is time-consuming. It demands experience, project management capability, knowledge of markets, and detailed understanding of not just the frontier of a field but also the direction in which it is expanding. There are no shortcuts, although there are ways of tapping into Western research networks and thereby telescoping the acquisition of knowledge and the development of products.[18] FDI is, of course, one obvious route, as are alliances with foreign companies.

A second approach is to increase incentives for R&D by the large state-owned enterprises and to encourage small collective-owned enterprises, private firms, and joint ventures to set up research facilities that cater to the needs of many small producers. Even in the mid-1990s, big state-owned enterprises have made minimal outlays on research and have minimal in-house capability. Testing, quality control, troubleshooting, new product development on a limited scale, and occasional reverse engineering define the range of enterprise activities. Few product and process innovations emerge from all this. Even the giant state-owned enterprises in Tianjin lack the strategy, managerial aptitude, or quality of the workforce needed to participate in the process of technological change, which is one of the prime determinants of a competitive strategy to attain international competitiveness.

Licensing arrangements offer other possibilities that strengthen medium-term prospects and build longer-term potential. Many enterprises in China are already exploring the full range of possibilities, and competitors in nearby Beijing are beginning to prod Tianjin's enterprises into action. To take one well-known example, Beijing's Stone (Si Tong) Group has emerged as a leader in a number of fields, including computer software, office automation (especially typewriters and cash registers), and electronic components. Stone Group has accomplished this by employing deft entrepreneurship and mobilizing scientific manpower:

nearly 70 percent of its employees are university graduates. In addition, it has entered into a number of fruitful joint ventures with Matsushita, Mitsubishi, and Mitsui to produce word processors, printers, and floppy disks (*Financial Times*, April 30, 1996). Stone Group's strategy of using abundant human capital, mainly from Beijing, to develop competence in a few technology-intensive fields is something that enterprises in Tianjin are beginning to emulate but must pursue more aggressively.

Colonizing Auto Industry Niches

Other industries already established in Tianjin could capitalize on agglomeration economies and the benefits from externalities, annex a large share of the expanding market in China, and be able to compete in the export sector. Among the most noteworthy is the automobile industry: Tianjin ranked sixth among the seven principal Chinese manufacturers of autos in 1994. This is a subsector with many linkages backward as well as forward. Tianjin's diversified industrial structure already encompasses many of the industries that support automobile production. For instance, steel, glass, petrochemicals, machine tools, electronics, and component manufactures are well established and could support an expanded auto industry. Some years ago, Tianjin, which was already assembling autos, made a big decision with respect to future output mix: it entered into a licensing arrangement with Daihatsu to assemble a minivan and a minicar, the Charade. In the process, Tianjin laid claim to two of the fastest-growing segments of the automobile market in China. The minivan is a practical and cost-effective vehicle for businesses wanting to transport passengers and cargo. The Charade is relatively simple to produce, ideally suited to China's narrow urban streets, and low priced. This puts it within reach of China's emerging middle class, which is composed of two-earner families engaged in either business or the professions. New, flexible process technologies and lean production methods make it possible for medium-scale producers to achieve unit cost levels comparable to those of large multinational corporations. The experience of Daihatsu (and also of Renault) has clearly shown that manufacturing for selected niches can be a viable strategy for medium-size producers.[19]

The Tianjin Auto Industry Corporation entered into a licensing agreement with Daihatsu in 1986. In 1988, 2,873 cars and 9,329 minivans were assembled. The number rose in 1996 to almost 88,000 cars. Production of both types of vehicles is projected at 150,000 in 1997 (Maxton 1994; Harwit 1995; "Toyota Targets Chinese Markets," *Financial Times*, November 16, 1995; "Long March to Mass Market," *Financial Times*, June 25, 1997). Both vehicles have been in heavy demand throughout China, and trends point to steadily rising sales. Minivans are also the preferred mode of transport in rural areas, where the roads and repair facilities are not suited for more sophisticated vehicles.

By 1996 sales of autos in China had risen to 1.6 million, of which 382,000 were cars, most of them manufactured domestically. By some estimates, the market for cars alone could double by 2000. Demand for minivans is also likely to increase rapidly. Undoubtedly the competition for such vehicles will be sharp because they are particularly suited to the profiles of likely buyers, whether individuals, enterprises, or taxi companies. However, Tianjin has the benefits that accrue to an early entrant, and it has a local manufacturing base that few cities in China can rival. Hence Tianjin could evolve into a major center for China's auto industry, and in certain respects it is offering a more attractive mix of products.

There are hurdles to be crossed, and these bring us back to weak agglomeration effects. First, Tianjin's partner in the automobile venture is one of the smaller Japanese producers. Daihatsu is partially owned by Toyota, which only recently began to assign substantial resources to widening the demand salient created by its subsidiary. Furthermore, the licensing arrangement with Tianjin Auto was quite frugal in transferring skills, process technology, design capability, and all the other factors that determine manufacturing strength. This will change with the increase in Tianjin's market share and Toyota's decision to enter the market.[20] The Japanese company set up a technical assistance center to explore opportunities for manufacturing components in the early 1990s. In 1996 it entered into a $250 million joint venture with the Tianjin Auto Industry Group to manufacture car engines, a prelude possibly to full-scale production of automobiles.

Parts production is the second hitherto missing element of agglomeration. Unlike Volkswagen, which has been instrumental in persuading its German suppliers to begin producing certain parts in the Shanghai area, Tianjin received little assistance from Daihatsu in attracting parts producers to the city. All 48 component producers are affiliates of Tianjin Auto, and because FDI in the production of auto parts has been negligible, less than 50 percent of the Charade is from locally sourced items. High value added items such as transmissions, electronics, and engines are still being imported. In fact, Tianjin Auto and the local industry bureaus have lagged significantly behind other major auto producers in China, both in the transfer of technology and in the domestic production of parts. This too is set to change because Tianjin Auto has entered into a dozen joint ventures to manufacture components such as oil filters, moldings, and mirrors. Toyota also appears ready to create a network of suppliers, much as Volkswagen has largely done in Shanghai.

The small size of engines used (0.98 liter) in both the Charade and the minivan, together with the poor quality of parts and materials required for automobile manufacturing, is a third hurdle that must be crossed. Production of 1.3-liter and even larger-capacity engines in collaboration with Daihatsu and Toyota will remove one of the deficiencies. But the problem of parts may take longer to solve. Although Tianjin has invested heavily in basic industries over the past four decades, improvements in quality have lagged behind growth in output, and this is immediately apparent from a casual inspection of the vehicles assembled by Tianjin Automobile in the first half of the 1990s. Because China's petrochemical industry is still not technologically on a par with those of more advanced countries, various products such as paints and sealants have poor resins. Quality problems also beset all rubber products. Locally produced glass is still deficient in certain respects, and the raw material continues to be largely imported. Cold rolled steel is now available from the modernized steel plant, but there is a dearth of zinc-coated, corrosion-resistant grades of the desired width.

The same problem applies to electronic components, from connectors to more sophisticated items. Some components are produced locally but fall far short of international standards. Such shortcomings stem in part from inevitable delays in assimilating technology, in establishing standards, and in creating a market environment, which induce firms to compete on grounds of technology and quality. In part also they stem from weaknesses in the production process that arise from the incentive structure embedded in the internal labor market of state-owned enterprises, work discipline and supervision, quality control procedures, and the availability of testing equipment, as well as the skill to put it to effective use. Of all these, work incentives and work organization on the factory floor are arguably the most important. Chronic overstaffing is a longstanding feature of state-owned enterprises in Tianjin, as it is in other cities. Combined with payment practices that do not recognize effort and skill and with lifetime tenure of the core workforce, they undermine motivation. Employees of state-owned enterprises function in a factory ambience where evidence of slack is widespread and rules of discipline can be fairly relaxed. Financial incentives to work harder or to upgrade skills are relatively modest. And the majority of employees are shielded from layoffs. Those state-owned enterprises that are now operating in buyers' markets have begun responding to competitive pressures by increasing the proportion of contract labor and reorganizing the workplace. But thus far the auto industry still faces excess demand, and many dysfunctional practices linger, slowing the ascent of Tianjin's auto industry along the learning curve. Productivity gains have not been fully realized, and vehicles still leave the assembly line with many defects.

Summary: Reforming for Growth

This brief examination of two industrial subsectors that could spearhead the future growth of Tianjin's economy indicates the breadth of choices at hand and draws attention to elements of industrial backwardness. Socialist development strategy was responsible for the wide industrial base and the experience accumulated by Tianjin. In this respect, it certainly enlarged the scope for agglomeration benefits and potential externalities. It also endowed Tianjin with a number of leading sectors, both actual and potential. Electronics and automobiles are among the two most promising. Together with industries that produce basic materials and are engaged in transport-related activities, they could give Tianjin the lead over other cities in north China, with the exception of Beijing.

Socialist development strategy isolated Tianjin from the technological spillover effects emanating from other countries. The autarkic, inward-oriented approach insulated the economy from fresh ideas, new techniques, and competition.[21] In this milieu, the system of planning, as well as the vertically integrated organizational structure of state-owned enterprises, dampened industrial dynamism. Furthermore, research with a commercial slant did not flourish, nor was the application of experimental findings given priority. Although scientific manpower was fairly plentiful, it was not used efficiently to advance the industrial fortunes of the city. The primitive state of the services sector meant that consulting, engineering, extension, and information services contributed little to agglomeration effects.

The compartmentalization of the workforce as a result of lifetime tenure in state-owned enterprises had macro- as well as micro-level consequences. At the macro level, it affected labor mobility and hence the flexibility of resource use. At the micro level, state-owned enterprises, faced with having to employ more workers than they needed, used labor inefficiently, made little effort to exert stringent work discipline, and in the interests of trouble-free relations, opted for minimal wage differentiation.

The transition from plan to market has enhanced Tianjin's autonomy from the central government, improved its growth prospects, and brought many possibilities for innovation within reach. However, new organizational structures are needed that efficiently use phycical and human resources, particularly the latter. As Landes (1991, p. 317) observed with regard to the industrial revolution in Germany, "reorganization of work entailed reorganization of labor: the relationships of men to one another and to their employers were implicit in the mode of production: technology and social pattern reinforced each other." Germany succeeded by creating organizations hospitable to emerging technologies. By contrast, the United Kingdom fell behind because organizational disabilities emerged: initially the social power of craft workers prevented factory owners from modernizing their facilities; later labor's ability to exercise its political voice prevented the dismantling of the work practices hindering innovation. There are lessons in this for China: the social organization in state-owned enterprises can be a major stumbling block, and micro-level restructuring and the political power of the urban, industrial workforce influence the content and pace of reforms overall.

Tianjin has been a late starter at serious micro-level reforms. By 1992 it had secured a fiscal arrangement with the central government that allowed the municipality to retain a larger proportion of revenues and shared most sales taxes with the central government. This system will increase Tianjin's share of total revenues.[22] Toward the end of the 1980s, industrial strategy had been sharpened and refocused on a core set of competencies that included the transport sector, certain basic industries, electronics, and autos. In order to build capacity in high-technology areas, Tianjin has created the development zone and is actively seeking FDI. Beyond that, the idea of a "Silicon Corridor" linking Tianjin with Beijing is arousing interest among the politicians and entrepreneurs who will see it to fruition. A multimodal transport network now links Tianjin with the immediate hinterland, but connections with more distant areas are poor. Hence the full benefits of transport investment remain to be realized.

One phase of enterprise reform, which encouraged the establishment of nonstate enterprises, has been pursued since the mid-1980s. But the reform of large state-owned enterprises gathered momentum only in the early 1990s. So far, the reform of labor contracting, the merger of enterprises, the setting up of umbrella corporations, and the closure of ailing state enterprises have yet to be molded into an effective strategy. Although some of the smaller loss-making state-owned enterprises are being closed, the tendency is to rely on mergers, which in the Chinese context entails transferring the staff and assets of one enterprise to another, usually in the same bureau.[23] State-owned enterprises are still absorbing the largest amount of capital, which otherwise could be used to finance private enterprises, and are responsible for more than 70 percent of all industrial losses in the city (see table 3.5).

However, Tianjin has attracted foreign investment despite its disadvantageous position compared with both Guangzhou and Shanghai. Unlike Guangzhou, whose proximity to and historical affinity with Hong Kong have proved to be a magnet for foreign investment, Tianjin was not particularly favored by any major source of investment.[24] And unlike Shanghai, Tianjin did not possess a wide range of industrial activities, a tradition of financial and producer services, a large pool of skilled labor, or a strong financial investment from the central government in recent years. In fact, Tianjin has to compete with its close neighbor, Beijing, which, as the nation's capital, can use its political muscle to poach potential investors. To overcome these handicaps, Tianjin has lured FDI with a combination of concessions and incentive policies. It has introduced measures to cut capital costs, reduce bureaucratic procedures drastically, and improve the quality of the infrastructure in the Tianjin Economic Development Area; provided postapproval services such as worker training and social insurance; and augmented fiscal incentives.[25]

Tianjin's experience, which is similar to that of other Chinese cities as well as East Asian economies, shows that a good incentives package, sound management, and high-quality infrastructure are key attractions for foreign investment. Incentives are particularly important for high-technology industries, which may be more dependent on them than other industries. City authorities could also provide direct financial assistance to multinationals involved in R&D activities. Other elements of a technology policy include forming a network of research institutions and helping establish linkages between suppliers and customers and between foreign and local firms.

Tianjin has yet to define a comprehensive program to reform these state-owned enterprises and their losses. But the city has a real advantage that Shanghai and Guangzhou can only envy: the availability of a large tract of undeveloped land around the city. Tianjin's infrastructure is also in relatively good shape because the 1976 earthquake forced the city to re-build itself. Once the expansion of both the port and the airport is completed, Tianjin will have the makings of a formidable transport hub for north China. If it is able to catalyze multimodal transport development in the hinterland, the city can become the center of a range of transport-induced activities, much like Chicago in the early decades of the century.

5

Guangzhou: The Pearl in the Delta

Of the three cities, Guangzhou easily has the most venerable historical record. It occupies the place where, legend has it, five genies riding on goats brought the first cereals to the inhabitants of the area. In memory of this event, Guangzhou is often referred to as Yang Cheng, or Goat Town, and a commemorative statue depicting a group of five goats (or rams; see Ikels 1996) was emplaced on a hill overlooking the city earlier in this century. The name Guangzhou dates back to the Wu dynasty, which ruled the area during the time of the Three Kingdoms (roughly around the third century). From ancient times to the present, Guangzhou's history is densely eventful. Long stretches of prosperity were interspersed with reversals, when war or dynastic change wreaked destruction or weakened the local economy.

Guangzhou's location in the Pearl River delta region is uniquely advantageous. The city is surrounded by some of the richest agricultural land in China, which has supported the cultivation of rice, sugarcane, vegetables, and the mulberry trees that sustain sericulture. Shanghai's location is no less advantageous, but it achieved prominence only in modern times, when the Yangtze delta region opened outward and began trading with the world economy. Guangzhou, in contrast, has been a regional market center and a port since the Han dynasty in the first century B.C. The coming together of international trade and local commerce made Guangzhou the largest city in China during the nineteenth century, but the inability to build an industrial base caused it to fall behind Shanghai. The relative backwardness of the economies ringing the South China Sea, through the first half of the twentieth century, also slowed Guangzhou's development. As the capital of Guangdong, a strategically vulnerable province near China's sensitive border with Viet-

112

nam, Guangzhou suffered neglect throughout the Maoist era. Choice industrial projects were almost never located in the southeastern coastal provinces.[1] Nor did the central government provide funds for infrastructure. Under these conditions, growth suffered, and by 1977 Guangdong ranked sixth in net material product per capita.[2]

Guangzhou's locational advantages became more prominent with the ending of the Vietnam conflict and the rising prosperity of Southeast Asia. Guangzhou's experience since 1978 is interesting, both because similarities with Shanghai and Tianjin deepen our understanding of certain fundamental forces driving urban development and because the contrasts draw attention to the richness as well as the complexity of the forces at work. This chapter analyzes seven factors that have a bearing on Guangzhou's performance: urban infrastructure; the politics of reform and its influence on resource availability; industrial structure and associated agglomeration economies and diseconomies; neighborhood effects emanating from buoyant economies along the rim of the South China Sea, kinship networks that bind Guangzhou to the economy of Southeast Asia, and the emergence of strong industrial growth poles in the Pearl River delta area; the role of transport; the labor market of the Pearl River delta region; and the rise of producer services in Guangzhou's economy.

Urban Infrastructure

Guangzhou was the sixth most populous city in China until the late 1980s and, in the early 1990s, the third largest urban economy in the country, surpassing Tianjin and trailing only Shanghai and Beijing. In 1993 Guangzhou also had the highest GDP per capita among all major cities in China, even ahead of Shanghai (table 3.2).[3] Guangzhou manifests the same problems facing many large cities in China, such as overcrowding, population density ranging from 27,000 to 55,000 persons per square kilometer, housing shortages, traffic congestion, and conflicts in land use (see Yeung, Deng, and Chen 1992). In Guangzhou, industrial land occupies the largest share of serviced urban real estate (more than 30 percent), and the concentration of factories is very high: more than half of all industrial enterprises in the municipality are located in the urban area. Guangzhou has enormous potential for upgrading the area bordering the Pearl River that is now cluttered with factories and warehouses. Within the central city, differences in the living environment and social status of districts are largely reflected in housing.[4]

A scarcity of housing has persisted for decades. The average living space per person was only 4.5 square meters in 1945. A trickle of investment raised it to a still meager 4.9 square meters in 1976. Investment in housing construction rose substantially in the late 1980s and in a handful of years pushed per capita living space to 8.5 square meters in 1993 and to almost 10 square meters in 1995. Annual investment of Y3 billion since 1993 has added a total floor space of more than 3 million square meters (FBIS-CHI-93158, August 18, 1993, p. 44). But the city is facing a new problem in the wake of a growing influx of migrant workers (see Ikels 1996).[5] More than any other district, the Huangpu cluster in the central city has the highest concentration of factory workers. The city will have to expand the market for rental housing to accommodate the demand for affordable housing and prevent social disorder associated with the unchecked influx of migrants. Low housing prices will be a major factor in holding down the increase in wages, as was the case in Hong Kong during the 1960s and 1970s.

Housing reforms already under way in Guangzhou are designed to deal with the problem of unmet demand and poor maintenance. A major goal of the reforms is to increase the private ownership of housing. The city has created a public housing fund, based on the Singapore Central Provident Fund model of matched employer-employee contributions (currently 5 percent of wages from each). It is also attempting to delink housing from work units. But the ultimate goal of treating housing as a commercial commodity to be produced, exchanged, and managed in response to market signals requires much institution building.[6]

Traffic congestion is also a problem. Although Guangzhou is still at the low end of per capita road coverage and total road length, it has the highest ratio of motor vehicles to population in China (Yeung, Deng, and Chen 1992). By the end of 1992, the city's 6 million residents owned some 320,000 motor vehicles, a fivefold increase from 1985. Together with more than 3 million bicycles and 2,000 public buses, Guangzhou daily struggles with incipient traffic strangulation. In this riverine city, water transport could play a vital role, but unfortunately it has been allowed to decline since the 1960s and now only accounts for 10 and 28 percent of passenger and freight traffic, respectively. This decline was mainly a result of limited mechanization of Huangpu harbor, but lack of funds and space for expanding the old harbor and ferry terminals has also contributed.

The city has responded to the increasingly severe traffic congestion by embarking on the construction of ring roads. It is tackling the grave shortage of public transport by building an 18.4-kilometer subway to be completed by 1998. The city will invest about Y35 billion by 2000 in road and bridge projects, including the subway. An expressway around the city and four new expressways in the downtown area will be constructed. Moreover, Guangzhou is ahead of other municipalities in its innovative approach to financing: transferring ownership rights to private companies of certain bridges, tunnels, and waterworks helps to ease the financial burden of the municipal government and provides new sources of funding for public utility construction.

The Politics of Reform: Why Guangdong Was First

As indicated in chapter 1, China's reform strategy as it was tentatively formulated in the late 1970s had two separate dimensions. First, it sought to respond to the dissatisfaction of farmers with planning and controls imposed through the communes and to release the full productive capabilities of the agricultural economy. Second, it sought to respond to the demonstration effect of increasing prosperity among China's immediate neighbors along the eastern rim in a manner that was ideologically defensible, that would be politically tolerated, that might generate large economic returns if it were to proceed according to expectations, and that could be contained and defused at acceptable cost were the experiment to fail.

Several factors decreed that Guangdong and Fujian would be at the forefront of China's attempt to modernize by carefully managing the opening of its economy. First, the two provinces were situated at a safe distance from the economic heartland and, although populous, played a marginal role in both agriculture and industry. A small dose of "opening and reform" could only improve matters and, with sufficient oversight, would not be explosive. Second, to succeed, any action had to win the backing of a neighboring economy with capital, technology, and international trading connections to share. This made the choice of a coastal province inevitable. Third, China was keen to enlist the support of economies and groups with which it could bargain on relatively equal terms. Hong Kong and Macao were obvious candidates because they were small, capital-rich, and already linked to China through trade and geopolitical circumstances. If Hong Kong and, through the island economy, countries in Southeast Asia were to serve as China's partners, then Guangdong and Fujian were the obvious candidates. Fourth, the two provinces possessed certain attributes that reformers could not overlook. The density of contacts with overseas Chinese was one consideration. If China were to attract FDI, only kinship ties and deep-rooted commitments to the homeland would negate the risks of investing. Furthermore, the Pearl River delta area was agriculturally rich and well endowed with labor that could be engaged in light industry. And then, there were the vestiges of a commercial tradition that had made the region wealthy in the past and, if revived, could do so again.

All these considerations tilted the balance toward the southeastern coastal provinces. However, politics had a large hand in the initial decision to experiment with reforms and in subsequent decisions to ensure that Guangdong benefited from the decentralization that governed the local availability of fiscal resources and from the freedom to interpret and implement central reform directives. Spillover effects from setting up the special economic zones in 1978 and opening up the Pearl River delta area benefited Guangzhou economically. In addition, the city gained, directly and indirectly, from the influence its leaders had with the central authorities.

In the late 1970s and the first half of the 1980s, Guangzhou enjoyed a close relationship with Beijing because of several important personal connections. It was granted a high degree of administrative autonomy well before other major cities in China. Some observers attribute this to the military and civilian ties of the late Marshal Ye Jianying with Guangdong. For a long time, Marshal Ye was the only major representative from Guangdong on the national scene. Born in Meixian, a small town in Guangdong, he served briefly as the first mayor of Guangzhou and later as governor of Guangdong before moving to a senior position in the central government. He emerged as the fourth-ranked member of the leadership hierarchy in the early 1970s and subsequently became one of the most powerful elder statesmen in the reform period (Sigel 1993). His son Ye Xuanping later became Guangzhou's mayor, deputy secretary of the Guangdong Provincial Party Committee, and then governor of Guangdong.[7] Guangdong also served as the power base for several other leaders who later achieved national prominence, including Tao Zhu, Zhao Ziyang, Wei Guoqing, Xi Zhongxun, and Yang Shangkun (see Vogel 1989; Cheung 1994b). With such contacts, Guangdong became one of the first provinces designated as a priority area for engaging in foreign trade and promoting foreign investment.

Arguably the most important incentive that the central government provided to Guangdong and Fujian was a special fiscal arrangement fixing the amount of revenue that each province had to transfer to the central government. Negotiated in 1979, this fiscal contract gave the two provinces the widest possible budgetary autonomy (Guangdong transferred 31 percent of its revenue to Beijing in 1979 and only 3 percent in 1984; see Sigel 1993; Cheung 1994a; Goodman and Feng 1994). The difference between the province's anticipated revenues and expenditures determined the sum to be transferred. Under the terms of the contract, central ministries ceased to issue mandatory targets and gave Guangdong full control over local spending. Ye Xuanping was able to extend the initial five-year fixed payment, remitting only Y1.2 billion to the central government each year, even though Guangdong's annual revenues topped Y10 billion after 1988. Thus Guangdong, and through it Guangzhou, stole a lead over other provinces whose fiscal contracts were commensurably less favorable. The fiscal contract was combined with measures that allowed Guangdong autonomy in formulating its own development plans, managing labor, and introducing price reforms.

Other actions enlarged Guangdong's financial decisionmaking powers, including the authority to establish its own financial institutions, engage in foreign exchange account business, and issue bonds overseas. After the Tiananmen event in 1989, hard-liners in Beijing proposed to take back the economic and fiscal autonomy enjoyed by Guangdong and a few other provinces.[8] But Ye Xuanping prevented such an outcome. Even after his formal departure from Guangdong in 1991, he continued to safeguard the province's interests. His capacity to do so was further enhanced by the important position of his brother-in-law Zou Jiahua, who served as minister in charge of the State Planning Commission and deputy premier.[9] The fiscal contracts negotiated in 1988 brought other provinces on a par with Guangdong, but the earlier political interventions put the province on the path to rapid development on which it continues at an unabated pace.

Industrial Structure and Agglomeration Economies

Guangzhou has already gained a foothold in a number of major subsectors, including clothing, textiles, consumer electronics, household durables, bicycles, motorbikes, and food processing. It has also begun exploiting backward linkages to metallurgical and petrochemical industries. There is ample scope for expansion and upgrading in all of these fields. In particular, garments, household electrical products, leather, and sporting goods industries might provide avenues for growth. Similarly, there are vast opportunities in food and cosmetics industries: the demand for custom-designed convenience foods will grow, requiring industrial enzymes, flavors, enhancers, and colors and encouraging the emergence of a biotechnology subsector.

Among the three cities, Guangzhou's industrial structure shows the lowest degree of specialization, as demonstrated by a lower level of Herfindahl indices than both Shanghai and Tianjin. The top 10 industrial subsectors accounted for 57 percent of GVIO in 1986 and 62 percent in 1993 (see table 5.1). In the mid-1980s the four leading subsectors in order of size were machine building, textiles, pharmaceuticals, and metallurgy. Machine building was by far the largest, with a fifth of output, followed by textiles, with 8 percent. Both of these have lost ground, and their shares were 14 and 5 percent, respectively, in 1993. The large gains in shares were registered by transport equipment, chemicals, leather products, and building materials. This represents Guangzhou's attempt to diversify into motor vehicles and motorbikes, chemical feedstocks, fibers for the textiles industry, and a wide array of light manufactures. The development of leather goods and clothing has strengthened export-oriented light industry. At the same time, the emphasis on transport, chemicals, and building materials increased the salience of heavy industry. Overall, heavy industry has gained in share, from a third in 1986 to 43 percent in 1993. Although the shift away from machine building represents a realistic assessment of Guangzhou's competitive strength relative to producers in other parts of China as well as overseas, the investment in autos—as distinct from motorbikes—and in chemicals suggests that the municipality remains uncertain about its areas of core competence for the long haul. Compared with Shanghai and Tianjin, Guangzhou has diffuse goals for industrial composition, which calls into question its otherwise impressive performance.

Several subsectors are gaining a stronger presence in Guangzhou's industrial economy, including petroleum processing and chemicals, transport equipment, and miscellaneous light manufacturing (see figure 5.1). The petroleum-processing and chemicals industries grew rapidly during recent years. Together they accounted for 11 percent of total GVIO in 1993, up from 8.6 percent in 1986. Chemicals are now the third largest industry in terms of output. The Guangzhou General Petrochemical Plant, with capacity to refine 10 million tons of imported sulfur-bearing crude oil, is being substantially expanded. If completed as planned by the end of

Table 5.1   Gross Value of Industrial Output in Guangzhou, Selected Years, 1986–93

| | 1986 | | 1991 | | 1993 | | Enterprises in 1993 | |
| | Billions | | Billions | | Billions | | | |
Indicator	of yuan[a]	Percent	of yuan[a]	Percent	of yuan[a]	Percent	Number	Percent
City total	17.80	100.0	53.68	100.0	100.25	100.0	5,261	100.0
Light industry	11.86	66.6	32.77	61.1	56.24	56.1	3,564	67.7
Heavy industry	5.94	33.4	20.91	39.0	44.01	43.9	1,697	32.3
State-owned								
enterprises	11.67	65.6	31.80	59.2	46.53	46.4	1,006	19.1
Collective-owned								
enterprises	4.53	25.5	8.54	15.9	16.22	16.2	3,081	58.6
Others	1.60	9.0	13.35	24.9	37.50	37.4	1,174	22.3
Top subsectors								
in 1993	10.11	56.8	32.42	60.4	61.71	61.6	2,657	50.5
Machine building[b]	3.63	20.4	8.20	15.3	14.11	14.1	746	14.2
Transport								
equipment	0.73	4.1	4.17	7.8	9.59	9.6	247	4.7
Chemicals	0.86	4.8	3.62	6.7	6.03	6.0	225	4.3
Metallurgy[c]	0.89	5.0	2.69	5.0	5.74	5.7	76	1.4
Textiles	1.42	8.0	3.07	5.7	5.03	5.0	264	5.0
Petroleum								
processing	0.67	3.8	2.97	5.5	5.00	5.0	3	0.1
Leather products	0.14	0.8	1.83	3.4	4.37	4.4	198	3.8
Building materials	0 40	2.3	1.45	2.7	4.19	4.2	258	4.9
Clothing	0.43	2.4	1.77	3.3	3.94	3.9	569	10.8
Pharmaceuticals	0.94	5.3	2.64	4.9	3.72	3.7	71	1.4
Herfindahl index		0.059		0.056		0.044		

Note: All numbers exclude village-run enterprises.
a. Current prices.
b. Includes machine building and electrical machinery.
c. Includes smelting and pressing of ferrous and nonferrous metals.
Source: State Statistical Bureau, *Statistical Yearbook of Guangzhou*, 1987, 1992, 1994.

Figure 5.1 Industrial Structure of Guangzhou, 1986 and 1993

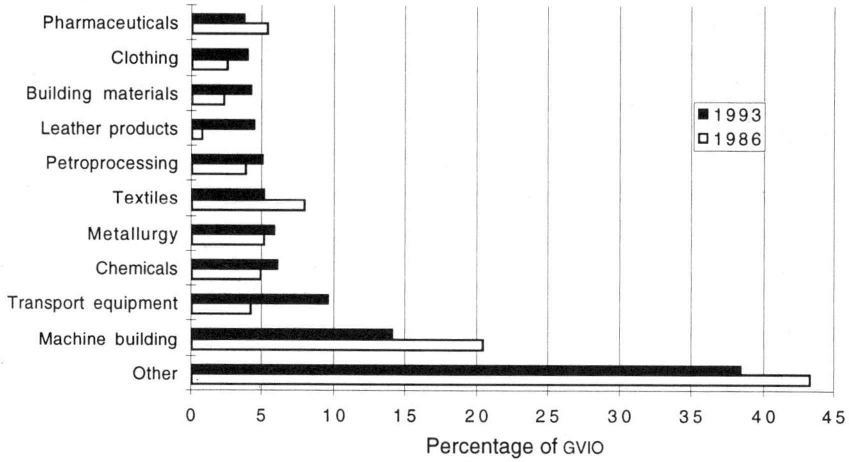

Note: GVIO, gross value of industrial output.
Source: Table 5.1.

this decade, the plant will be able to produce high-quality lead-free gasoline, diesel oil, and kerosene for use in aviation. In addition to domestic sales, it will export its products to Singapore and other countries in Southeast Asia (FBIS-CHI-94111, June 9, 1994, p. 50).

Guangzhou's transport equipment industry got an early boost from a joint venture with Peugeot to produce passenger cars. But Peugeot's decision in 1995 to halt production of its 505 sedan suggests that the market for midsize cars is already too crowded and that smaller players face an uphill battle.[10] Motorbikes might be better suited to Guangzhou's capabilities, and the market prospects are brighter (penetration rates are 3 to 5 percent) than for midsize sedans, although competition from large producers in Chongqing, Jinan, Shanghai, and Luoyang is strong. China produced 7.8 million motorbikes, mostly in the 100-cubic-centimeter range, in 1995, and capacity distributed across 140 producers is nearly 10 million units. By the end of the century, estimated demand could be as high as 12 million, a huge market for assemblers and component makers alike.[11] The collaborative venture with Honda that began in 1984 gives Guangzhou an opportunity to become a major player. However, only through aggressive marketing, improved technology, and expanded capacity can Guangzhou ensure that it is one of the top five dominant producers five years from now.

Guangzhou's approach is similar to that of Japan. Earlier in the century, Japan relied on its well-articulated and efficient bicycle industry to gain entry into the manufacture of motorcycles. Guangzhou's bicycle industry, led by the Five Rams Company, had already established a network of suppliers with the sophistication required to produce parts for the motorbike subsector (certain engine electronics and instrumentation were still being imported in 1995 and may still need to be imported). This company has also shown initiative in linking up with defense suppliers to arrange for technology transfer in the area of metallurgy and carbon-fiber composites. No doubt they will need a few years to reach acceptable standards of quality, but the experience of Taiwan (China), and even Pakistan, indicates that once the skills are present, movement along the learning curve can be rapid.

Differences in the structure of output are also evident in miscellaneous light manufacturing, which is considerably larger in Guangzhou than in Shanghai or Tianjin (and even larger in Guangdong as a whole). Here is the strongest evidence that Guangzhou is following the export-oriented path pioneered by Hong Kong and Taiwan (China). Guangzhou's light industry is labor-intensive, has low skill requirements, and emphasizes design and product diversity so as to facilitate the penetration of international markets. Examples of this type of manufacturing include toys, shoes, and sporting equipment. Guangdong has avoided the problem of low income elasticity for these goods by displacing Hong Kong and, to a lesser extent, Taiwan (China) with the help of suppliers who have consciously relocated production from these economies to southern Guangdong. Guangzhou, and more generally Guangdong, has followed the standard "stepladder" or "flying geese" pattern of export development (Yamazawa 1990, p. 13). Entering at the bottom of the technology spectrum, they have taken over production of the simplest goods with the largest labor component. Guangdong has only just begun the transition to higher-quality, more skill-intensive goods and still has a long way to go (Bateman and Mody 1991). Growth of miscellaneous light manufactures also characterized Shanghai during the past decade. Rapid increases in garments, shoes, printing, sports goods, and handicrafts have been responsible for a portion of Shanghai's growth. However, in both Shanghai and Tianjin this process is less advanced than in Guangzhou.

Food processing may well become a profitable pursuit for Guangzhou. The region around Guangzhou yields an assortment of produce, only a small percentage of which is processed, compared with 70 percent in Brazil and 83 percent in Malaysia. As a result, waste is still substantial. Processing of fruits and vegetables is likely to be an important growth industry, which will spur investment in storage facilities and packaging. The market for nonalcoholic drinks throughout China is enormous and still largely untapped. Compared with the annual per capita consumption of 16 liters in Hong Kong, the average Chinese consumes just 4 liters of nonalcoholic drinks. Firms such as Vitasoy from Hong Kong have already established joint ventures in Shenzhen, and beverage production in Guangzhou, with or without foreign participation, could certainly expand and find markets throughout China as well as overseas.

But the tasks of enlarging market share and moving upscale into items with a higher value added call for investment in services to raise skills, enhance quality, improve the access of small businesses to financing, and increase the level of design and marketing capacity. For instance, training can augment the productivity of garment workers and their stitching skills. Garment manufacturers with support from municipal authorities could add training facilities, as the Thai Garment Manufacturers Association has done. Likewise, raising the standards of university courses and establishing design institutes sponsored by the industry or the government, as is the case in Hong Kong and Japan, can address deficiencies in design. Quality is also a function of equipment, and small enterprises often have difficulty obtaining sufficient credit to purchase the latest machinery. Although informal arrangements and urban credit cooperatives satisfy much of the need, the infrastructure of financing is still backward.

Guangzhou's state sector is rather different from that of Shanghai in that small-scale state enterprises have played a much more important role in production, providing more than half of the city's GVIO. The city is restructuring municipally owned state enterprises by transforming property rights and attracting foreign investment. In early 1994 it selected 50 loss-making state-owned enterprises for a two-year trial restructuring. Under this program, firms will move out of prime sections of the city to make way for real estate development. Proceeds from land leasing will be used to pay the debts of these enterprises.[12] Other enterprises owned by the municipality are being offered to foreign investors, who can purchase them outright or enter into joint ventures with the Guangzhou authorities. In this way, it is hoped that problem enterprises will be put back on their feet, their technology improved, and their production facilities modernized.

Guangzhou has also been the most active in cultivating the nonstate sector, especially joint ventures and cooperatives. Ease of entry (and exit) by smaller nonstate enterprises offers the best chances to build robust networks of subcontractors, absorb new technology, and enhance the competitiveness as well as the flexibility of the local economy. As they have done in Korea and Taiwan (China), state enterprises can continue to dominate the upper reaches of industry, where capital intensity and scale economies are significant. Elsewhere, the flexibility of nonstate enterprises can be a tremendous asset. All three cities need to reverse the vertical integration that characterizes large state enterprises, but Guangzhou took an early lead in building a base of potential suppliers.

The changing structure of ownership is heartening and indicates that the role of the market is on the rise. In the mid-1980s, state-owned enterprises generated two-thirds of Guangzhou's industrial output, a large proportion even though it is below the ratios registered by Tianjin and Shanghai. By 1993 this had diminished to 46 percent, but so, interestingly,

Table 5.2 Foreign Trade in Guangzhou, 1985 and 1990–93

Indicator	1985 Millions of U.S. dollars	1985 Percent	1990 Millions of U.S. dollars	1990 Percent	1991 Millions of U.S. dollars	1991 Percent	1992 Millions of U.S. dollars	1992 Percent	1993 Millions of U.S. dollars	1993 Percent
Total exports	413.3	100.0	1,442.9	100.0	1,840.7	100.0	2,456.8	100.0	3,482.2	100.0
Trading companies	314.5	76.1	543.3	37.7	621.1	33.7	607.4	24.7	474.4	13.6
Light industrial products	116.2	n.a.	182.6	n.a.	193.8	n.a.	190.9	n.a.	137.6	n.a.
Crafts	37.0	n.a.	53.8	n.a.	48.0	n.a.	46.0	n.a.	35.1	n.a.
Textiles	54.1	n.a.	75.8	n.a.	88.7	n.a.	75.7	n.a.	61.9	n.a.
Chemicals	7.7	n.a.	15.7	n.a.	13.9	n.a.	13.0	n.a.	13.3	n.a.
Machinery	1.6	n.a.	9.0	n.a.	11.6	—	15.2	n.a.	14.8	n.a.
Equipment	2.0	n.a.	18.3	n.a.	47.0	—	50.0	n.a.	36.8	n.a.
Industrial enterprises	36.9	8.9	440.2	30.5	523.8	28.5	634.4	25.8	909.7	26.1
Foreign-invested enterprises	11.6	2.8	349.2	24.2	559.7	30.4	1,073.3	43.7	1,416.3	40.7
Processing/assembly plants	50.3	12.2	110.2	7.6	136.2	7.4	141.7	5.8	542.6	15.6
Others	0	n.a.	0	n.a.	0	n.a.	0	n.a.	139.2	4.0
Total imports	—	—	671.6	100.0	1,178.9	100.0	1,746.9	100.0	2,485.1	100.0
Trading companies	—	—	114.1	17.0	153.9	13.1	187.8	10.8	238.5	9.6
Industrial enterprises	—	—	226.1	33.7	265.5	22.5	361.0	20.7	413.7	16.7
Foreign-invested enterprises	—	—	328.8	49.0	756.1	64.1	1,191.8	68.2	1,473.3	59.3
Processing/assembly plants	—	—	2.7	0.4	3.5	0.3	6.2	0.4	359.6	14.5
Commodity trade balance	—	n.a.	771.3	n.a.	661.8	n.a.	709.9	n.a.	997.1	n.a.

— Not available.
n.a. not applicable.
Source: State Statistical Bureau, Statistical Yearbook of Guangzhou, 1992, 1994.

had the share of collective-owned enterprises (table 5.1). The big gainers were joint ventures and private enterprises, whose share increased four-fold, from 9 to 37 percent, underscoring the sheer volume of FDI in Guangzhou and its dramatic impact on the industrial system. Prospects for continuing reform of state-owned enterprises may depend on the maturing of the still embryonic social security system. So long as jobs are abundant and few state employees are being laid off, a state-supported social security system is not essential. However, an accelerated closure of state-owned enterprises and the concomitant loss of welfare services could engender labor unrest and in turn rising labor costs. In this regard, Shanghai has acted faster than Guangzhou in devising a framework for providing social welfare outside of state-owned enterprises.[13]

Guangzhou's growth performance puts it ahead of the two other cities in some respects. Its efforts to restructure, which have been pushed ahead more forcefully by reforms, have substantially enlarged the share of nonstate enterprises, as well as service industries. Guangzhou's hospitality toward foreign investors has provided funding for industry and promoted export activities, enabling the city to achieve a high ratio of trade to municipal output.

Where Guangzhou is weakest is with regard to industrial focus. In the light manufacturing sector it has areas of specialization, such as leather goods, but overall the impression is less positive. The city is being pulled in several different directions, spreading resources thinly across subsectors, such as autos and chemicals, where its comparative advantage is uncertain.[14] Some industries should either be pursued comprehensively, with a long-term vision and the willingness to commit a large volume of capital, or be left alone.

The robustness of Guangzhou's economy and its competitive strength are also apparent from export trends. Exports were valued at $413 million in 1985. By 1993 they were almost $3.5 billion, a more than eightfold increase yielding a net surplus of approximately $1 billion on the trade account (see table 5.2). More than half of the exports were light manufactures produced by joint ventures and enterprises processing or assembling items on contract. Such activities have multiplied all across Guangdong and Fujian. Guangzhou, because of its size, industrial base, port facilities, and services, has emerged as a manufacturing base that foreign investors find especially attractive.

Neighborhood Effects

The overwhelming importance of neighborhood effects is arguably the most remarkable feature of Guangzhou's development. These derive from three separate sources: FDI primarily from Southeast Asia, proximity to Hong Kong, and growth of the Pearl River delta economy. The roots of FDI in Guangzhou lie in the emigration of Chinese to Hong Kong and to other countries in the region. A trickle before the mid-nineteenth century, emigration mounted rapidly after the Qing authorities relaxed the ban in 1890. A hundred years later, in 1990, roughly 37 million Chinese were living overseas in 136 countries and economies, with two-thirds residing in Indonesia (20 percent), Thailand (16 percent), Hong Kong (15 percent), and Malaysia (15 percent). Including Singapore and the United States raises the ratio to more than 75 percent (Poston, Mao, and Yu 1996). A majority of the emigrants are from southeastern China, and many of them have retained their ties with the cities and villages of their birth. Even during the Maoist period, when contacts were difficult to sustain and travel to China was problematic, overseas Chinese kept alive their relations with kinfolk whenever possible by sending money and packages. This large, interconnected, entrepreneurial, and wealthy Chinese diaspora is the conduit for much of the FDI in China and the force behind neighborhood effects (*Financial Times*, August 16, 1995).

The turning point for Guangdong and for its capital city was Central Document No. 50, issued in 1979, which not only formalized the generous new fiscal contract but also enabled the province to add operational content to its latent ties with Hong Kong and other economies of Southeast Asia. Under the terms of the agreement with the central government, Guangdong retained 30 percent of foreign exchange in excess of a fixed amount of $20 million from export processing, compensation, trade, and joint ventures. This was 5 percent over the level allowed to other open regions. The province was granted greater authority to conduct foreign trade and to create investment entities so as to bring in foreign capital. Two later documents, No. 41 (mid-1980) and No. 27 (1981), encouraged Guangdong to pursue enterprise, labor, and price reforms so as to maximize benefits from the "opening to the outside world." Financial measures permitting, the ability to issue stocks and bonds so as to absorb foreign capital strengthened Guangdong's hand yet more (Cheung 1994b).

With the blessing of the central government and the latitude to manipulate policies so as to induce FDI, Guangdong moved quickly to breathe life into cross-border relationships. Businessmen in Hong Kong, seeking opportunity and some relief from rising land and labor costs, were quick to reciprocate. For all the initial uncertainty, the attractions of shifting some production facilities into Guangdong were exceedingly powerful. The absence of language barriers, the ease of dealing with kinfolk, and the convenience of being a short truck drive from Hong Kong outweighed the headaches caused by red tape, the avarice of local authorities, and the problems of operating in a country that had adopted a posture of studied aloofness for 30 years.

In an amazingly short span of time, economic considerations triumphed convincingly over political reservations, over ideological resistance to the seeping in of capitalism, and over the many day-to-day annoyances of doing business in the China of the early 1980s. Starting with the four Special Economic Zones, FDI diffused into Guangdong. Soon it spread throughout the delta and especially to Guangzhou, which created an Economic and Technological Development District in 1984, initially covering an area of 7 square kilometers that by 1996 had expanded to 50 square kilometers. Between 1979 and 1993 Guangzhou actually received $3.0 billion in FDI, three-quarters of it from Hong Kong (see table 5.3; about 64 percent of all foreign investment in Guangdong Province was in Guangzhou and Shenzhen). By the end of 1993, there were nearly 5,000 joint ventures in Guangzhou, with a gross output of Y30 billion and exports of $1.4 billion (FBIS-CHI-94104, May 31, 1994, p. 49).

The effect of this great wave of capital was far-reaching for Guangzhou and the entire Pearl River delta.[15] Guangzhou and the surrounding region acquired a modern industrial base of light industry composed mainly of joint ventures, collectives, and private enterprises.[16] By the close of the 1980s, 7,000 joint ventures were operating in the Pearl River delta, while another 20,000 local factories were working with Hong Kong businessmen in various kinds of subcontracting relationships. Nearly 6 million workers, mostly in Guangdong, were employed in these businesses by 1994, compared with about 615,000 manufacturing workers in Hong Kong itself. Moreover, the number of manufacturing workers in Hong Kong has been declining in absolute and relative terms, from 42 percent of total employment in 1980 to 20 percent in 1991 (Wong 1991; Sung 1991). Thus, the export of jobs from Hong Kong has made possible the rapid growth of manufacturing employment in Guangdong. Hong Kong itself has already made the transition from being a significant manufacturing center to serving as the financial and commercial focus of a manufacturing network that spans the Pearl River delta. In 1978, 75 percent of Hong Kong's exports were manufactured in the colony; by 1989 the figure was only 39 percent. The share of employment in commercial, financial, and real estate services increased from 25 percent in 1980 to 33 percent in 1990.

Despite rising land and labor costs, foreign investors continue to enter Guangdong in droves. Provincial planners expect high costs in the open coastal areas to push processing/assembly and other labor-intensive industrial activities gradually out of the Pearl River delta and into more remote areas. In 1992 all major cities in Guangdong were declared "open" to promote foreign investment. But weak transportation and distribution links to the mountainous areas have inhibited most firms from moving out of the delta. Foreign-invested enterprises in Guangdong still rely heavily on Hong Kong affiliates for marketing, repair, and other support services, which are rarely available domestically or at least are not available cheaply (see Brudvig 1993).

The spillovers from Hong Kong and later from Taiwan (China) as well as other economies have covered a wide spectrum. Most immediately, FDI was the source of capital manufacturing technology and market outlets.

Table 5.3 Foreign Investment in Guangzhou, Selected Years, 1979–93

(millions of U.S. dollars)

Indicator	1979	1980	1985	1990	1992	1993	1979–93
Contracted foreign investment	23.58	249.05	701.75	554.26	4,710.80	7,047.64	16,320.92
Loans	0	0	159.82	50.67	155.71	175.66	938.80
Direct investment	19.70	247.94	515.75	471.83	4,496.54	6,836.34	14,963.90
Equity joint ventures	0	0	70.73	107.06	526.67	444.83	1,918.73
Contractual joint ventures	19.70	247.94	445.02	242.27	3,661.13	6,034.09	12,017.34
Wholly foreign-owned	0	0	0	122.50	308.74	357.42	1,027.83
Other	3.88	1.11	26.18	31.76	58.55	35.64	418.22
Leasing	0	0	0	14.55	46.01	25.09	132.16
Compensation trade	3.88	1.11	6.09	4.79	2.40	2.22	107.87
Assembly/processing	0	0	20.09	12.42	10.14	8.33	178.19
Utilized foreign investment	9.84	30.13	157.82	267.37	728.80	1,463.92	4,151.06
Loans	0	0	39.37	66.43	155.71	175.66	907.88
Direct investment	1.65	12.87	103.89	180.87	554.20	1,278.28	3,019.50
Equity joint ventures	0	0	29.64	85.05	244.84	332.80	991.20
Contractual joint ventures	1.65	12.87	74.25	60.31	210.67	796.92	1,681.34
Wholly foreign-owned	0	0	0	35.51	98.69	148.56	346.96
Other	8.19	17.26	14.56	20.07	18.89	9.98	223.68
Leasing	0	0	0	7.65	15.42	3.61	39.36
Compensation trade	0.56	3.63	7.15	3.77	0.52	0.50	75.25
Assembly/processing	7.63	13.63	7.41	8.65	2.95	5.87	109.07

Source: State Statistical Bureau, *Statistical Yearbook of Guangzhou,* 1994.

In less than a decade, Guangdong had acquired a large and dynamic industrial sector, which was responsible for 9.5 percent of China's manufactured exports in 1993.[17] A province not known for its industrial performance and whose growth rate barely reached the average was transformed into an industrial powerhouse and became one of the three fastest-growing provinces in the country.

The longer-run effects of Hong Kong's participation and the FDI entering the province are equally significant. First, industrialization and contact with foreign engineers, technicians, factory supervisors, and others have sharply raised labor skills. Second, many economic institutions—legal, regulatory, for propagating information, and for selling standards—have been absorbed into the life of the province, squeezing out earlier socialist practices. This has made Guangdong a leader among China's modernizing provinces. Third, neighborhood effects have given rise to an irresistible reform dynamic. Greater integration with the international economy by way of Hong Kong has created pressure for more reform. Each step forward gives rise to demands for more change, which wears down the residual political resistance (from supervisory bureaus, state enterprises, and more conservative elements in the party) to the extension of market institutions. Fourth, Hong Kong is the source not only for the bulk of FDI, but also for a full suite of producer services critical to the effective functioning of joint ventures and the export of products assembled in Guangdong (see Enright, Scott, and Dodwell 1997).

Although financial services are at the top of the list, industry and trade would be helpless without marketing insurance, brokerage, and transport services that see goods from the factory gate to their overseas customers, most commonly via the port in Hong Kong (increasingly, seaborne freight is being channeled through other ports, such as Shekou, Yantian, and Zhuhai; see Chu 1994). China's long isolation from the world of international trade in manufactures and its relative industrial backwardness made it necessary for Hong Kong businesses to provide training in quality control, to supervise production closely, to train key factory personnel, to arrange for professional inspection of items before they are shipped, and to send skilled technicians to repair equipment (three Hong Kong firms do the bulk of inspections in the Pearl River delta area). As the scale of cross-border activities mounted in the 1980s, the supply of such services rapidly grew in volume. Toward the end of the decade, more than 50,000 people from Hong Kong were crossing into Guangdong each day, mostly to service industrial activities.

Hong Kong has been the main gateway for capital, skills, information, and services into Guangzhou (Sung 1991). Other economies, such as Taiwan (China), Thailand, Singapore, and Indonesia, have also invested in the province. Although their shares are smaller, these rapidly growing economies have generated other kinds of spillover benefits. Together they constitute a large and highly competitive market for Guangzhou's industry. Collectively they had a gross national product

(GNP) of $675.0 billion in 1992, and their total trade, exports plus imports, amounted to $685.2 billion, which has increased 10.5 percent annually since 1985.[18] Because Chinese businesses dominate the industrial scene even in countries where the majority of the populace is not Chinese, there exist ready-made channels through which enterprises from Guangdong can acquire market contacts, gather market intelligence, and strike up alliances. Redding (1992, p. 21) has mapped the spread of these alliances and the diffusion of Chinese capital throughout Southeast Asia. He notes that:

> Chinese have been holding various international meetings in recent years. These gatherings are significant in that they transcend the traditional family, geographical, and business ties of overseas Chinese. . . . They are aimed at building a global network of expatriate Chinese and Chinese enterprises. Furthermore, the recent modernization and diversification of Chinese businesses are combined. It seems that the international conference is the place where Chinese enterprises create the new network for becoming an international company by making the best use of the traditional networks which have been created in the past. It is easy to think, therefore, that recent international conferences are harbingers of moves to create a strategically more broadly based worldwide network that would replace the traditional network which has lost some of its vitality and resilience because of generational change. If that is the case, the presence of Chinese networks in the world economy, not just in the regional economy, will become a factor of decisive importance.

The size of the Southeast Asian market means that there are scale economies to be exploited in certain export industries. Economies that have access to an abundant supply of low-wage labor and are able to invest in large-scale modern facilities can gain the upper hand. Guangdong Province can marshal the labor, and it commands a substantial investable surplus. This permits a rapid supply response and the achievement of scale economies. As service industries clustered around Guangzhou mature, Guangdong's overall productivity and competitiveness will increase even more, adding to its power in the region. Thus the size of the potential market has feedback effects that the economy around Guangzhou can use to gain in strength.

The region lying beyond China's southern periphery is exerting a profound influence on Guangzhou, shaping its development, and regulating the pace of growth. But the Pearl River delta economy is of considerable consequence as well, and its evolution is also leaving an imprint on Guangzhou. The so-called open region of the Pearl River delta has an area of 45,005 square kilometers and contained 17.2 million persons in

1993. The delta as a whole was responsible for close to 59 percent of Guangdong's gross product, with industry accounting for much of its preponderance (see table 5.4). Factories in the Pearl River delta produced almost three-quarters of Guangdong's industrial output and an equivalent percentage of provincial exports. Within the delta, Guangzhou is the largest city in terms of population and industrial output, but manufacturing centers have grown around it in the counties of Dongguan, Foshan, Zengcheng, and Zhongshan, not to mention the thriving special economic zones of Shenzhen and Zhuhai (see figure 5.2). Each produces a range of manufactures, though in most instances there is some specialization. For instance, Foshan is especially noted for the assembly of consumer electronics, textiles, and toys, and Dongguan has a reputation in ceramics and clothing. In a little more than a decade, FDI and the opening of the economy to trade have transformed largely rural counties into thriving industrial districts with clusters of networked firms whose competitive strength equals if not surpasses that of other producers in Southeast Asia.

The drive for wealth in the Pearl River delta is most striking in Dongguan, a metropolitan area of 2 million persons that includes 29 surrounding townships. The local economy has grown about 20 percent annually since 1979. To lure bigger enterprises, Dongguan has put up factory buildings, which it rents to manufacturers from Hong Kong and Taiwan (China). It now has more than 7,000 processing/assembly manufacturing and "compensation trade" enterprises in which foreigners have invested (migrants from Dongguan account for a sizable share of Hong Kong's population—650,000—and Dongguan was the first to attract investment from Hong Kong; see Fitzgerald 1996).[19] In 1993 production of household appliances, textiles, foodstuffs, pharmaceuticals, building materials, and machinery pushed GVIO to Y21.5 billion. Dongguan is improving its infrastructure as well as human resources. Since 1979 it has invested Y6 billion in infrastructure, including the rapid conversion of the port into a container terminal. It is building a Y1 billion, 186-megawatt power plant. Dongguan will benefit tremendously from the new rail connection between Guangzhou and Kowloon because the double-track line runs through eight towns in the county. It is also forging direct relationships with universities and other educational institutions in other parts of China.

Since the early 1980s Foshan has emerged as an important industrial area focusing on consumer durables, textiles, aluminum products, and electronics (Foshan's position as a significant commercial town and administrative unit dates back to Ming times; see Faure 1990). Some of China's best-known brands are produced there, and GVIO in 1993 was Y76.7 billion. It also manufactures electronic equipment, textiles, and construction materials, in part in the Foshan high-technology industrial development zone. Transportation links have fueled the growth of

Table 5.4 Macro Indicators for Guangdong Province and Pearl River Delta, 1993

Indicator	Guangdong Province	Pearl River delta region					
		Open economic region[a]	Guangzhou city proper	Shenzhen Special Economic Zone	Zhuhai Special Economic Zone	Total	As a percentage of provincial total
Population (millions)	65.82	17.20	3.73	0.52	0.31	21.75	33.0
Area (square kilometers)	180,000	45,005	1,444	328	121	46,897	26.0
Gross value of agricultural and industrial output (billions of yuan)	613.64	230.44	68.26	43.69	17.12	359.51	58.6
Gross value of industrial output (billions of yuan)	523.74	211.56	66.59	43.62	16.81	338.57	64.6
Exports (billions of U.S. dollars)	27.03	8.23	0.81	5.77	0.95	15.76	58.3
Utilized foreign investment (billions of U.S. dollars)	9.65	3.92	0.28	1.11	0.52	5.84	60.5

a. Composed of 28 counties and municipalities, excluding the city proper of Guangzhou and the Special Economic Zones of Shenzhen and Zhuhai but including the counties administered by Guangzhou, Shenzhen, and Zhuhai.

Source: State Statistical Bureau, *Statistical Yearbook of Guangdong,* 1994; *Statistical Yearbook of Guangzhou,* 1994.

Figure 5.2 Guangzhou and Its Environs

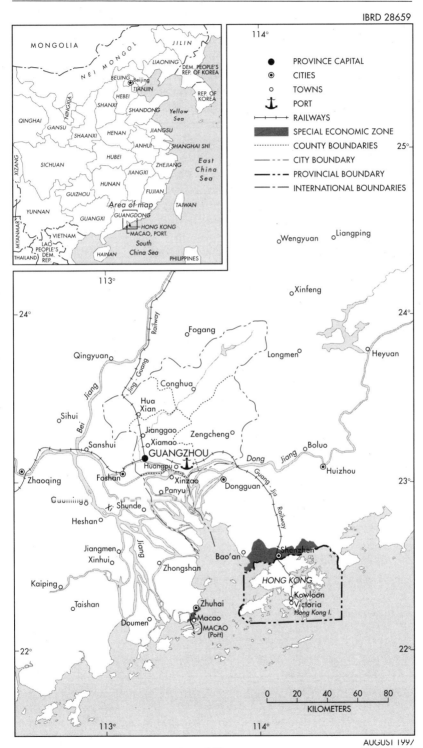

IBRD 28659

LEGEND:
- ● PROVINCE CAPITAL
- ◉ CITIES
- ○ TOWNS
- ⚓ PORT
- ⊢—⊢—⊢ RAILWAYS
- ▓ SPECIAL ECONOMIC ZONE
- ············ COUNTY BOUNDARIES
- —·—·— CITY BOUNDARY
- ▬▬▬ PROVINCIAL BOUNDARY
- —··—··— PROVINCIAL BOUNDARY
- —·—·— INTERNATIONAL BOUNDARIES

Foshan, and new highways to Zhuhai and Guangzhou are strengthening its links with the rest of the delta area. A daily direct train offers service from Hong Kong to the new railway station in Foshan. The adjacent container port at Lanshi, just 9 kilometers from Foshan railway station, has an annual capacity of 2 million tons.

The economy of Guangzhou complements and competes against the manufacturing establishments sprouting in nearby counties.[20] Guangzhou's lead in the sphere of producer services allows it to support the industrial push in the nearby cities. Because it is the main port of the region, it has the best sea, air, and rail links to other parts of China as well as the outside world. Whereas cities such as Wuhan have found that their interests as open and autonomous cities conflict with those of the provincial authorities (Hubei), Guangzhou remains very much the administrative center of Guangdong, as it was in the past. It is not just the largest industrial city in the region, but one with several roles that have taken on a greater importance as the Pearl River delta has become industrialized. The rise of Dongguan, for instance, has had spillovers for Guangzhou: demand has grown for transport and other services available in the city, local manufacturers have increased their clientele in the neighboring countries, and provincial administration has become much more significant.

The element of industrial competition and some collaboration is also noteworthy. Enterprises in Guangzhou, especially state-owned enterprises, are under far more competitive pressure from producers in the area. State-owned enterprises are being driven to restructure their operations and to use their reserves of skilled and trained staff to compete, if not in terms of price, then on the basis of quality and innovation. Other enterprises must offset the higher land and labor costs of operating from Guangzhou by improving their productivity. In any event, competition from the hinterland has beneficial macro and micro consequences. At the macro level it helps drive the tempo of reform in Guangzhou. Already among the front-runners with respect to reforms, Guangzhou has been compelled by intraprovincial circumstances to strive even harder to create an efficient economy keyed largely to market signals and to develop financial instruments, technical skills, and producer services so as to enhance the competitive position of local firms.

Transport-Induced Development

Continuing economic prosperity will require the province to expand transport capacity, including that of the airport, seaport, connecting road, and water system, because transport-dependent light industry and trade are the lifeblood of the delta area's economy.[21] Guangzhou harbor, the third largest seaport in the country, is undergoing expansion in a bid to attract a greater volume of international marine traffic. With more than

70 berths, 34 of which are able to accommodate 10,000-deadweight-ton ships, it handled 65 million tons of goods in 1993. Starting in 1996, the port authority began investing Y750 million over a five-year period to dredge the mouth of the harbor and add 9 million tons of cargo-handling capacity annually. Moreover, an entirely new port zone is to be built before 2005 to raise the port's annual handling volume another 40 percent (FBIS-CHI-94171, September 2, 1994, p. 36). China's first container route, between Guangzhou and Shanghai, was inaugurated in November 1993. A ship capable of carrying 235 containers is plying between the two cities five or six times a month. This has relieved pressure on the overloaded rail system. Moreover, the new port at Yantian near Shenzhen and Hong Kong is emerging as a major transshipment terminal for coal and containers.

Guangzhou airport is the third largest in the country and one of the busiest.[22] The city has proposed building a new facility instead of expanding the existing Baiyun airport, which is located 40 kilometers away from the city center. The local authority is allowed greater flexibility to choose the location and size of the airport and to share management responsibility and profits. Guangzhou will also permit foreign funds to be invested in the new international airport in Huadu. Foreign sources may provide as much as 60 to 70 percent of the $1.15 billion that the airport is estimated to require. A company will be created to construct the airport, which will be listed on either the Shanghai or the Shenzhen Stock Exchange.

In the Pearl River delta, infrastructure facilities, such as highways, deepwater ports, and airports, are constructed at a much higher density than in other regions in China (Nanyang Commercial Bank, Ltd. 1992). Within 100 kilometers of the Pearl River estuary, there is a high concentration of ports, including Guangzhou port, the four ports of Shenzhen, the two ports of Zhuhai, and six others. Three more ports are under planning or construction. In addition to passenger transport, these ports are mainly used to ship goods to Hong Kong for reexport. There are two international airports in the delta, Guangzhou and Shenzhen, and four domestic ones in Foshan, Huizhou, Jiangmen, and Zhuhai. With completion of the Guangzhou-Shenzhen-Zhuhai and Huizhou-Shenzhen freeways, most of these airports will become part of an effective multimodal network.[23]

However, the surface transport network is not as well developed, inhibiting door-to-door delivery, which is advantageous for light industries. Although the density of road networks and inland waterways in Guangdong is higher than the national average, there is still a severe shortage of transport capacity, which is compounded by outmoded technology and high costs. Roads are heavily congested in the fast-growing areas because road capacity has not expanded in line with the growth of traffic in recent years. Growth rates of total road traffic in the province have averaged an estimated 20 to 30 percent a year since 1980. In particular, there is a lack of class 1 and 2 roads, as well as expressways. The mixed use of roads by motor vehicles, tractors, bicycles, and pedestrians, without separation, exacerbates the situation. Congestion and road conditions greatly reduce speeds and consequently increase the costs of operating a vehicle. Moreover, many trucks are of 1950s vintage, and the introduction of new equipment is poorly planned. For instance, the use of modern heavy trucks is causing rapid deterioration of pavements because few roads were constructed to handle such loads.

To deal with these problems, the Guangdong authorities have launched two initiatives. One is an intensive program to upgrade the road system to class 1 or class 2 standards. Another is the heavy emphasis on investment in highway construction using both domestic and foreign sources (Luk 1994). The Shenzhen-Guangzhou highway, by Hong Kong's Gordon Wu, is the most notable instance of foreign investment in infrastructure. Highways will play an increasingly large role in the future because the fast-growing industries in the province will need the speed, flexibility, and door-to-door delivery that only road transport can provide.

Although roads are receiving attention, construction and improvement of inland waterways continue to suffer neglect. The condition of water channels, which ranges from poor to good, limits long-haul shipping. Despite having several thousand kilometers of navigable inland rivers, the Pearl River delta area has not increased its use of water transport. In addition, many river ports are not equipped with modern handling facilities, and loading and unloading are often done manually. Because of outmoded technology and limited port capacity, state-owned ships achieve a utilization rate of only about 20 percent (see Harral, Cook, and Holland 1992). Recently, larger barges, barge trains, and container barges have increased their services, and efficient handling equipment has been installed in several locations. Outside the delta, inland river transport tends to specialize in bulk goods such as construction materials, cement, and fertilizer. Channel dredging could allow larger vessels upstream and extend the navigation season. But thus far, inland waterway transport is not a priority for investment in the eyes of provincial authorities, and opportunities to alleviate a critical bottleneck are being allowed to slip.[24]

Labor Mobility

Guangzhou, as a pioneer of reforms among the three cities, is also an appropriate place for observing the state of labor markets. From early on, the city recognized the need to enhance labor mobility and to expand the authority of enterprises over labor market decisions. A series of measures have been introduced, particularly after 1986, to revamp the "iron rice bowl" system and to improve labor productivity, including labor contracting and wage reform. Two of the most successful changes in matching people with jobs have been the circulation of information about job openings and the policy that applicants must take exams (Vogel 1989). A municipal labor service company was set up to facilitate recruitment and serve as a training center (see chapter 6). To accommodate migrant workers, a system of temporary registration was also established to regulate entry into the municipality and to help enforce a system of annually renewed employment contracts.

Although local labor is plentiful, it is unlikely that the expansion of industry and construction could have proceeded at the rate actually attained without voluntary and induced migration from poorer parts of the province as well as farther afield.[25] Rural people from Hunan, Guangxi, Sichuan, and deeper in the interior have flocked to Guangdong, whose prosperity is a byword in China. Many of them find their way to Guangzhou to work in factories, in construction sites, and in the myriad formal and informal service industries. Factory managers, taking a practical approach, frequently send supervisors to recruit young workers from distant villages once a few migrants from these places have established a good reputation. Given the nature of factory work, fresh blood sustains productivity and fills the gaps left by locals who graduate to less demanding jobs or begin to press for higher wages.

The existence of unskilled and semiskilled migrant labor has sustained elastic labor supply conditions that have allowed Guangzhou to retain its industrial competitiveness. But the city and its sister counties have also relied on the experience of technical staff, who are drawn by attractive salaries from Shanghai, Tianjin, and Liaoning Provinces. These people have made good Guangzhou's deficiencies in factory operation, plant engineering, repair work, and a host of engineering tasks associated with rapid industrialization. According to a 1987 population survey, technical personnel accounted for close to one-third of male migrant workers (see Li and Siu 1994). In fact, the flow in skills was on such a large scale that Shanghai authorities attempted to curtail it starting in the early 1990s. Migrant labor is also more highly educated than Guangdong's population as a whole: 62 percent have a junior high school education or above compared with only 36 percent of the general population in Guangdong (Fan 1996).

The magnitude of intraprovincial migration is remarkable, in fact larger than interprovincial movement, and was estimated at around 2.5 million in 1990. Close to two-thirds of this movement is from rural areas, particularly in the mountainous periphery, to cities and towns. As may be expected, the majority of migrant workers end up in the Pearl River delta region. Major destinations include Shenzhen, Guangzhou, Dongguan, Foshan, and Zhuhai (in that order). The eastern part of the delta—Shenzhen and Dongguan—attracted the most migrants during the 1980s. Both cities capitalized on their proximity to Hong Kong and concentrated on developing processing/assembly industries and operations, which are highly labor-intensive by nature. Estimates of how many migrants, from both within and outside the province, are present in the

Pearl River delta area tend to be imprecise, but by 1990 they were close to 2 million, with Guangzhou accounting for half that number (see Sawada 1992). Since then, the number has risen, possibly to 2.5 million or 3 million, and is likely to continue inching upward as the attractions of a large prosperous metropolis exert their inexorable pull.

The Rise of Producer Services

Another noteworthy feature of structural change in Guangzhou relates to services. Possibly because the central government allowed Guangzhou greater leeway than either Shanghai or Tianjin, the percentage of services in municipal output was greater than in the other two cities. In fact, Guangzhou is the only large city in China where the tertiary sector dominates. The increasing extent of market-directed development has brought about a further growth in share, with the result that Guangzhou's economy is structurally balanced and in a somewhat better position to realize productivity gains. Retailing, fast food, and tertiary business are set to continue their strong growth. In 1992 Guangzhou ranked third in retail sales after Beijing and Shanghai; it also recorded the largest throughput of foreign visitors—2 million—of any city (*Business China*, November 1, 1993, pp. 8–9).

From the second half of the 1980s, there was a steady increase in the import of consulting services from Hong Kong as Chinese firms started taking more initiative in the areas of design, product innovation, research, and streamlining of the production process. Real estate development and the building of better urban infrastructure also generated its own needs for architectural, engineering, and consulting services. Within less than a decade, enterprise managers, party bosses, city mayors, urban planners, and officials in the myriad bureaus realized the necessity of developing a producer-services sector to sustain manufacturing industry. Initially, there was the ingrained ideological resistance to services, which were viewed as unproductive. Where possible, the tendency was to spend money on hardware but to skimp on services. Experience eventually drove home the irrationality of this attitude, and the use of imported producer services increased. In due course, domestic suppliers learned the tricks of the trade, and import substitution began in earnest, with Guangzhou emerging as the focus for these activities. Guangzhou's edge over other candidates in the region derives from its being the provincial administrative center, a major port, and the second largest recipient of FDI in the delta region (where Shenzhen is the largest recipient). But municipal authorities also were quick to see the possibilities and to call for the acquisition of skills that would allow Chinese professionals to enter service industries. Although Hong Kong is likely to retain its dominance during the balance of the 1990s, the intensive development of this sector in Guangzhou is certain to erode Hong Kong's role as a provider of services to firms in Guangdong.

One example of a service activity largely neglected in China's socialist economy is packaging. Chinese enterprises, unassailable in seller's markets, were oblivious to the need for attractive packaging and unwilling to sort and pack items to suit consumer demands. However, in the competitive international market, slipshod packaging was a serious drawback, and Hong Kong expertise proved essential. Sung (1991, p. 133) observed that "packaging is not a particular[ly] capital- or skill-intensive activity . . . and repackaging Chinese goods in Hong Kong [went against the grain of entrenched practices]. A good example of reexports arising out of sorting [was] the labor-intensive sorting of Christmas decorations into variety packages." This is now being shifted to China, with Hong Kong firms providing the expertise and the Chinese investing in "imported packaging machinery to remedy past negligence."

Universities in Guangzhou were among the first in the country to seek commercial outlets for their academic research. This may be related to the deep-seated business culture and the early introduction of market mechanisms into the local economy. For instance, the South China Engineering University developed a robot production line for assembling ceiling fan motors, the first of its kind ever designed and manufactured completely by China itself. The university was also one of the first units to start research into robots.

Summary

Whether it is growth or reforms, Guangzhou is the front-runner of the three cities. It continues to benefit from spillover effects from the delta area and abroad. The network of overseas Chinese has extended its potential economic reach deep into Southeast Asia, giving the city access to capital and making it part of the trading network that embraces one of the most dynamic economic regions in the world. Infrastructure development in Guangdong and in Guangzhou—with the help of foreign capital—is strengthening the all-important communication links with the hinterland, other parts of China, and external markets. At the same time, special rules governing the fiscal and foreign exchange regimes have been terminated. Guangzhou is on a level playing field with the other cities, but it has a head start and no longer needs an extra push.

Starting with fewer resources and less industrial capability than the other two cities, Guangzhou has used the advantages of neighborhood to strengthen its economic position. These neighborhood effects are partly an accident of geography—Hong Kong is close by, and it is an economic powerhouse—and partly an outcome of historical conditions that drove the Cantonese to emigrate. Partly also they derive from the sequencing of China's reforms and the political *guanxi* (connections) that were instrumental in giving Guangdong the autonomy to pursue policies deemed too radical initially for the rest of the country.

Reviewing Guangzhou's performance, and juxtaposing it with that of the other cities, highlights two contrasts. First, Guangzhou's agglomeration economies are weaker, it has fewer industrial options, and its longer-term growth prospects are less clearly defined. Second, the neighborhood effects, although mostly positive thus far, could turn against the city. On the first point, Guangzhou's narrower industrial base, smaller stock of human capital, and more limited education infrastructure restrict its opportunities. Moreover, the city has not yet adopted a coherent development strategy that will keep it near the front of the pack well into the next century. Although it has tackled the problems of the state sector more forcefully than the other two cities, Guangzhou has not yet closed this difficult chapter from the past. The many loss-making, inefficient state-owned enterprises exert a serious drag on the municipal economy, and their partially reformed circumstances have undoubtedly shaved perhaps 1 to 2 percentage points off Guangzhou's annual growth rate during the last 10 years.

Shanghai, and, to a lesser extent, Tianjin dominate their immediate neighborhoods. Shanghai is China's leading industrial and financial center, and Tianjin is an industrial power and the greatest port of the region. Guangzhou also is a major port, but it competes against two other world-class ports—Hong Kong and Yantian—that share the business generated in the region. Similarly, as a middleman, a financial sector, and a supplier of producer services, Hong Kong is far ahead of Guangzhou and will probably retain that position after 1997. Thus, Guangzhou might be constrained by the presence of such a redoubtable contender in a sector where scale economies, an early start, and a reputation are important.

The industrial field in southeast China is crowded, and several cities are approaching Guangzhou's level of industrialization. As industrialization spreads inland, Guangzhou will be exposed to competition from centers where labor and land are cheaper and the costs of urban overhead are much lighter. With so many cities vying for a place, Guangzhou will have to play its industrial cards with some dexterity and be on the lookout for promising niches. Agglomeration and neighborhood effects will still be a factor in the future, but their significance will be less. The major reforms will also have had their effect by the end of the decade. In the future, the gains in productivity, mobilization of resources, innovations, and improvements in the urban environment will depend on the effective combination of many micro-level policies.

Similarities, Contrasts, and Lessons: Three Cities and Others

6

China's urban development is both very old and relatively recent. Many of China's cities, including the three that occupy the center stage in this study, were established centuries ago and were important players in their corner of the world. What might be described as modern urban development in China is a phenomenon of this century and one that initially embraced a relatively small number of cities, the majority lying on the eastern seaboard. This first stage lasted through the mid-1930s, when internal turmoil halted modernization. The urbanization that resumed after 1952 was both limited and in certain respects one-dimensional: cities were viewed as a necessary evil for promoting industry. By the mid-1980s, as reform and external contacts chipped away at the socialist image of the city, these preconceptions were seen as outdated, and China's cities braced themselves for rapid expansion, a diversification of functions, and a fundamental change in spirit and in autonomy. The past 18 years have provided only a taste of what is to come. But already the direction of change is becoming apparent, and Chinese cities are both learning about the problems of rapid urbanization and devising instruments to cope with them, using the advantages of size, of hinterland, of location, and of acquired industrial capability.

The three preceding chapters situate Shanghai, Tianjin, and Guangzhou within a specific historical-geographic context and a framework of developmental possibilities. They seek to provide a sense of place and to convey a perspective on how these cities have begun adjusting to an unforgivingly competitive world, where the rewards are a function of ceaseless effort and are no longer simply assigned by central planners in Beijing. It is a world in which budget constraints are hardening and municipalities themselves must bear a large share of the costs of bad policies.

This chapter operates along two planes: the first is comparative, and the second is concerned with models of municipal development synthesized from a broad range of experience. In earlier chapters we frequently juxtapose and contrast the performance of the three cities in particular areas. Here we look more systematically at the economic record and perceived strategies. We then examine forces that will drive urban change in China during the balance of the 1990s and into the next century. The concluding section explores the relevance of and lessons from the international experience for the three cities.

Three Cities Compared

Shanghai, Tianjin, and Guangzhou have much in common, including certain trends in development. All three are, first and foremost, industrial cities to varying degrees. Their economic center of gravity is in the manufacturing sector. Second, each city has a distinctive geographic location within the regional context: they are on or near the coast, they have large and busy ports, and they are well served by the hinterlands around them. Third, as was typical for major industrial centers in China, the three cities have concentrations of state-owned industry, which are slowly being whittled down as enterprise reform continues to make headway. Fourth, because of the large share of state-owned industry, which sustained a workforce enjoying lifetime tenure, and tight restrictions on labor mobility, the labor market in these cities was subject to many rigidities. These are diminishing but still interpose barriers to change. Fifth, all three belong to the select group of "open" cities that have spearheaded China's "opening to the outside world" and have taken the lead in introducing reform. Sixth and final, the three cities have received a substantial volume of FDI and have benefited from spillover effects emanating from neighboring economies. In these respects, they are comparable and relatively well matched. They are also, to a considerable extent, representative of other large industrial cities of China such as Chongqing, Fuzhou, Hangzhou, Ningbo, Qingdao, and Wuhan.

In other respects, the three cities diverge from one another in ways that draw attention to size, industrial composition, location, share of state industry, and reform initiatives. Of the three, Guangzhou has consistently grown the fastest (see table 3.1). During 1952–78, its GDP increased at an annual rate of 9.5 percent, with Shanghai in second place at 8.8 percent and Tianjin bringing up the rear with a growth rate averaging 7.3 percent. In the 15-year period after the start of reforms (1978–93), Guangzhou maintained the lead with a growth rate of 11.3 percent, which was somewhat above the national average, while Shanghai and Tianjin grew at a roughly similar pace of 8 percent, more than 1 percentage point below the national average. Industrial performance was broadly similar, with Guangzhou once again leading the group during 1952–78, albeit not by a wide margin. But after the start of reforms,

Guangzhou's lead widened substantially, with GVIO rising annually 15.7 percent compared with 9.1 percent for Shanghai, although part of this might be traceable to biases in measurement.

Guangzhou's superior performance in the prereform era was the outcome, most probably, of greater economic autonomy and the smaller share of centrally managed state industry. Unlike the other two cities, Guangzhou was less subject to central direction, less bound by plan targets, and not forced to serve as a vehicle for generating state revenues. It did not receive major state-funded investment projects, but by the same token neither were its development and fiscal policies tightly regulated by Beijing. Although both Shanghai and Tianjin started out in the mid-1950s with a commanding lead over Guangzhou in per capita GDP, this gap no longer exists.

During the reform period, Guangzhou also went further in dissolving large, inefficient state enterprises. By 1993 state-owned enterprises accounted for less than half of the city's GVIO and only 20 percent of all industrial enterprises (see table 5.1). Its trial enterprise restructuring program made headway by transferring property rights of more than 50 loss-making state-owned enterprises to shareholding or foreign ownership. As a result, joint ventures and cooperatives multiplied and by 1993 produced close to 40 percent of municipal GVIO. By contrast, Tianjin was the slowest to reform its state-owned enterprises, and by 1993 the state sector still accounted for close to 60 percent of production. In particular, Tianjin lagged behind in devising a workable program of state-owned enterprise reform, whereas Shanghai recently moved forward with an acquisition and merger program.

There are other differences as well, which are only briefly summarized here. Both Shanghai and Tianjin have an industrial base that is broader and stronger than that of Guangzhou, with Shanghai decisively in the front. These cities enjoy more generous agglomeration economies deriving from the breadth of their industrial base, although during the 1980s they suffered relative to Guangzhou with respect to the scale of the services sector. When various aspects of subsectoral performance are compared, Shanghai dominates Tianjin and Guangzhou in profitability and productivity across six major industries (see table 6.1). Interestingly, Guangzhou is ranked second in the majority of industries, suggesting that its relatively small share of the state sector, its more competitive market environment, its greater FDI, and better developed producer services outweigh Tianjin's industrial reach and agglomeration economies.

Shanghai's indicators of costs are by and large the lowest, with Guangzhou again in second place and Tianjin at the bottom of the list. It is only with respect to the competitiveness of wage rates that Tianjin has an edge over the others, a reflection of greater control over prices and the relative slowness of the reform process. When all the indicators are pulled together, the index of overall performance favors Shanghai in each of the sampled industries except one—transport equipment—where Tianjin seems to have an advantage. In other subsectors, Tianjin ranks above Guangzhou in metallurgy and electronics, which seems very plausible from the evidence presented in earlier chapters. Guangzhou is ahead in textiles, a testimony, no doubt, to the heavy FDI in that subsector. It also has an advantage in chemicals, again possibly because of investment in new plant. The higher ranking in machine building may reflect Guangzhou's greater specialization and market orientation, which offset steeper wage costs and relative lack of accumulated experience in the sector (see figures 6.1–6.6).

Two of the cities, Shanghai and Tianjin, are starting to confront the problem of an aging workforce. Compared with the national urban average, Shanghai's population in 1990 was the most mature (see figure 6.7). Persons above 50 years of age, both male and female, accounted for close to 20 percent of the municipal population, against the benchmark

(*Text continues on page 149.*)

Table 6.1   Industrial Comparative Advantages in Shanghai, Tianjin, and Guangzhou, 1988–92 Average

Industry	Profit (PT/GVIO)	Productivity (GVIO/OVFA)	Cost TPC/GVIO	Cost Wage rate (thousands of yuan)	Index[a]
Textiles					
Shanghai	0.12	2.86	0.80	2.92	0.19
Tianjin	0.01	1.93	0.92	2.27	0.13
Guangzhou	0.03	2.60	0.82	3.60	0.15
Machine building					
Shanghai	0.17	1.89	0.82	3.28	0.17
Tianjin	0.06	1.47	0.89	2.55	0.13
Guangzhou	0.07	1.96	0.94	3.98	0.15
Metallurgy					
Shanghai	0.12	5.17	0.84	3.58	0.27
Tianjin	0.10	4.88	0.86	3.26	0.25
Guangzhou	0.11	3.28	0.76	4.05	0.20
Basic chemicals					
Shanghai	0.16	2.40	0.79	3.95	0.19
Tianjin	0.12	1.62	0.86	2.63	0.15
Guangzhou	0.18	1.79	0.75	4.96	0.17
Transport equipment					
Shanghai	0.18	2.91	0.83	3.62	0.21
Tianjin	0.10	4.34	0.88	3.11	0.24
Guangzhou	0.10	3.39	0.89	4.72	0.21
Electronics					
Shanghai	0.08	2.65	0.91	2.99	0.18
Tianjin	0.06	1.71	1.04	2.43	0.15
Guangzhou	−0.10	2.69	0.91	3.35	0.12

Note: PT, profits and taxes; GVIO, gross value of industrial output; OVFA, original value of fixed assets; TPC, total production costs.
a. Index equals {[(PT / GVIO) + (GVIO/OVFA) / 10] + [(TPC / GVIO) / 5]} / 3.
Source: Survey of Industrial Enterprises, conducted by the Policy Research Department, World Bank, and the Department of Economics, Brandeis University.

Figure 6.1   Textiles Industry in Shanghai, Tianjin, and Guangzhou, 1988–92

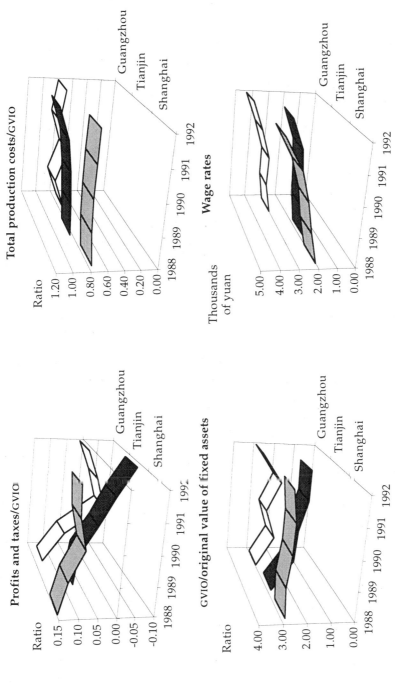

143

Source: Survey of Industrial Enterprises, conducted by the Policy Research Department, World Bank, and the Department of Economics, Brandeis University.

Figure 6.2   Machine-Building Industry in Shanghai, Tianjin, and Guangzhou, 1988–92

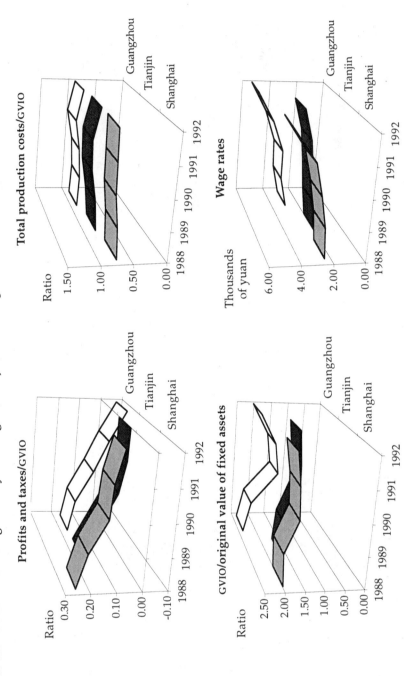

Source: Survey of Industrial Enterprises, conducted by the Policy Research Department, World Bank, and the Department of Economics, Brandeis University.

Figure 6.3 Metallurgy Industry in Shanghai, Tianjin, and Guangzhou, 1988–92

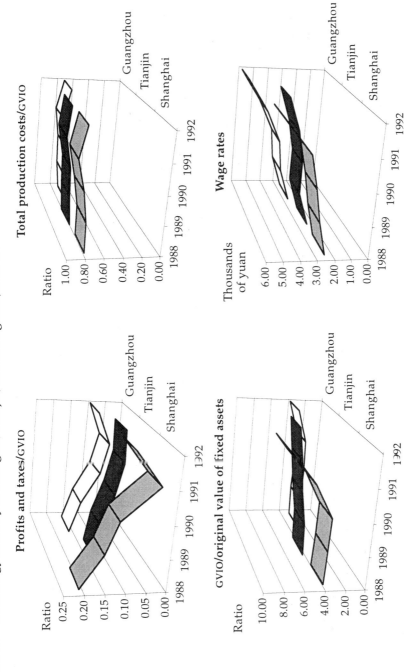

Profits and taxes/GVIO

Total production costs/GVIO

GVIO/original value of fixed assets

Wage rates

Source: Survey of Industrial Enterprises, conducted by the Policy Research Department, World Bank, and the Department of Economics, Brandeis University.

Figure 6.4   Chemicals Industry in Shanghai, Tianjin, and Guangzhou, 1988–92

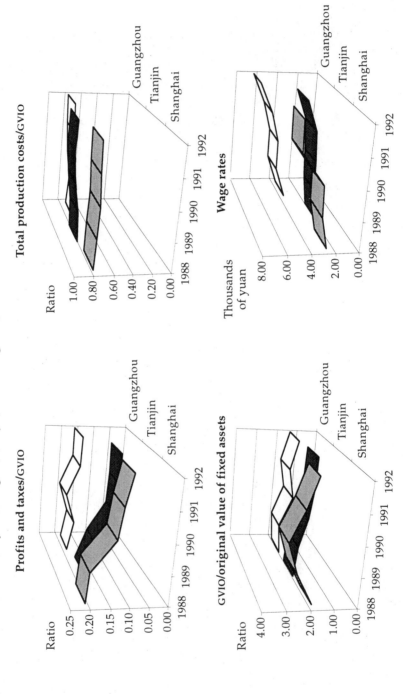

Source: Survey of Industrial Enterprises, conducted by the Policy Research Department, World Bank, and the Department of Economics, Brandeis University.

Figure 6.5   Transport Equipment Industry in Shanghai, Tianjin, and Guangzhou, 1988–92

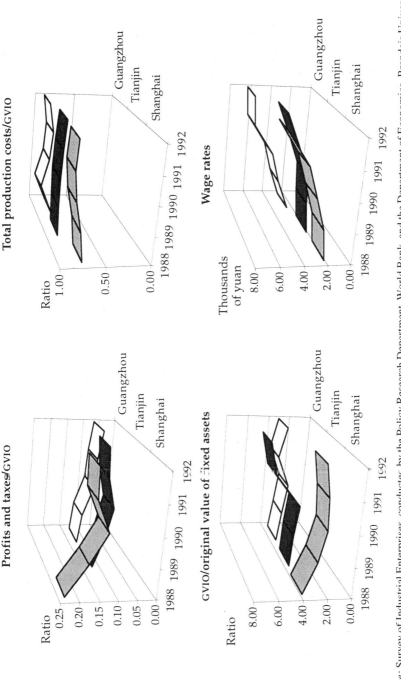

Source: Survey of Industrial Enterprises, conducted by the Policy Research Department, World Bank, and the Department of Economics, Brandeis University.

Figure 6.6   Electronics Industry in Shanghai, Tianjin, and Guangzhou, 1988–92

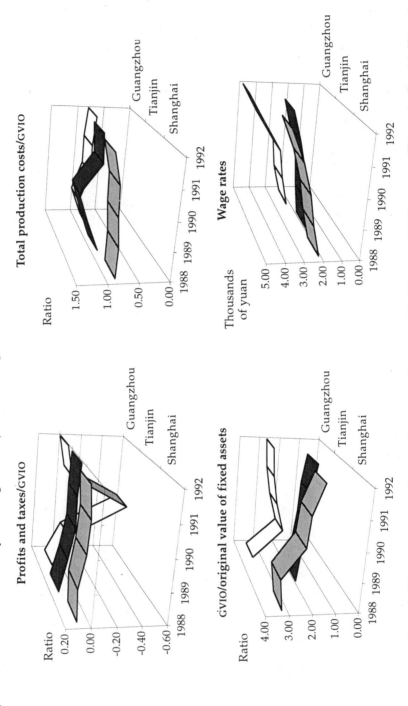

Source: Survey of Industrial Enterprises, conducted by the Policy Research Department, World Bank, and the Department of Economics, Brandeis University.

of about 12 percent at the national level, 14 percent in Guangzhou, and 16 percent in Tianjin. Shanghai also has the lowest birthrate of the three cities, while Guangzhou has the highest, well above the national average (as shown in the size of the 0–4 year age cohort; see table 6.2). A low birthrate, unless offset by continuing migration of young workers to Shanghai and some emigration of retirees, will lead to a significant increase in the share of older age cohorts in the population. The aging workforce will sharpen the demand for a viable long-term social security system that will eventually displace the coverage provided by enterprise-based schemes and will allow the majority of municipal residents to enjoy some coverage. Fortunately, Shanghai has begun to devise such mechanisms, whereas Guangzhou as well as Tianjin have yet to move beyond the trial stage, even though Guangdong has initiated several programs elsewhere in the province.

However, patterns of convergence are emerging among the three cities and are most apparent in sectoral concentration. By 1993 the largest four subsectors in all three cities were metallurgy, machine building, transport equipment, and chemicals (except in Shanghai, where chemicals ranked fifth, behind textiles), though with slightly different sequences. Such a convergence can be a double-edged sword: it encourages healthy competition, but it also diverts limited resources from going to the most efficient producer. Despite a wide industrial base and decreasing level of overall concentration since 1978, the top four subsectors in Shanghai and Tianjin are beginning to enlarge their rela-

Table 6.2   Demographic Profiles of Shanghai, Tianjin, and Guangzhou, 1990–91
(cumulative percentages)

Age cohort	All cities, 1990[a]		Shanghai, 1990[a]		Tianjin, 1991		Guangzhou, 1990	
	Male	*Female*	*Male*	*Female*	*Male*	*Female*	*Male*	*Female*
0–4	7.9	7.9	6.4	6.3	7.0	6.8	8.4	8.2
5–9	15.1	15.0	13.2	13.1	15.4	14.7	16.7	16.4
10–14	21.8	21.7	18.3	18.1	22.5	21.9	24.9	24.5
15–19	31.3	31.3	23.9	23.4	29.3	28.3	33.0	32.5
20–24	42.8	42.2	31.6	30.1	37.7	36.6	44.3	42.8
25–29	53.9	53.0	41.6	39.6	48.2	47.1	55.7	53.1
30–34	63.5	62.4	54.2	51.7	57.8	56.8	64.3	61.7
35–39	72.1	71.2	65.3	62.0	68.2	67.1	72.9	70.3
40–44	78.3	77.2	72.8	69.0	75.3	74.2	77.9	75.2
45–49	83.0	82.0	77.6	73.7	80.3	79.4	82.9	80.2
50–54	87.7	86.7	82.0	78.3	84.7	84.0	87.3	84.5
55–59	92.0	90.9	87.5	84.1	89.3	88.7	91.6	88.9
60–64	95.2	94.0	92.0	89.2	93.2	92.7	94.4	92.0
65–69	97.4	96.4	95.5	93.3	96.1	95.7	97.2	95.1
70+	100.0	100.0	100.0	100.0	100.0	100.0	100.0	100.0

Note: Urban population includes city-administered counties and agricultural population.
a. Based on 1990 population census.
Source: State Statistical Bureau 1992b; *Statistical Yearbook of Shanghai,* 1992; *Statistical Yearbook of Tianjin,* 1992.

Figure 6.7 Urban Life Cycle: Population Pyramids for All Cities of China and for Shanghai, Tianjin, and Guangzhou, circa 1990

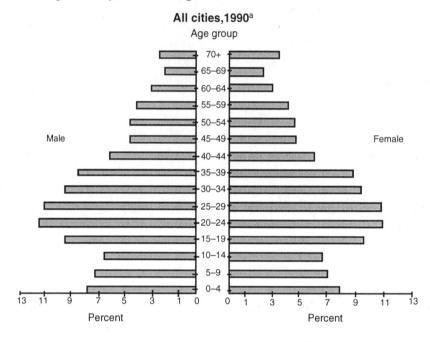

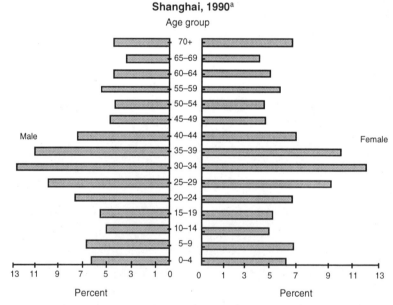

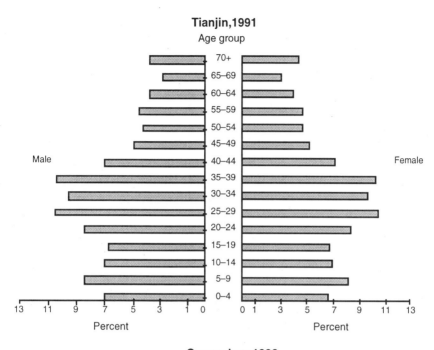

Tianjin,1991

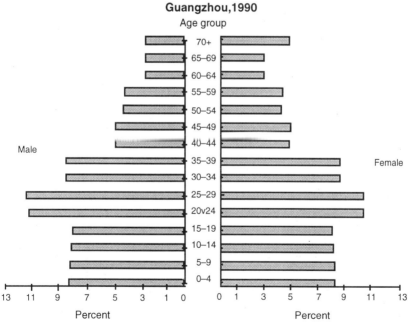

Guangzhou,1990

Note: Urban population includes city-administered counties and agricultural population.
a. Based on 1990 population census.
Source: State Statistical Bureau 1992b; *Statistical Yearbook of Shanghai,* 1992; *Statistical Yearbook of Tianjin,* 1992.

tive shares. By 1993 they accounted for close to 55 percent of GVIO in Shanghai and 51 percent in Tianjin. Moreover, each of the three cities is striving to develop service industries, particularly financial and producer services. Shanghai has the potential to become a world-class financial center, whereas Guangzhou might pursue trade-related services, and Tianjin is well positioned to develop transport-induced activities.

All three cities, Tianjin in particular, are facing increasing competition from secondary cities in their hinterlands. For instance, during the period from 1985 to 1991, Shijiazhuang became a serious contender with Tianjin in both textiles and clothing industries (see table 6.3). Foshan is challenging Guangzhou in textiles and electronics; in fact, its electronics production surpassed that of Guangzhou in 1991. Dongguan is another contender in both clothing and electronics industries. Of course, all three cities are still clinging to their advantages in such large industries as machine building, chemicals, metallurgy, and transport equipment. However, only Shanghai is likely to remain competitive across these subsectors over the longer term.

The 1980s were a period of ferment. The retreat from planning and centralized management induced each of the three cities to redefine its relationship with the center and to begin chalking out a modernization strategy, which would be implemented largely by itself. All three cities are starting from a broadly similar situation with regard to urban infrastructure: urban amenities are poor, transport and communication links are quite weak, housing is scarce, and the environment is heavily pol-

Table 6.3   Shares of Gross Value of Industrial Output of Selected Subsectors in Shanghai, Tianjin, and Guangzhou and Secondary Cities in the Hinterlands, 1985 and 1991
(percent)

City	Textiles 1985	1991	Clothing 1985	1991	Machinery 1985	1991	Electronics 1985	1991	Chemicals 1985	1991
Shanghai	14.4	9.3	15.6	8.2	12.6	10.8	16.1	10.3	11.9	8.2
Tianjin	4.1	2.8	5.0	2.5	3.9	3.5	5.4	4.0	5.0	5.2
Guangzhou	1.3	1.4	2.0	2.2	2.0	2.2	3.1	1.4	1.7	2.7
Hinterland										
Shijiazhuang	1.7	1.8	1.6	1.5	0.7	1.0	0.6	0.8	0.7	0.7
Tangshan	0.5	0.4	0.6	0.4	0.5	0.4	0.0	0.0	0.4	0.2
Qinhuangdao	0.1	0.1	0.2	0.1	0.1	0.1	0.0	0.0	0.1	0.0
Wuxi	3.6	2.3	1.3	0.9	2.4	1.5	4.5	2.2	1.4	0.7
Suzhou	4.8	1.5	2.2	0.5	1.9	0.8	3.1	1.5	2.1	1.0
Ningbo	1.7	0.9	1.8	1.0	1.0	0.5	1.1	0.5	0.4	0.4
Foshan	1.4	0.9	1.4	0.6	0.4	0.3	1.8	1.7	0.3	0.4
Zhanjiang	0.1	0.1	0.1	0.4	0.1	0.2	0.1	0.4	0.1	0.2
Dongguan	0.1	0.3	0.3	0.8	0.1	0.3	0.0	0.9	0.1	0.1

Source: State Statistical Bureau, *China: Urban Statistical Yearbook,* 1986 and 1992; *Statistical Yearbook of China,* 1987.

luted. The funds to remedy these problems are almost equally scarce, but each city is relatively well placed to mobilize fiscal and financial resources and to attract foreign capital. The three cities have unexploited agglomeration and neighborhood economies that they can use, and all are beginning to do so, with Guangzhou displaying the most energy. Likewise, much momentum remains to be derived from enterprise and urban land reform. Guangzhou was the first to initiate reforms, and this is reflected in its growth rates and productivity. Now Shanghai and Tianjin are attempting to catch up. Developing producer as well as other services and modernizing the infrastructure are clearly a priority for Guangzhou and Shanghai and, to a lesser extent, for Tianjin, whose future growth is dependent to a greater degree on its role as a regional transport hub. Above all, each city has begun tackling the matter of industrial strategy in a piecemeal fashion, but the time is approaching when a comprehensive reappraisal is called for.

Driving Forces for Urban Change in China

Urban modernization in China is a river that is fed by numerous streams of greater and lesser significance. It is neither necessary nor feasible to give each its due because attending to the major ones is adequate to depict the big picture. Beyond that, analyzing urban modernization from several vantage points can impart a sense of China's urban dynamics in the final years of the twentieth century, a sense, moreover, that is filtered through the accumulated experiences of cities in other countries. Because this study emphasizes the industrial facet of urban development, we highlight three factors that are currently driving urban change in China and will remain pivotal for at least the next decade and more. They are industrial organization and urban industrial networks, urban finances, and the labor market.

Industrial Organization and Networks

Two forces are propelling the growth of industry in urban China: the emergence of many new firms, which are generally quite small, and the creative restructuring of large state-owned enterprises and collective-owned enterprises.[1] The emergence of new firms is the outcome of buoyant entrepreneurship and the fortuitous coming together of many relatively specialized enterprises into networks that distantly mimic similar constellations in industrial countries. The creative restructuring of state- and collective-owned enterprises is expressed in several ways:

- Vertical disintegration whereby a big industrial concern is divided into a core unit and affiliated subsidiaries, which provide inputs and subassemblies to the mother enterprise but also to other producers

- The formation of corporate groupings that bring together firms into formal networking arrangements in which overall financial control and strategic functions are centralized in a parent holding company

- Loose alliances that permit rationalization of production, joint financing of activities subject to externalities, and agreement over rules of market behavior along with cooperation among firms.

Industrial networking has its intellectual antecedents in Alfred Marshall's view that the matrix of production is a region or an industrial district and not a firm. Networking is a means of pooling information, capital, expertise, and infrastructure and is a mode of insurance. It lowers entry barriers by providing new start-ups with a bundle of essential ingredients.[2] Thus a dynamic, networked, industrial community has many layers. At one level, there is the layer composed of social or kin-based overlapping relations, which entangle the individual with the ties of reputation, family, and friendship. Local banks, credit societies, and informal savings societies embedded in the networks depend critically on the flow of information. While most small start-ups in China and elsewhere draw mainly on personal savings of the entrepreneur or resources obtained from the community through various relational mechanisms, the growth of small enterprises is frequently a function of the availability of credit from local institutions of finance.

At another level of the network, there are circuits that transmit R&D. Powell and Smith-Doerr (1994, p. 387) note that "bonds of professional membership greatly expedite the formation of collaborative R&D networks. The sense of common association with a technological, intellectual, or scientific community is a glue that thickens cooperation. This membership in scientific or industrial associations is ongoing, occurring outside of commercial relationships; thus members monitor individuals' behavior and reputation." Interfirm movement of individuals helps knowledge circulate and stimulates a trade in information, which is the key to an innovative milieu. "When [an] R&D network brings firms together, the sharing of different competencies can generate new ideas."

Services constitute still another layer. These cover a broad spectrum. At one end there are technical colleges and vocational institutes that infuse networks with skills. At the other there are testing facilities and organizations that generate information on technical standards enforced in foreign markets and the translation of tenders advertised overseas (World Bank 1994a). In sum, the layered nature of networks and the involvement of enterprises at many levels—resource exchange, information, board of directors—account for the effectiveness of the ones that work best. Networking arrangements are particularly suited to certain kinds of industries where production on a small scale, specialization, and collaboration between geographically clustered firms not only is efficient but also promotes innovation.

Industrial modernization and restructuring in the three cities require forms of organization that will ensure gains in efficiency and technology sufficient to put China's firms on a par with those of its more advanced East Asian neighbors. How industrial organization evolves will depend on a host of factors, in particular administrative, legal, and institutional initiatives pursued in each city. International experience, although remaining short on industrial specifics for individual countries, is increasingly unanimous on the broad guidelines. Major elements include industrial groupings, mergers, joint ventures, and subcontracting.

Industrial groups in which a major enterprise exerts strong financial and strategic control over the members have certain advantages. Unlike alliances, groups need not materialize through some lengthy organic process but can be created rapidly, with the precise details regarding management and financial control determined over time. Given current administrative arrangements in China, the deliberate creation of groups (or corporations, which include a smaller number of enterprises) through the joint action of municipal or provincial agencies saves time and permits a linking together of enterprises drawn from different jurisdictions. Groups can have a definite subsectoral focus, in order to cultivate a basic competence and streamline the production system. The experience of automobile assemblers in Japan and the initial results achieved by the group headed by Second Auto Works (Changchun) suggest that when the core enterprise can provide able leadership and other members are fully committed to its goals, industrial groups can tap deep reserves of dynamism.

The use of groups as a vehicle of industrial policy confronts two realities. Large-scale restructuring and modernization of industrial subsectors by means of centralized planning are not feasible. Likewise, the market cannot efficiently guide macro changes in the structure of industry or major investment decisions with a long-term strategic purpose. An intermediate organizational form is needed that is capable of making and implementing strategic choices and coordinating the actions of multiple participants. But the organization must partake fully of the market milieu and reserve some independent decisionmaking role for the various enterprises subsumed within the group.

One of the most ambitious efforts in this sphere, which embraces enterprises from all cities, is the Chinatron Corporation. This electronics giant, which brings together such enterprises as Great Wall Computers (Tianjin) and Panda Electronics, is attempting to concentrate R&D, training, electronics, and machinery engineering within a single corporate structure.[3] Chinatron represents an initial effort to create a viable corporate grouping, and it mirrors the organizational weaknesses of other corporations created in the three cities. By and large, differentiating between administrative units and corporations is still difficult. Often only the name is changed, with the structure and functions of the old bureau remaining intact. Even when the bureau and corporation are separate and distinct, the former retains control over major divisions and personnel management. The idea of setting up autonomous corporations to restructure enterprise clusters and stimulate market competition is a good one, but so far evidence of true autonomy is sparse and few corporations have gone far in rationalizing plant or closing obsolete facilities.

Among other corporations created in the three cities, a typical example is the Wanbao Corporation of Guangzhou, founded in mid-1988, which produces refrigerators, fans, and washing machines.[4] Wanbao is made up of 26 enterprises, each consisting of an independent accounting unit with its own contract. During the early 1990s, it began to remake itself into a holding company and to work on the precise legal, structural, and managerial implications of such a transformation. To be successful over the medium term, the corporation must achieve autonomy from direct administrative supervision, while remaining accountable for its performance to shareholders and stakeholders. Wanbao, much like other state enterprises in transition, is attempting to define the nature of ownership and to ascertain the hardness of budget constraints in the environment of reform. Much depends on the degree of competition. Only if competitive pressures become more severe will the corporation be induced to use autonomy to ensure that its various operations satisfy the test of long-run profitability. Clearly, measures that increase market competition must proceed hand in hand with attempts to change industrial organization.

Mergers offer yet another path to rationalizing production capacity within more or less optimally sized units and to lessening market uncertainty by increasing market concentration. Free market advocates see mergers as a way to bring productive assets under the control of the most efficient managers and to internalize certain transactions within a larger whole that cannot be conducted efficiently through market dealings. The common tendency is to merge a failing enterprise with a stronger one. In a number of instances, this is a surrogate for bankruptcy. It is a means of salvaging usable physical and human capital. To the extent that mergers achieve this purpose, they prune obsolete or inefficient capacity and maximize the returns from industrial resources. But using mergers to maintain inefficient and loss-making firms in production not only perpetuates waste and maintains obsolescent production capacity but also compromises the health of the successful enterprise, which has to take on new managerial and production burdens, operate multiple facilities, sacrifice funds that might otherwise be used to upgrade its own plant, and bear the cost of assimilating the culture of a company in decline. For reasons of administrative and financial convenience, mergers have, thus far, been the preferred route to restructuring, especially in Shanghai and Tianjin.

Empirical research conducted in industrialized economies on the results of horizontal mergers is equivocal at best, while research on conglomerate mergers is negative. Even where mergers are the market-driven outcomes of voluntary and well-informed decisions, half or more pull down the profitability of the merged entity from the level achieved by each individual firm prior to the union (George 1991). Changes in ownership that reduce organizational slack can bring the performance of moderately inefficient enterprises close to the average, but this requires two to three years at least, and performance is likely to deteriorate initially (Lichtenberg 1992).

Another problematic side to horizontal mergers is their effect on industrial concentration. Views on this have tended to change, with much stress being placed on scale economies, the minimum efficient scale of R&D, and the investment outlay required to sustain competitiveness in industries with short product cycles and high tooling costs. Nevertheless, the dangers of excessive oligopolistic power loom large. The importance of scale economies can also be overplayed. In a wide range of industries, medium-size firms are as competitive and innovative as large companies, if not more so (Freeman 1982; R. Howard 1990; Pratten 1991; for a historical perspective, see Mowery and Rosenberg 1989). In Germany and Italy, the "backbone" enterprises are midsize specialist firms (Rommel and others 1995).

Restructuring in the sense of technological modernization can also be sought by way of joint ventures with domestic or foreign partners. These have become a commonplace in industrial economies and are increasingly widespread in China as well. Four concerns motivate firms to enter into joint ventures. First are the advantages of sharing product or process technology. Second is the ability to spread risks in the development of complex new products involving large outlays. Third is the possibility of market access. Last is the ability of firms to pool complementary strengths. One partner might have labor and a choice production site, while the other might have the capital and marketing apparatus to permit full use of the existing plant.

The success of joint ventures depends on balancing the benefits and reconciling differing operational philosophies. It calls for perseverance by both parties, a fairly high degree of organizational flexibility, and a willingness to weather the inevitable frictions. Over the past 10 years or so, foreign investors have entered into many joint ventures with Chinese partners. They have infused capital, technology, organizational change, managerial skills, and marketing expertise into a handful of important manufacturing subsectors: automobiles, clothing, and electronics. One striking instance is the Xerox Corporation of Shanghai, which has followed an effective strategy of training 60 suppliers in production and materials handling so that they can meet quality and delivery standards. Xerox has expended several million dollars in this effort, with the Shanghai Economic Commission providing supplementary funding.

Most joint ventures have encountered start-up problems having to do with style of management, complexity of labor relations, low degree of formalization in operating procedures, and quality of infrastructure. Industrial enterprises in China also have to cope with the thickets of bureaucracy that surround an industrial enterprise in China (China-European Commission Management Institute 1990; World Bank 1991c;

Pearson 1991). Foreign investors entering into a joint venture with a state enterprise often have difficulty coping with the overhead and complexities of personnel management that arise from the far-ranging social responsibilities of the enterprise. Overstaffing and permanent employment pose one set of problems. But the enterprise must also take care of family records, health care, education of dependents (frequently also the employment of wives and children), housing, and public security. Usually the Chinese partner attempts to keep a tight grip on personnel management and finances, which tends to frustrate the foreign company's efforts to improve labor use and financial accountability. The majority of joint ventures are eventually able to overcome the teething difficulties and turn a profit after a few years, but not without a struggle. Joint ventures yield promising results only when the foreign partner is committed and the Chinese partner is fully prepared to be flexible; to adapt technology, soft as well as hard, to local circumstances; and to modify work practices so that they begin to approximate those found in market economies.

The activity of agglomerating, creating alliances, establishing groups, merging, and setting up joint ventures can introduce organizational changes, some positive and others less obviously beneficial. Among the organizational changes, one of the most far-reaching is the role assigned to subcontracting. The utility of subcontracting within certain manufacturing subsectors has undergone a fundamental reappraisal. Earlier in the century, when the industrialized countries were pushing toward maturity, major corporations preferred a high degree of vertical integration within giant facilities (Chandler 1990). This was the era of managerial centralization and scale economies. It not only shaped the corporate sector in Europe and the United States but also proved attractive to the centrally planned socialist economies. Eastern Europe and the former U.S.S.R. embraced giant, vertically integrated production complexes that promised managerial and scale economies. They exported this organizational strategy to China, which diluted it by emphasizing decentralized development and retained vertical integration while tempering very large-scale production and tight control from the central government to allow for Chinese realities. There is a long tradition in China's enterprises of setting up subsidiaries so as to employ relatives and children of staff. In recent years, the tax system has reinforced the incentive to do this. To minimize tax obligations, a state enterprise often finds it advantageous to create a largely tax-exempt collective to produce a profitable new product rather than to manufacture the item on its own premises.

The larger state enterprises in the three cities buy components from subcontractors, most of which are located within the municipal boundaries, although firms in Shanghai have dealings with affiliates in nearby provinces as well. Nevertheless, the scale of subcontracting is fairly small by Japanese, Taiwanese, and now even U.S. standards, averaging about 20 to 30 percent among the large state enterprises. It is conspicuously low among major machinery producers, who stand to gain the most from subcontracting. Enterprises and bureaus confront a number of problems. Smaller subcontractors, unless they happen to be located nearby and are closely supervised, cannot meet delivery and quality standards. Because of China's transport constraints, regular delivery from distant suppliers can be difficult to arrange. And when a supplier in another province or municipality receives a contract, the local finance bureau loses tax revenue. These problems can be resolved, but they require initiatives on the part of both the bigger firms and the supervising bureaus.

China's major municipal centers already possess the institutional and cultural essentials of successful subcontracting. They have a tradition of networking between enterprises and a strong belief in the binding significance of informal long-term relations. Furthermore, as revealed by the experience of coastal provinces, the Chinese extended family can be the enterprising nucleus for dynamic small-scale enterprises (On the role of the family in building businesses in Hong Kong, see Redding 1990.) People do possess the business acumen and skills to set up small firms. The family provides the organizational glue and a mechanism for mobilizing funds. Interfamily and community networks help to generate business opportunities, thereby lessening the degree of market risks. Enterprise reform that encourages the vertical disintegration of larger firms, the full exploitation of new information technology, and the building of networks would help local industry to exploit other strengths and draw closer to international competitors.

Urban Finances

Urban industrial restructuring is costly. Both international experience and the lessons from China's own efforts over the past decade are unequivocal on this score. To achieve their dual objectives of urban modernization and industrial restructuring, all three cities must devise suitable policies to ensure that an adequate volume of financing is forthcoming for these activities. Making provisions for the necessary funding is a precondition for the successful implementation of an urban-industrial strategy. This is especially critical at the current juncture: cities are still facing an uncertain tax base; revenue transfers to the central government, although lower than in the past, remain sizable; mounting competition is squeezing the profits of enterprises; and investable surpluses are diminishing.

Even as traditional sources of funding decline, new opportunities are appearing in both fiscal and financial spheres. New taxes and user charges can restore the revenue base. Moreover, the progressive development of capital markets can mobilize a larger volume of local savings as well as resources from elsewhere in the economy. Because fiscal-financial reforms are still at an early stage, the full resource potential of the cities and the neighboring regional economies has yet to be utilized. Once that is done, the problems of restructuring will appear far less formidable.

Each of the municipalities operates under a slightly different set of fiscal rules, but two principles apply to all. First, none of the municipalities can legally establish its own taxes or other formal sources of revenue. The central government imposes taxes, sets rates, and then assigns revenues to the local authorities. Second, within each of the municipalities, budgetary revenues accrue separately to central and municipal authorities (and, in the case of Guangzhou, to provincial authorities as well). In general, central government revenues come from enterprises or entities under central government jurisdiction: for example, railroads, the banking system, and a few industrial subsectors. Municipal governments have no direct control over these revenues.

Although local fiscal authorities have no formal authority to create new avenues of financing, they have usually been able to find new types of financial resources that they can control more effectively. For instance, in the early 1990s fiscal authorities in each of these cities created a "revolving fund" that was used for small-scale investments, predominantly in industry. Ordinary fiscal grants for industrial investment were transformed into repayable loans, and both repayment of principal and interest payments were channeled into the revolving fund, gradually building available resources. Loans were made at interest rates equal to, or up to a point below, bank interest rates, typically for periods of around one year. Such funds are operated in a legal gray area, in the face of opposition from officials in the banking system (perhaps as a result, statistics on the funds were uniformly imprecise in the three cities).

Municipal fiscal authorities are clearly in a difficult position. They are caught between two important economic trends. On the one hand, traditional sources of revenue are declining as the monopoly profits of the state industrial sector are competed away. On the other hand, the growing need for municipal infrastructure, education, urban amenities, and social security is placing new demands on local budgets. Thus far, municipal authorities have resolved this conflict by reducing the share of revenues turned over to the central government and by drawing on new financial sources to fund industrial investment. Nevertheless, they continue to be squeezed between conflicting demands on their resources. Unable to provide large amounts of direct finance, municipal fiscal authorities have fostered the restructuring process through a variety of tax breaks and concessionary policies.

Concessionary tax policies are typically coordinated by the municipal economic commission. They include exemption from product and value added taxes for up to two years for items that are new to the municipality, subsidization of interest on loans, permission to repay loans from before-tax income, remission of import duties on imported materials and equipment, accelerated depreciation (30 percent additional) for projects in accord with national industrial policy, and generous expense provisions for small investments associated with restructuring. These concessionary policies can be an important aid to the restructuring process, but municipal authorities find it difficult to restrict their use to those cases where tax relief is genuinely required. In Guangzhou, 80 percent of tax rebates were given to the city's 20 centrally controlled enterprises. Tax concessions frequently threaten to become a general form of subsidy, rather than targeted restructuring assistance. More significant, in financial terms, is the rebate of the value added tax on exports, which is automatic rather than discretionary.

Financial constraints are not the sole, or even the primary, obstacle to industrial restructuring. In many cases, fiscal authorities are willing to conduct restructuring programs but face obstacles from industrial bureaus or concerns about employment. All three cities face difficult tradeoffs caused by the relatively high tax burden that state-owned factories currently bear. Because Guangzhou's economy and fiscal revenues are growing overall, fiscal authorities in Guangzhou are willing to bear substantially more risk, lowering tax burdens temporarily on individual firms in the knowledge that the money could be raised subsequently from vibrant sectors of the municipal economy. By contrast, growth and structural change in Shanghai and Tianjin were slower, which made it difficult, until recently, for fiscal authorities to bear that kind of risk, because they had difficulty identifying the alternative sources of tax revenue. Although Guangzhou has succeeded in defining a more flexible policy for itself, the dilemma facing the three cities underscores the obstacles that high tax burdens impose on restructuring. It may also illuminate a key feature of restructuring: the more rapidly it progresses, the more resources will be available to carry it out. Growing economies can undertake restructuring more easily.

Bank credit has emerged as a major source of financing. Over the past decade, China's industrial financing shifted from budgetary grants and retained funds (internal financing) to bank credits. China increasingly resembles market economies in which surpluses generated in the household sector are loaned to the enterprise sector to finance a large portion of investment. However, in the current partially reformed state of China's economy, a large proportion of loan financing is channeled through the state banking system, which is still subject to a high degree of government control, exercised in part by the earmarking of loanable funds for specific purposes. One such purpose is industrial restructuring. According to one estimate, the government earmarks two-thirds or more of the total amount of bank fixed investment lending (both capital construction and renovation investment), mainly for state-owned enterprises. Thus, although bank loans are a significant financial resource, they are allocated administratively by various levels of government, which limits the efficiency with which they can be used. The current system of allocating bank loans retains some of the practices embedded in the old system of administrative allocation of investment, which is responsible for the problems of industrial restructuring that are so pressing today.

The banking system is now capable of moving substantial funds across provincial boundaries. As a result, the cities have also attracted a certain amount of portfolio investment, at least in the form of bank deposits. Nonresidents of the municipality hold more than 10 percent of total household savings deposits, in the case of Shanghai, reflecting the superior convenience and confidentiality of holding savings in a major urban center. Similar shares are reported for the other cities. The superior productivity of coastal regions and the greater flexibility of economic policy outside the major cities enhance the attractiveness of these areas. So the development of new financial instruments sets the pace at which coastal cities are able to attract capital from other regions. Stocks and, especially, bonds have already demonstrated their attractiveness to Chinese households. Household saving is extremely high, but the range of assets available to households is still quite narrow (overwhelmingly concentrated in savings deposits). As the range of available assets expands, the coastal cities should be able to tap these sources.

Another new option may lie in the use of venture capital.[5] Venture capital is different from other forms of capital in that institutionalized venture capitalists provide equity rather than debt financing and frequently take an active role in managing the enterprises they finance. In the United States, for example, many new companies and technologies, including Apple Computer, Fairchild, Intel, and Sun Microsystems, would not have been launched nor would they have attained commercial success so quickly without such capital.[6] The major centers of venture capital include Silicon Valley, New York City, and the Route 128 corridor outside Boston, where such capital has been used mainly to establish high-technology enterprises. In Silicon Valley, the archetypal start-up was formed by a group of friends and colleagues with an innovative idea that they could not realize in their current workplace. They initiated a business plan and sought funding from local venture capitalists. The expanding local circle of university researchers and consultants provided additional assistance (see Saxenian 1994).

Venture capital would be conducive to the development of new technologies and enterprises because venture capitalists often bring technical skills, production experience, and networks of contacts, in addition to their equity investment. Geographic proximity and the existence of a critical mass of researchers can be a further advantage. An expanding network of special suppliers and service providers also facilitates the start-up process. Both Shanghai and Tianjin could use much more venture capital to finance technological innovations and enterprises.

Labor Market

Labor market flexibility, by enhancing productivity, can impart greater momentum to industrial change. Restructuring becomes a positive sum game where the winners compensate the losers and thereby retain their support. China's major cities are appropriate laboratories for observing the state of labor markets and for devising policy measures that will assist not just industrial restructuring but also the larger purpose of self-sustaining urban development.

All three cities recognize the need to enhance labor market mobility and to expand the authority of enterprises over labor market decisions. The "iron rice bowl" not only has tied the hands of employers but also has sharply circumscribed the ability of workers to quit and has bound them in a dependent relationship in which employers are responsible for almost all their living needs (Walder 1991).[7] Although local governments are no longer obligated to find jobs for all graduates and enterprises are not required to accept those being placed, labor authorities and work units are still subject to employment imperatives and recruitment plans. Labor reforms in a city such as Shanghai have enlarged a graduate's choice of jobs: an individual is no longer assigned to a unit. Likewise, an enterprise need not accept a candidate selected by the labor bureau but can recruit directly and only later notify the labor bureau. However, the greater degree of choice has increased frictional unemployment among school leavers (World Bank 1992b). Managing the transition in labor markets and relocating workers displaced by the merger or, in rarer instances, the closure of enterprises pose serious problems (middle-age female textile workers in Shanghai and Tianjin are especially hard to place in new jobs). They constitute one of the major challenges facing each city. This recognition has motivated a range of reforms intended to make the labor market more flexible.

The purpose of the labor market reforms, introduced in stages since 1986, has been to improve labor productivity and industrial efficiency by gradually dislodging permanent employment and state allocation of jobs. The introduction of labor contracting has been accompanied by somewhat greater scope for employee discharge, usually for disciplinary reasons, and by "waiting-for-employment" or unemployment insurance. Second, although fixed-term contracts should increase labor mobility, they may be insufficient to address the larger goal of enhancing labor market flexibility in the three cities. Chinese enterprise managers indicate that the hiring of contract workers has not fundamentally altered labor-management relations, despite the large changes, at least on paper, in job security. Even if worker contracts were much more prevalent, the degree of job insecurity desirable from the standpoint of labor productivity is hard to define against the historical background and expectations of permanent tenure. Too much job security, as well as too little, can damage worker productivity. Therefore, the mere existence of a contract may not be a sufficient incentive to raise productivity. Anecdotal and circumstantial evidence points to the automatic renewal of long-term contract workers, though the extent of this phenomenon is not known (Liu 1989; Davis 1988). Rigid job definitions and work rules, which are rarely observed and therefore keep multiplying in a bewildering array, are essentially untouched by the contract system.

Broadening job assignments and enhancing worker mobility within a given enterprise is another approach to enhancing labor flexibility. Narrowly delineated career paths severely restrict the ability of enterprises to respond quickly to changing technologies, production processes, new competition, and shifting demand. Highly circumscribed worker and managerial assignments make sense primarily in mass production systems and where trainability of the workforce is a concern. This is why traditional job security and wage structures are based on narrow work rules in the United States. But the resulting work patterns generate neither the skills nor the incentives to seek flexibility. Generalized skills cannot develop where the adaptation and innovation such skills make possible do not have ready outlets. They develop when there is an existing skill base and when workers have opportunities to upgrade their skills in specific directions that are determined within the enterprise.

Labor use in Chinese enterprises is highly compartmentalized; workers are trained in a narrow specialization. In this context, the presence of a labor overhang in China's urban sector further complicates efficient labor allocation within and between firms. Authorities in the three cities, though conscious of the rigidities in labor use, are faced with the tradeoff between underemployment and open unemployment. Over the medium term, they have opted to absorb surplus labor in service operations (such as catering, retailing, repair and maintenance works, grounds maintenance, guest house operation, and cleaning services) within the firm. This service employment is being generated either from existing operations, which are now run as stand-alone subunits within the enterprise and are required to be fiscally independent, or from new activities that are being started especially for this purpose.

Industrial restructuring involves the breakup, regrouping, birth, and demise of individual industries and industrial sectors. Almost no part of this process is devoid of implications and consequences for education and training. The quality and quantity of the initial training of new entrants to the labor force influence turnover costs in enterprises. Recurrent vocational training, either on the job, within the enterprise, or on leave from the enterprise, has important effects for incentives and technology absorption. The retraining of workers, either to respond to shifts in production within the enterprise or to facilitate employment after the enterprise closes, influences internal and external labor mobility and the pace of industrial restructuring. Finally, the retraining of older workers affects decisions about retirement and the cost of pension benefits for society.

The vast state-sponsored education and training establishment in China is of a socialist pedigree. Whether it is at the level of the central, provincial, or municipal government, of the industrial bureau, or of the enterprise, the sheer number of layers and the volume of educational services imparted are impressive (for details on China's educational and vocational education system, see World Bank 1986, 1987). At one level, with respect to training policies and programs, the three cities must consider whether they simply need to do more of what they are doing and perhaps do it better. At another level, and in the context of industrial restructuring, they need to consider more fundamental questions that do not yet command much attention. These are questions about the inherent uncertainty of the demand for skills during the process of industrial transition, about the potential for mismatching skills unless flexibility is built into decisions regarding training, about the relative value of vocational and on-the-job training, and about the incentives for training under different labor market conditions.

Several factors will increase the uncertainty about the composition of demand for skills in the three cities: demographic trends, the opening up of China's markets to international competition, the likely narrowing of industrial specialization, and technological change. This greater uncertainty will make planning for the requisite skills all the more difficult. Very likely, greater emphasis will have to be placed on devising flexible training arrangements and on-the-job training, with the responsibility for this devolving more on enterprises than on planning agencies, and on determining and anticipating the required mix of skills.[8]

Urban Prospects: International Experience

This section paints a broad canvas but examines it from a particular angle, thereby filling out and extending the earlier discussion. It deals with the economies of cities worldwide but is concerned with those few characteristics that must economically explain success, failure, or resurgence. It uses a few cities as examples of these qualities and, from their experience, extracts a handful of lessons germane to the three Chinese cities. These refer to cities in ascendance, troubled cities able to sustain a level of performance, and cities attempting comebacks.

Lesson 1

The clustering of industries in and around a particular city often occurs simply through a historical accident, thereby creating new urban centers (Krugman 1990; Scott and Angel 1991). Examples are the carpet industry in Dalton, Georgia, the shoe industry in Massachusetts, and the tire industry in Akron, Ohio. These cases are all drawn from the United States, but similar ones abound in Europe. Aggressive entrepreneurship by individual communities, states, or provinces seeking to woo industries has also influenced the geographic distribution of industry. Local politicians have frequently been decisive in steering industry to their city by tirelessly extolling its virtues and by using a variety of instruments; tax relief, quality of infrastructure, and creation of science parks are among the most common. The science park adjacent to Stanford University—the genesis of Silicon Valley—is now famous (Scott and Angel 1991). The first company to locate there was Fairchild Semiconductor, which subsequently spawned almost 50 independent spin-off firms. These became the core of a vertically desegregated production complex, which includes every aspect of microchip production from basic research, production, and testing equipment through bonding material, silicon wafers, and photomask, all the way to metal plating deposition and etching services. The agglomeration economies from such clustering have been very significant. North Carolina's Research Triangle, which is a highly successful research park, is built on the research and institutional foundations provided by the universities of Raleigh, Durham, and Chapel Hill, the standard-bearers of the second most lavishly funded state university system in the United States. The growth of an industry producing packaging and boxing machines around Bologna, Italy, followed a similar pattern. The first two or three factories were set up between 1920 and 1950. These became the source of technical and entrepreneurial skills that have spawned nearly 300 small and medium-size specialized firms occupying a variety of niches within the packaging industry (Capecchi 1989).

Across the Pacific, Tsukuba Science City, near Tokyo, represents the Japanese government's attempt to establish a major center for research that would provide a nucleus for high-technology manufacturing. Approved by the cabinet in 1963, construction was begun in the early 1970s, and a substantial research infrastructure was in place by the late 1980s at great public cost. Tsukuba has certainly emerged as a hub of scientific research composed largely of public institutions. However, the vertically integrated structure of laboratories and the isolation of city from industry—both factors present in China—have limited the spillover benefits. Tsukuba might be finding its stride in the mid-1990s, but the gestation period was exceedingly prolonged and the return on public investment questionable (Castells and Hall 1994).

Another arguably more successful venture initiated by the Japanese government is located in Kyushu. Politicians closely connected with powerful central government ministries made rural Kyushu into Japan's Silicon Island (Calder 1988). Governor Hiramatsu Morihiku, formerly a key figure in the Ministry of International Trade and Industry, set in motion forces that contributed to industrial success: he mobilized local support and funding and persuaded the central government to defray the start-up costs of high-technology industrialization by financing infrastructure and much of the cost of retraining the local workforce. Once the government had been won over, its own championing of Kyushu prompted businesses to act. Finally, the need for human capital was met through the creation of a network of training institutes, universities, and research centers, such as the Kyushu Institute of Technology and the Fuzzy Logic System Institute, both in the former coal mining town of Iisuka.[9]

Two of the newly industrializing economies have also set up their own versions. Some 90 kilometers from Taipei, Hsinchu Industrial Park stands next to two major universities and the government's Industrial

Technology Research Institute. And Korea's Daedok Science Town, 160 kilometers from Seoul, is home to 55 research institutes, whose findings are enticing industry to the area.

Lesson 2

It is becoming increasingly evident that reputable universities with extensive science and engineering programs are necessary for industrial health, especially with regard to technologically advanced activities. However, synergistic interaction with important government or corporate research establishments provides an additional spur. The aircraft and electronics industries around Los Angeles and along the M4 auto route near London could hardly have arisen without the research infrastructure built up by government funding. A significant part of this funding was earmarked for defense purposes but generated substantial spillovers into civilian sectors, primarily through the movement of personnel (see Block 1988; Castells and Hall 1994). Thus, in several notable instances, government funding has determined the industrial future of cities not only through the money channeled into physical infrastructure but also through the sums poured into research, whether in universities or in public sector establishments. Even where the direct transfer of technology from defense-related research has been meager, civilian industry has profited indirectly from the training imparted to a vast body of professionals, the experience engendered, and the pure knowledge propagated. The potency of these externalities is evident all along Route 128 out of Boston.

Successful cities have capitalized on these trends in production, in organization, and in services. To stay ahead, they have also achieved workable tradeoffs in two other areas: public finances and regulation. Cities compete with one another for industry by exempting companies from certain local taxes. However, if nontax revenues do not offset a narrower tax base, infrastructure and services—important attractions for industry—suffer. A balance has to be struck, and cities that offer the winning combination are unusually efficient with their expenditures and ingenious in persuading the private sector to fund a variety of capital projects. Regulations can contribute to a city's livability, for instance, by sustaining high environmental standards, as in parts of California. They also can saddle companies with expensive red tape. In market economies where capital is mobile, institutional arbitrage ensures, within limits, that industry moves to those cities where the regulatory framework is most advantageous. Such competition is an important check on the scope of regulation and discourages the unwanted interference of local authorities (see Siebert 1991).

Lessons 1 and 2 are extremely relevant for the three Chinese cities. They underscore the importance of good urban infrastructure and environmental conditions. They draw attention to the role of premier universities. And they suggest that local as well as central governments should at least prime the pump by adequately funding research facilities and encouraging the commercialization of research. Both lessons also highlight the significance of increasing private sector involvement in supporting research and tertiary education, in stimulating interaction with researchers, and in promoting entrepreneurship that builds high-technology industry. Municipal authorities in Shanghai could pour money into public research institutes, but spillovers into industry require initiative from the business sector.

Lesson 3

A city is most vulnerable when its economy is dominated by a single firm with a relatively narrow specialization. Should the company's business decline because of a secular trend in demand or falling competitiveness, this very quickly affects the urban economy. There are many examples of this in western Europe and North America, most conspicuously with respect to cities dependent on producers of basic metals, ships, transport equipment, and textiles. For example, centers of steel production all across northern Europe and Japan have had to contend with a steady ebbing of business activity since the mid-1970s (see Houseman 1991). The practice followed by German steel manufacturers in the nineteenth and early twentieth centuries of purchasing large tracts of land and controlling local politics so as to prevent other industries from challenging their monopoly over local labor markets became a severe handicap for the Saar region when the retreat of steel increased the demand for alternative employment.

Old industries such as steel, textiles, and shipbuilding, which have a long history and have employed successive generations of workers in a particular location, exercise a profound influence. The labor force becomes inbred and wedded to the company through multiple points of contact. Social networks and local traditions breed intense loyalties, which discourage workers from seeking jobs farther afield. The need to support increasing numbers of unemployed is an additional drain on the economy, which compounds the effects of soft demand for the principal manufactured product.[10]

Cities where a single firm is the main economic axis represent an extreme case. More common is the concentration of multiple producers, all operating within a narrow industrial segment, such as the hard-hit centers of the textile industry in the British Midlands. Battered by foreign competition, a once-proud manufacturing establishment has now been reduced to a small handful of vertically integrated corporations occupying some of the more capital-intensive segments. The eclipse of textiles was a blow for cities whose economic life revolved around this industry. It was only a little less serious for areas in which textiles shared the spotlight with another major industry, such as machine tools.

The disquieting aspect of this experience is that in many instances the failure of one industry has not been counterbalanced by the rise of another. Furthermore, even when an industry, for example steel, has been effectively downscaled, the prolonged orchestration of local policies and substantial grants from central governments are required to salvage the affected urban economies (Rodwin 1991). Hill and Fujita (1993) describe how Japanese steel companies have ameliorated the effect of closure in Kamaishi and Kitakyushu without being able to offset the drastic reduction in jobs in the local communities. Financing from the central government has eased the pain of severance and unemployment, but regional policies have rarely succeeded in reversing the decline. Shanghai and Tianjin have already lost jobs in the textile and light consumer industries. Restructuring of state-owned enterprises and competition from elsewhere in China will undoubtedly force some other subsectors to shrink. The experience of other countries shows that resisting such pressure is costly. Instead, local authorities should work with the enterprises to cushion the shock and relocate displaced workers to other enterprises. Thus the emphasis must be on encouraging industrial diversity and putting in place labor market mechanisms that enable displaced workers to find alternative employment.

Lesson 4

Old and troubled industrial cities are populated by firms that survive by cutting costs and postponing capital expenditure. Most of them are resigned to being technological laggards and are disinclined to open or exploit new niches aggressively. By and large, the labor force is composed of older or female semiskilled workers whose geographic and occupational mobility is often limited. Because of unionization and conditions peculiar to local labor markets, average wages are often high in relation to the level of skills. Furthermore, the capacity to augment skills either within companies or through urban training institutions might be poorly developed. Aging infrastructure can be another drawback. Whether in education, telecommunications, housing, or recreation, older cities frequently lag behind. All this plus an unpleasant environment discourage the inflow of capital, entrepreneurship, scientific talent, and young workers.

These conditions are not by any means irreversible, but once the competitiveness of the foremost industrial players begins to wane, their difficulties infect the finances of the city and shrink the fiscal base. This in turn adversely affects the supply of services and investment in social overhead, unless the city is in a position to tap other sources of funds. Ultimately, the factor preventing cities from staging a comeback is the paucity of capital with which to invest in infrastructure and clean the environment. The early stages of decline are caused by the erosion of industrial capability. In today's world, this is principally a technological failing, with the term being interpreted broadly to cover not just product and process but also the organizational innovations conducive to efficiency. The future of steel and machine tools is as closely tied to technological increments as is the future of electronics.[11] Both industries, especially machine tools, need to forge links with producers in neighboring subsectors so that a concerted effort can yield product diversity as well as productivity gains.

Lesson 5

Some cities have managed to restructure their industrial bases and to sustain steady growth. This is most evident in the newly industrializing economies, and, in most cases, the outcome has been encouraging. Take the example of Hong Kong. Its early success as a center of low-end manufacturing exports is quite unusual in that it chose to specialize in only a few stages of the production process. Because of the small size of the capital goods sector, which is limited by the dearth of land and natural resources, and the government's noninterventionist industrial policy, Hong Kong lagged behind other newly industrializing economies in technological innovations and R&D capacity. By the late 1970s and early 1980s, the price competition from some lower-cost countries in the region was seriously challenging Hong Kong's advantage. With the opening up of China, the city restored the competitive advantage of its labor-intensive light manufacturing by relocating production facilities to the mainland. By the early 1990s, between 80 and 90 percent of Hong Kong's electronics establishments had moved across the Shenzhen River.

Hong Kong's process of "deindustrialization" is often regarded as positive because it facilitated the expansion of financing and trading activity, which in turn sustained full employment. The share of the industrial sector in employment (including manufacturing and construction) fell from 50 percent in 1980 to a mere 36 percent in 1991, while that of the service sector rose from 48 to 63 percent. Every branch of the service sector, including financial services, trading services, transportation, and communication, experienced steady growth in employment (Ho and Kueh 1993; Ash and Kueh 1993). Real wage growth in the service sector was also much higher than in the manufacturing sector. Hong Kong now has perhaps the most service-oriented economy in the world.

Lesson 6

The city-state of Singapore took a related but contrasting route. In the 1950s and 1960s Singapore relied on its cheap labor to produce for export markets, particularly in the electronics industry. Although knowledge-based industries such as electronics require a large contingent of technically qualified personnel to design the product, integrate production equipment, and maintain and supervise the production process, the bulk of the workforce is composed of unskilled and semiskilled labor. The elastic supply of such labor has buttressed manufacturing capability in and around the science parks. It also explains the rise of the electronics industry in Hong Kong and Singapore, cities not especially well endowed with scientific manpower but with an abundance of semi-skilled workers and factory-level technicians.

As its labor advantage diminished in the 1970s, the Singapore government took drastic measures to restructure the economy. One important element was the technology policy, which emphasized basic education for the entire population, strong fiscal incentives for foreign investment in R&D, disincentives for low-end processing, reduction of capital costs of foreign investment, and organization of local research institutions.[12] These policies enabled Singapore to hold on to the large multinationals in the electronics industry and to become a center of high-technology production. Singapore is now the world's largest exporter of computer hard-disk drives, with a 60 percent share, and is the fifth or sixth largest exporter of computer products overall. The technology policy, which pushed Singapore up the learning curve, has successfully maintained the city-state's competitiveness and its attractions for multinational corporations.

Another element of its success consists of regional cooperation, with its hinterlands, in industrial development. Such efforts include a sectoral and technical division across Singapore, Johor in Malaysia, and the Riau Islands in Indonesia (K. C. Ho 1994; Lim 1993). Land and labor constraints require the low value added, labor-intensive stages of the production process to be subcontracted or relocated to Johor or Riau. Singapore also serves as a regional headquarters for multinationals with production facilities in the region, offering transport and communication infrastructure, a range of financial services, and a good urban environment.

Singapore's approach finds an echo in the strategy of Korea's capital city, Seoul, which is being challenged by new industrial cities such as Ansan, Kumi, Pusan, and Ulsan, despite its historical dominance in a number of trade-oriented industries (Park and Markusen 1995). Even within the capital region, Seoul was losing to the suburban areas, as demonstrated by a relatively large reduction in industrial jobs in the former and gain in the latter (Park 1993). To meet the challenge, Seoul in the late 1970s launched a concerted effort to attract high-technology industries. Within 10 years, four-fifths of all such activities were located in the vicinity of Seoul (as against 58 percent of total manufacturing) in spite of a government-sponsored effort to disperse R&D centers throughout the country. Side by side with the spread of high-technology manufacturing, the rapid growth of consulting, technical, and computer services sustained Seoul's growth.

Lesson 7

Urban-industrial decay is by no means a one-way street. City governments have been able to work with corporate management to revive old industries and attract new ones. In most cases, it has been a multipronged effort, but there are instances where a city has retained a modicum of dynamism by building on its base as an international supplier of services.

Earlier in this century, New York's economy was dependent on the manufacture of clothing, food processing, the printing industry, and its role as a transport hub (Glazer 1991). These activities financed the development of an efficient infrastructure, the growth of urban services, and the founding of a university system that remains one of the best in the country. Between 1950 and 1994, New York lost over 700,000 manufacturing jobs (Moss 1997). By the 1960s the city's economic focus had shifted to services, and it slowly consolidated its claim to being the premier financial center. Vestiges of past manufacturing activities remain, most notably in fashion garments, but for the past three decades, New York has derived its prosperity from services—financial, professional, tourism-related, and cultural—supported, in turn, by communications facilities of high quality. Between 1979 and 1989 the city also benefited from the surge in defense spending, both directly and as a result of heightened industrial activity in Connecticut (Netzer 1997).

New York has been able to live off services for several reasons (Piore and Sable 1983). First, it stands at the apex in the world of finance (albeit with increasing difficulty). As a result, the city was a logical site for corporate headquarters that, in turn, have pulled in a range of legal, consultancy, and real estate services.[13] Second, New York is well endowed with skills. Its universities not only nurture local talent but also draw in some of the best minds from around the world. Third, the city's cultural resources are exceedingly rich, keeping alive its attractiveness in spite of endemic urban blight. Fourth, its principal competitors in the 1990s are equally high-cost cities in Europe and East Asia, some of which lack New York's other attributes.

The experience of cities as diverse as New York, Baltimore, London, Amsterdam, and Dortmund suggests that sustaining dynamism or finding a second wind are critically dependent on three factors. First, the political leaders and opinion-makers of the city must crystallize and endorse a vision of the future that is acceptable to businessmen and common taxpayers alike. For such a consensus to form, the tenor and participatory nature of local politics and trustful relations between key political figures are important assets (Richardson 1991). Second, public and private sectors must collaborate so as to spread the burden of cost and risk. By drawing in the business community, a city can be sure that the money spent to attract industry is going to the right places. Industrialists have quite specific concerns that might be related to labor or physical infrastructure or quality of the environment, as indicated by the experience of Pittsburgh, Rochester, Research Triangle in North Carolina, Utah Research Park, and Silicon Valley. Access to university faculty, the ease of recruiting professionals, the degree to which the university is responsible for administering the research park, and the provision of amenities appear to be the critical factors. The more directly these concerns are addressed, the greater is the impact.

Third, the actual implementation of projects has in some notable instances been most efficacious when it was made the responsibility of quasi-public bodies (de Jong 1991). These can join public interest with private initiative. Quangos, as they are called, can rely more fully on the economic calculus to neutralize political concerns that dilute the effects of public schemes. The justly acclaimed Inner Harbor development in Baltimore is an example of deft political inception and efficient realization by a quasi-public body, which put forward a project credible enough to draw federal funding.

Lesson 8

The above lessons for three Chinese cities are based mainly on the experience of large cities in the industrialized economies. However, Shanghai, Tianjin, and Guangzhou also have much to learn from major urban centers in lower-income and newly industrializing countries. Cities such as Bangkok, Bombay, Karachi, Manila, and Seoul do not have to cope with decline or recovery. They are struggling with explosive population growth that is placing immense burdens on an infrastructure unable to keep up with demand. In many of these cities, municipal politics are murky, administration is weak, crime is rampant, and local revenues fall far short of requirements (Asian Development Bank 1997).

Although a city such as Seoul has enjoyed respectable growth, led first by industry and more recently by a combination of industry and producer services, other large cities in lower-income countries have turned in a less robust economic performance. This weakness stems from the inability to increase rapidly the number of relatively well paid jobs in manufacturing and producer services. One constraint is the quality of the infrastructure (energy and water supplies as well as transportation and housing services). Another is the transaction costs of doing business. There is too much red tape, taxes and fees are often excessive and unpredictably chaotic, local officials are extortionate, and criminal mafias thrive largely unchecked by the authorities. A third constraint that derives from the first two is that the quality of the physical and institutional environment deters FDI, negates agglomeration economies, and interferes with the functioning of dynamic industrial networks that strive to compete and give due attention to technological gains. The Bangkoks and the Bombays are expanding cities, but their growth is seemingly involuntary, propelled more by population than by a strategy that seeks to promote a mutually reinforcing mix of industry and services under environmentally sustainable conditions.

The lesson here relates to the quality of municipal leadership, administration, development strategy, and governance. Megacities in developing countries can thrive only if they retain the initiative and have clear strategic goals and the political determination to implement them. Cities that allow themselves to be engulfed by myriad problems and then struggle to survive have a bleak, crowded, possibly unsustainable future.

Summary

An important difference between the three Chinese cities and declining cities in developed market economies is their degree of industrial specialization. As noted above, cities in market economies are particularly vulnerable when they depend on a single manufacturing sector. By contrast, the three cities possess extremely diversified manufacturing sectors. Although this has hindered specialization and the focused use of resources, it protects the municipal economies from the decline of an individual subsector and allows them to explore different industrial options. Thus, the task of industrial restructuring takes on a different slant. Rather than trying to move out of a single declining industry, the three cities might allow a range of noncompetitive industries to shrink in relative size. The difficult but nonetheless crucial task is to identify the growth industries and producer services that will serve as the basis of restructuring and will absorb labor and capital from declining industries.

The experience of reviving cities in industrial countries shows that no industrial sector is intrinsically obsolete, even at high wage levels. Some textile and garment producers flourish in Germany, Italy, Japan, and the United States. Thus, it is impossible for planners to determine the shape of future restructuring from first principles, even when those principles are firmly grounded in economic logic. It is impossible to say that Shanghai's textile industry will not survive and prosper simply because Shanghai's wage and skill levels are higher than those in the interior of China. Nor can it be said that coastal regions will necessarily succeed in a particular high-technology sector because they share the same factor endowments. Municipal planners succeed best when they work in concert with markets.

Urban modernization, or revival, takes place when city planners provide effective support for industrial restructuring by developing municipal infrastructure and improving labor and capital markets, while allowing market demand to pick the winners and losers in the process. This is particularly important in the coastal cities. Some declining industries will effectively "downsize" into competitive and flexible "niche" producers. Some will disappear completely. And some apparently declining industries will surprise everyone and turn into engines of dynamic growth for the future urban economy. The objective of the three cities should be to allow these surprising trends to emerge without obstruction.

A Map of the Future

Aristotle believed that the ideal city contained just 5,000 people and that a settlement with more than 100,000 inhabitants could no longer be considered a city. Times and opinions have changed. In 1995 the largest city in the world—Tokyo—had a population of 27 million, and 21 megacities had populations in excess of 8 million. There were only two megacities in 1950. Urbanization has slowed in industrial countries to 1 percent a year or less but is projected to continue at rates of 3.5 percent and more in developing countries. It is fastest in Africa and Asia, where urbanization ratios are between 30 and 35 percent. By 2015 there are likely to be 33 megacities, 27 of them in the developing world. In addition, the number of cities with populations ranging from 1 million to 10 million will have risen from 270 in 1990 to 516 in 2015 (World Resources Institute 1996).

Recent trends suggest that China's rates of urbanization will be among the highest in the world, possibly in the range of 4 percent a year, and that between one-half and two-thirds of China's populace will be living in towns and cities within a couple of decades (see Kojima 1995). Already in 1995, both Shanghai and Tianjin were classified as megacities, Shanghai occupying sixth place and Tianjin occupying thirteenth. Guangzhou will officially catch up in the near future, although in reality it may already be a megacity. Thus one of the biggest challenges for the three cities will be to absorb the flood of migrants without experiencing a paralysis of services and a sharp deterioration in living conditions.

But each city can only do so much in the face of relentless migration. Only a nationally coordinated strategy for urban development can ensure a degree of regional balance and ease the pressure on the main coastal centers. For this reason as well as many others, China will need to have a strong central government and efficient mechanisms for fiscal sharing so that poorer but densely populated interior provinces benefit from progress elsewhere (on the range of problems to be solved in the interests of sustainable development and the necessity for local-central cooperation, see Drakakis-Smith 1995).

In the two decades that have elapsed since the start of reforms, Shanghai, Tianjin, and Guangzhou have managed to achieve substantial growth. If they are to emerge as China's world-class cities, each will have to sustain this momentum. If growth falters, reforms now under way will also falter. Problems carried over from the past will not be solved decisively. The challenges that lie in the future will be evaded. For the majority, life in the cities will become brutish.

Strategy in Capsule

Earlier chapters present many suggestions as to what might be done. Here we will push our ideas further. The principal messages emerging from theory and experience are that the three Chinese cities must continually strengthen the municipal economy, make full use of the benefits of agglomeration and scale, tighten their links with the hinterland, and, where possible, develop transport facilities to expand the surrounding economic "catchment area." Successful cities are active traders that use trade relationships to enhance competitiveness as well as to capture the gains from spillovers. These broad messages have a number of implications for the cities:

- Put municipal finances on a sound footing, maximize resource mobilization from within and outside the municipality, and arrive at the most favorable fiscal arrangement with the central government in the context of an agreed revenue-sharing framework

- Enhance the competitiveness of state enterprises using all available avenues so as to increase the growth stimulus derived from these entities, limit the fiscal burden imposed by loss-making firms, and contain the accumulation of nonperforming assets in bank portfolios[1]

- Fully exploit human resources and FDI to build a technologically robust industrial system, particularly through the transfer and diffusion of technology

- Modernize the infrastructure so as to improve municipal services, the quality of the environment, and linkages both with the hinterland and with overseas markets

- Concentrate on areas of core competence but at the same time build the capacity to diversify into new areas, particularly producer services; that is, view comparative advantage in dynamic terms.

Municipal Finances and Resource Mobilization

The quality and pace of urban growth depend on how a city manages its own finances, how it pursues institutional development to generate resources, and the skill with which it conducts financial relations with the central government and with outside investors. The local finances of the three cities, although improving, are far from transparent or rationally organized. Tax reform that suitably restructures the taxes under municipal control, fees, revenue from land leasing, and income from municipally owned enterprises is a priority for calibrating revenue effort to the exigencies of modernization. At the same time, a host of outlays and tax expenditures (which refer mainly to tax exemptions) need to be appraised so as to derive the maximum benefits from spending. Financial management must be tightened by way of planning, designing revenue instruments, scrutinizing expenditures, maintaining careful accounts, and subjecting these to vigorous auditing. For Shanghai and Tianjin, fiscal relations with the central government, and in Guangzhou's case with provincial authorities, must balance the requirements of governments with the at times overwhelming medium-term development goals of municipalities aggressively competing with one another.

All three cities are pursuing financial deepening at varying speeds, and the new infrastructure of institutions, banks, and finance houses will improve the mobilization of resources from within the municipalities and other parts of China. Shanghai has the lead in this area, but Guangzhou stands to benefit from the Pearl River delta–Hong Kong nexus. Tianjin lags behind but could develop the regional financial market in conjunction with Beijing.

FDI has emerged as a major source of capital for the three cities over the past four years, and it could remain so for some time. However, it needs to be cultivated more attentively than has been the case thus far. Even though municipal and central government authorities fully realize the importance of FDI, investors are still facing a great deal of uncertainty. They continue to be entangled in red tape, corrupt practices are undiminished, legal recourse is ill-defined, and negotiating practices are exhausting. By all accounts, the environment for FDI can test investors to the limit. To an extent, hard bargaining and stringent conditions are desirable, but all parties would gain from an efficient and equitable legal system, less red tape, and clearer, binding rules that keep corruption in check.[2]

Taking the State Sector into the Twenty-first Century

Reform, market competition, interfirm linkages, and FDI have all had a hand in improving the condition of state enterprises in the three cities.

They have contributed to better management, innovation, efficient production, success in the export market, and streamlined organization. The municipal authorities have hardened budget constraints where possible, allowed a few enterprises to go bankrupt, promoted mergers, financed modernization, and encouraged share ownership so as to prepare enterprises for corporate autonomy.[3] But all too many enterprises are struggling to break even, and many run large deficits that are financed either from the budget or through bank lending.

Although the pace of change quickened in the first half of the 1990s, resistance to enterprise reform has scarcely abated. Such resistance can be reduced, but this requires attending forcefully to four institutional barriers. First, there are the many bonds that tie workers to enterprises and transform enterprises into social communities—so-called total institutions—whose closure can become an economic event with traumatic social consequences. Second, there is the relationship between the enterprise and its municipal supervisory bureau, a body with a vested interest in maintaining the status quo because of the power and resources under its direction. Third, there is the larger municipal goal of self-sufficiency, a hangover from the past, which breeds resistance to the closure or migration of industry, even when this would cut subsidies and improve long-term prospects. Finally, there is the planning framework, still residually in place, which is geared to preserving a certain industrial proportionality through the balanced allocation of resources. Planning, as currently practiced, cannot readily accommodate the downsizing or geographic displacement of industry. It encounters difficulties when the goal is to close obsolescent facilities or redeploy resources. In theory, the ability to orchestrate macro changes with an eye to long-term objectives is the principal advantage that planning has over markets. In practice, the potential gains from planning are largely nullified by procedural rigidities, the political opposition to restructuring that alters incentives and threatens jobs, and the inability of a few planners to assimilate the vast body of relevant information, which the market is designed to process.

The experience of other countries teaches us that drastic action is generally sparked by a serious crisis. None of the three cities is in the grip of such a crisis. However, all three face opportunities, some of which could slip away if action is long postponed. The system of planning can play a useful role, but it must define strategic choices and supplement market forces in the active promotion of state enterprise reform by corporatizing larger enterprises and privatizing smaller ones.[4] The current approach to industrial reorganization through mergers and the formation of groups remains, substantially, an administered process, which often does not precisely define the legal, financial, accounting, and managerial rules. In a large number of instances these administered solutions do not improve productive efficiency or arrange for the exit of failing enterprises.

Some of the most ambitious efforts to combine firms also risk introducing the problems associated with excessive concentration in an economy where market competition is just beginning to surface.

Where the interest of efficiency and long-term modernization can be served, mergers have a role. But if they are viewed largely as an instrument for lightening the burden of fiscal subsidies, their effects could be deleterious. An enterprise that is a chronic loss-maker, with little by way of salvageable assets, should be closed.

Administrative reform that reorients the function of planning, attempts to prune the number of supervisory agencies, and converts the remaining ones into regulatory bodies that take many of the cues from the market is a long and difficult step. So also are measures aimed at changing the organizational characteristics of industry through exit, merger, and the formation of groups. These will be hardest to institute if many participants view them as negative-sum solutions. If bureaucratic pruning, closure of firms, or industrial streamlining result in widespread unemployment, any moves will encounter resistance even if the unemployed are generously compensated. Only the firm prospects of a job, offering rising real wages in a rapidly expanding economy (or, possibly, generous redundancy allowances), are likely to allay the fears of individuals whose jobs must be sacrificed for the greater good. A better unemployment insurance program can temporarily ease the pain, but it is not a solution.[5] Hence, growth and reform strategies are tied inextricably together.[6]

Human Capital, Foreign Direct Investment, and Technology Transfer

Recent experience in China and several decades of development in East Asia have highlighted the fruitfulness of agglomeration economies in an urban market environment that fully harnesses human capital by encouraging the entry of smaller firms and stimulating technological change. Small and medium-size firms entering industry and services will decisively influence the longevity of existing lines of activity and the successful introduction of new lines of business. To flourish, such enterprises need entrepreneurial talent. There is no dearth of such talent for the light consumer industries, but as the three cities continue moving up the ladder of technological sophistication, entrepreneurs with higher-order technical skills will be in demand. For instance, Tokyo derives some of its industrial strength from numerous small-scale, high-technology companies run by skilled craftsmen and technicians. These use the applied research from local laboratories to produce small quantities of pilot or specialty products, often for larger corporations. Once these products have won consumer acceptance, their manufacture can be shifted to bigger facilities in regional centers (see Hill and Fujita 1993).

To build the requisite pool of skills, Shanghai can attempt to follow the example of Taiwan (China). A very large number of Taiwanese have received graduate degrees in science and engineering in the United States. Many have also acquired work experience in technology-intensive firms. This group of professionals is now the entrepreneurial backbone of Taiwanese industry, especially in subsectors such as computers, telecommunications, microprocessors, and biotechnology. Not only are they responsible for many of the new start-ups, but they also enable companies to absorb new techniques on the shop floor, support much of the R&D effort that underlies Taiwan's export drive, and serve as a conduit for technology transferred from leading firms in the United States. Because the average Taiwanese engineer earns a third of what his U.S. counterpart earns, product development costs are lower, and this enables Taiwanese firms to compete against large corporations in the industrialized countries.[7]

In the United States and Japan, Chinese students outnumber students of all other foreign nationalities. They are heavily concentrated in the sciences and engineering. Many are now working in manufacturing industries or conducting research, thereby adding a valuable empirical dimension to their theoretical knowledge. In the second half of the 1990s, a third generation of Chinese students is enrolling in U.S. universities, with those of the first generation, who remained abroad, well into their professional careers. China is, therefore, building up a pool of valuable entrepreneurial and technical skills overseas. A significant percentage of current and former students are from the three cities, and many others would, no doubt, welcome the opportunity to work in these cities under appropriate circumstances.

Creating the conditions that would make it feasible for Chinese trained abroad to contribute directly to the modernization of manufacturing activities in the state sector, to establish enterprises, and to conduct research should be a priority. This would be a highly effective means of importing state-of-the-art technology, production skills, and marketing contacts into the three cities. It would augment the pool of young entrepreneurs, who will be responsible for steering China's small and medium-size industry sector into regions of advanced technology.[9] Furthermore, these returnees are likely to bring back the dynamic, commercially oriented research culture and modes of professional communications (facilitated by nationwide computer networks) that flourish in Japan and the United States. This culture and system of communication are absent in China but are badly needed if China is to use fully the technical resources that could give it a decisive edge over its competitors.

A few Chinese laboratories are attempting to recruit overseas, but so far the culture of China's scientific institutes inhibits commercially oriented research, communication between researchers, and the translation of applied research into marketable products. Money and facilities are part of the problem, but the isolation of Chinese laboratories, the lack of mobility of researchers, and the absence of interdisciplinary work are serious obstacles even in a city such as Shanghai. The state-established "key laboratories" are better endowed with higher-quality researchers, but the fields of investigation remain narrow. Shanghai has attempted to introduce interdisciplinary research by way of the Center for Life Science, which is the nucleus of a research network linked with other key laboratories. This effort will gradually break down the walls separating institutes from one another and from the commercial world. The retirement of thousands of senior scientists, once they reach the age of 60, will clear the way for younger, often better-qualified researchers imbued with a different ethos. Improved communication by way of the Internet is also linking China's R&D establishment to that of the world. Starting with just 1,000 users in April 1994, when connections were first set up, the number had risen tenfold by mid-1995.

Another strategic concern relates to the current and future role of neighboring economies in the modernization of the three cities.[8] There is no doubt that the great surge in industry and exports in the Guangdong-Fujian region is closely linked with the shift of export processing and other manufacturing activities from Hong Kong and Taiwan (China) to southern China. In addition, this shift has provided Chinese producers with financial, brokerage, packaging, consultancy, repair, and other services essential for raising the level and quality of industrial production, as well as for channeling China's goods into foreign markets. For a variety of reasons having to do with geography, official policy, kinship ties, and municipal receptivity to low-technology processing, much of the investment originating in or funneled through places such as Hong Kong has entered Guangzhou or its hinterland. The process of industrial transfer of hardware and software is by no means complete. Guangzhou should continue to compete aggressively for foreign investment and to give undiminished attention to the growth of trade because doing so is the surest way of inducing local producers to maintain a desirable cycle of innovation.

The surge in FDI that commenced in 1992 has greatly increased the influx of capital into Shanghai and, to lesser extent, Tianjin. The appreciation of the yen will most likely continue to induce Japanese firms to invest in China and to develop China's capabilities for exporting to third countries, selling in the Chinese market, and producing for Japanese consumption (*Far Eastern Economic Review,* March 31, 1994). Korean manufacturers are also under pressure to invest in their trading partners so as to sustain corporate growth and counteract rising domestic wages.[10] These two countries and Taiwan (China) will be major sources of capital and technology for the three cities.

Southeast Asian countries are also likely to figure prominently in the development of infrastructure, commercial property, energy, and light manufacturing. For instance, Choroen Pokphand (CP) from Thailand is already well established in Shanghai, having invested in the Ek

Chor Company, which produces 300,000 motorcycles drawing on technology licensed from Honda. CP is building a modern plant in Pudong that will double its capacity in 1996. In fact, CP might be the single largest investor in China, having entered fields such as food grains, petrochemicals, and property development by way of 130 joint ventures (see Lever-Tracy, Ip, and Tracy 1996; *Far Eastern Economic Review*, January 23, 1997).

Alongside the growth of Thai and Indonesian investment, there is also a substantial flow of capital from Singapore. With a surfeit of capital and circumscribed prospects for local expansion, Singapore businesses are targeting projects in China. What Singapore has to offer, aside from capital, is the creation and management of technological parks. A government-owned company called Singapore Technologies Industrial Corporation is working with the Wuxi municipal authorities on an integrated industrial park that had attracted 20 foreign companies by mid-1995.[11]

The first wave of FDI during the period 1980–91 was predominantly in industry (70 percent), and it enabled China to expand its capacity for light manufacturing and to enter export markets. China received very little sophisticated technology during the first wave but benefited immensely from the learning imparted with respect to production methods, organization, quality control, labor training, and marketing (see Chen, Chang, and Zhang 1995; Hobday 1995). All these helped to deepen the foundations of industry, exposed Chinese industries to international market competition, and forced enterprises to make good their deficiencies in a brief period of time. The first wave focused on the southern provinces, which absorbed well over half of all FDI through 1990 and transformed rural industry.

A second wave that has been gathering force since the early 1990s promises to transfer much more capital, to raise the technology quotient, and to distribute capital more evenly across subsectors. This investment is also more likely to be centered on the major cities, if they are ready to take the initiative themselves. Foreign investors are emphasizing automobiles and electronics but are equally prepared to enter petrochemicals, metallurgy, telecommunications, and imaging equipment, to name just a few. Partnerships with foreign firms are necessary if the three cities are to participate in the technological race.

The extent to which technology transfer takes place, spillovers are exploited, and industry is rendered technologically sophisticated will depend on the building and deployment of human resources. The strategy of expanding and leveraging municipal research establishments with the help of long-term research-sharing arrangements with foreign corporations has a high payoff. Widely diffusing the improved process technology and organization that a few firms have acquired would also telescope the learning process. For instance, to help small firms master new technology, specialize, and produce complex parts of requisite quality,

Japanese prefectural governments have used various support schemes and set up research laboratories. Similar action would contribute to the emergence and dynamism of networks of small firms in China's potential industrial centers. Having clear goals for industrial competitiveness and technological capability would facilitate the articulation of industrial policy mechanisms for transferring technology and the strategy with respect to FDI (Morris-Suzuki 1994).

To take an example, future development of urban transport in its totality is likely to be the single largest investment decision made by any one of these municipalities, spanning manufacturing, energy, infrastructure, services, and environmental management. From a long-term perspective, the most efficient, environmentally sustainable strategy would be to take aim at the technology that is likely to prevail by the turn of the century, by which time the potential market for autos in China will be large. Environmental and energy concerns are forcing the leading auto companies to invest seriously in lean-burn engine technology, very light-weight aerodynamic vehicles, and battery propulsion.[12] Once these achieve commercial viability, they could gradually change the face of the auto market. These technologies are best fitted for China's urban conditions and would provide urban inhabitants with low-polluting transport easily accommodated in crowded cities. Strengthening the automobile production and research base with a view to technological leapfrogging might be the most attractive course to follow. This requires moving quickly from the 1970s technology of the Santana-type autos closer to the frontier of the field and ensuring that foreign investors are under sufficient competitive pressure to transfer the latest technology to China and to enlarge the local capacity to participate in innovation.

Although alliances can shorten the learning process and permit technological leapfrogging, Brazil, India, and Korea have had mixed experience with the transfer of technology. To be advantageous for the local partner, partnerships with foreign firms will have to develop the local partner's research capacity to absorb foreign innovations quickly, as well as its ability to contribute home-grown innovations. Alliances that are a one-way street reduce the local partner to a subsidiary. Thus the scale of domestic effort will determine the gains to be realized from relationships with overseas corporations (see Evans 1995).

Infrastructure

Even at this early stage of motorization, Guangzhou and Shanghai are beginning to suffer from traffic congestion and vehicular pollution. During rush hour, traffic slows to a crawl. Expanding the road network—an exceedingly expensive proposition—can arrest the trends temporarily but, as other Southeast Asian cities have discovered, investment in roads and the most stringent efforts to regulate traffic (as in Singapore) only push back the day of reckoning, sometimes by not very much. As congestion mounts, the benefits of automobility ebb rapidly for individuals and commercial users. As more and more vehicles are tied up in traffic jams, average speeds decline to between 5 and 10 kilometers per hour, and haulage and taxi companies are forced to increase fleet size and hire more drivers. This only serves to compound the problem.

Housing construction on the periphery of cities such as Shanghai, and the dramatic growth in the number of small businesses that do not provide adjacent residential accommodation, have meant increasing separation of home and workplace. This has greatly increased the number of commuters. Side by side, the presence of migrant workers, who rely mainly on public transport, has led to crowding on buses and demand for vehicular transport such as taxis and vans (see Gaubatz 1995). In Shanghai and Guangzhou motorized vehicles outnumber bicycles, and mixed traffic conditions result in congestion at all hours of the day. To avoid Bangkok-type gridlock, each city will have to work with factories and real estate developers on a transport plan that will improve the situation even as population pressure mounts in the decades ahead.

Transport planning must be coordinated with the assimilation of communications technology. Such technology is making it far easier to connect economic activities while allowing them to be physically separated. It is also making it convenient to relocate from downtown headquarters certain "back office" service activities that do not require face-to-face contact (for a detailed discussion of the possibilities opened up by new technologies, see U.S. Congress, Office of Technology Assessment, 1995). Modern telecommunications and computerized merchandising systems backed up with commercial delivery (as in Paris) can diminish individual shopping expeditions. These are initiatives for the long term but must be factored into city telecommunications development plans. Together such initiatives can reduce the pressure on high-cost, congested urban areas and curb the growth of traffic. With the costs of computer equipment falling precipitately, it is not difficult to imagine that, by 2000, Chinese homes and offices will have a MINTEL-type facility with a telephone hookup. The extraordinarily rapid expansion and deepening of China's telecommunications network in cities such as Shanghai, Beijing, and Guangzhou could ease the task of urban planners.

More urgent perhaps, if only because of the length of planning and lags in execution, is the construction of subway systems for intracity commuting and surface railways that link up suburbs as well as nearby urban centers. Shanghai is well on its way to building a subway network, and Guangzhou has also embarked on one. The full play of agglomeration effects and close interaction with the hinterland make it imperative to modernize transport and communications infrastructure within and around the cities.

This requires an intensive effort to develop modern surface rail networks, which are the fastest, cheapest, safest, and least environmentally damaging form of transport. The severity of land constraints in the crowded delta areas makes the dedicated two-track high-speed railway line for a system such as the ones used in Japan and Europe enormously attractive. Such a line has the same capacity as a six-lane superhighway, and a passenger traveling on such a train consumes half as much energy per kilometer (1 megajoule; Eastham 1995).

Rapid rail technology is evolving continuously as one country after another perceives the congestion, pollution, and land availability dilemmas and turns to the railway to satisfy the growing need for intermetropolitan transport. Several steel wheel on rail technologies are available, and Mag-Lev trains are being tested. Any choice must be based on an educated guess of what the state of the art will be in 10 years. As Korea has discovered, it can take up to 20 years to go from conception to the start of service. The time to begin planning and obtaining the support of nearby cities is now (see "Train Delayed," *Far Eastern Economic Review*, November 28, 1996). Only a cross-modal effort, using the very latest technologies, will ensure that Chinese cities are effectively linked to their hinterlands and to one another.

Producer Services

China has come to recognize more fully the contribution that services make to growth and employment. On June 16, 1992, the central authorities and the state council issued a strongly worded directive to accelerate tertiary sector development, which all three cities have embraced enthusiastically. Although the initial focus is on retail and financial services, the long-term growth prospects span a broader range of possibilities (see Harris 1995 for a discussion of Bombay along similar lines). Shanghai, in particular, could tap some very powerful trends if it makes the right policy decisions, upgrades infrastructure, and enjoys good fortune. Besides the standard producer services—finance, insurance, consulting, and information—several other areas could prove more lucrative for Shanghai. These are tertiary education, health, and entertainment.

The demand for higher education is sure to mushroom in the years ahead, along with research activities. Shanghai's university system is among the strongest in China (matched only by that of Beijing), and the city could well emerge as the center of learning, comparable to Boston in the United States. As China's population ages and becomes more affluent, it will consume more hospital-based services. This growth, some of it wasteful, has proceeded inexorably in industrial countries and is already apparent in China. Once again, Shanghai's hospitals are among the best, associated as they are with the nation's finest teaching institutions. They also have an edge in terms of capital equipment and laboratories. Again, like Boston or possibly Houston, Shanghai could set up a huge medical establishment with backward linkages to industry.

The writing of software and making of movies are already established businesses in Shanghai, but the production of electronic and nonelectronic media entertainment is still quite small. Future prospects are bright, and the potential earnings can be large, if the experience of centers on the U.S. West Coast is a guide. The limits to what the service sector can achieve in Shanghai will be set not by opportunities but by the ambition, talent, and energy of Shanghai's inhabitants. On a lesser scale, Guangzhou–Hong Kong is likely to emerge as a giant in the service sector, stronger even than Shanghai in producer services, especially finance and information, but possibly less so in education and health. The Jin-Jing-Tang region, taken as a whole, may be the third major hub of service industries in China, but Tianjin alone might have difficulty matching the performance of the other two cities. Future development of the service sector may hinge on the nature of transport and telecommunications, which pool the region's diverse resources.

Looking perhaps two decades into the future, it is possible to see these cities distancing themselves from actual production and concentrating on R&D, design, and marketing, activities which add the most value, while leaving the actual manufacturing to others (Rappaport and Halevi 1991). Both Singapore and Taiwan (China) are moving in this direction. Whereas today the major enterprises of the three cities count their wealth in tangible assets, in the world of tomorrow intangible assets—intellectual resources—will be the key to success.

Summary

Economic strategy in the three cities can have a number of strands. In closing, we touch briefly on four of them. First, thoughtful, long-term industrial planning that is well informed by technological possibilities on the horizon is essential. It should tailor action to a vision of what the city wants to be 15 or 20 years in the future. Second, while making adequate preparations to realize distant goals, the city should maximize its own pace of growth, using its current strengths to overcome the many frictions inherent in transforming the state sector and embracing fresh possibilities.

Third, the quality of the urban environment is becoming a vital ingredient of future prosperity. The emergence both of high-technology industry and of the services supporting it depends on the successful use of policies to control pollution and enhance the quality of cultural, recreational, and housing facilities. The cultural endowment of these cities is superior to that of most other urban centers in China, but it badly needs refurbishing. Other facilities and environmental conditions are relatively poor. Migration to these cities, the increasing scale of industry, and the spread of industrialization will put further pressure on environmental quality. This is clearly a priority area for future investment (see Lam and Tao 1996). Stricter environmental standards will be costly for industry as well as utilities. Certain producers may be forced to close down or relocate elsewhere, but the long-term industrial gains will be sizable. Pulling in technologically sophisticated activities will constitute only part of the benefits. The attempts to satisfy new rules will also bring into existence an industry and a range of skills for which future demand is likely to be very strong. These include solid waste and landfill management, air quality control, and sewage and water treatment (see Serageldin, Barrett, and Martin-Brown 1995).

Fourth, growth over the medium term, and the realization of future goals, will depend on integration with the international industrial system, so as to tap foreign capital, technology, and markets. China can be more effective than most other countries because it has the potential market and the manpower, skills, and work traditions that matter. But the country is still some distance from matching, if not improving on, the legal framework, the business practices, and the political ambience of some of its neighbors.

The world is becoming a small, economically integrated, and intensely competitive place. There are going to be winners and losers. No matter what perspective one adopts, whether national or municipal, the winners will share certain attributes: they will mobilize investable resources most fully, they will be the most flexible in adapting institutions and using the benefits of agglomeration to achieve economic results, and they will make the most strenuous efforts to use neighborhood effects to realize scale economies and maximize technological gains.

Notes

Chapter 1

1. Yang (1996a) maintains that such dissatisfaction and the push to change had its roots in the Great Famine of 1959–60. For an overview of the first decade of reforms, see Riskin (1987). On the grassroots pressures that triggered agricultural reforms, see Kelliher (1992). Perkins and Yusuf (1984) trace the evolution of the household responsibility system and the parallel dismantling of communes. Little (1992) assesses agricultural change in considerable analytical depth. For the effects of reform on agricultural productivity, see Lin (1992).

2. According to Naughton (1995b), China's reform has moved in unexpected directions, and China's policymakers did not expect rural industry to grow at the rates it did.

3. Urban growth in developing countries in general seems to have displayed a relatively smooth pattern since the late nineteenth century, similar to the timing of urban growth in China. It started slowly, accelerated as the industrial revolution hit full stride, and then slowed down. As a group, cities in developing countries achieved their peak rates of growth in the early 1970s, a time when China's leaders still had an antiurban bias. Between 1960 and 1980 these cities grew at an average rate of around 4 percent. Urbanization rates in 1960 and 1970 were about 15 and 18 percent, respectively, for low-income developing countries and 37 and 50 percent for the rest. See Williamson (1992); World Bank (1981, 1994b).

4. Urban population includes agricultural population within the city proper; see State Statistical Bureau, *China: Urban Statistical Yearbook,* 1990; *Statistical Yearbook of China,* 1995.

5. Shanghai and Guangzhou serve as the axes of two of China's four "metropolitan interlocking regions" (see Zhou 1991). According to Zhou, each zone has (a) at least two cities with more than a million people serving as growth poles, (b) important ports, (c) well-developed lines of communication between the main centers, (d) numerous small and midsize cities along the transport

corridors, and (e) intensive economic interaction between urban and rural areas.

6. State Statistical Bureau, *Statistical Yearbook of China,* 1995. The calculation of gross value of industrial output (GVIO) of the three cities includes city-administered counties and village-run industrial enterprises.

7. Externalities can be static or dynamic, and their relevance varies from industry to industry. Henderson, Kuncoro, and Turner (1995, p. 1068) describe "static externalities [as] localization economies in which a firm benefits from local firms in the same industry and [as] urbanization economies in which a firm benefits from overall local urban scale and diversity. Dynamic externalities deal with the role of prior information accumulations in the local area on current productivity and hence employment. . . . [D]ynamic externalities may be Marshall-Arrow-Romer economies that derive from a buildup of knowledge associated with ongoing communications among local firms in the same industry, or Jacobs economies, which derive from a buildup of knowledge or ideas associated with historical diversity." See also Rotemberg and Saloner (1990); Scott and Storper (1990); Krugman (1991, 1992, 1993); Petrakos (1992).

Chapter 2

1. The names of cities and phonetic conventions changed after 1949. For instance, Canton was changed to Guangzhou, Peking to Beijing, Foochow to Fuzhou, Amoy to Xiamen, Hankow to Wuhan, and Nanking to Nanjing. We use the older names and spellings when writing about the earlier period and the new system thereafter. For personal names, we use the new system throughout. Also, on July 1, 1997, Hong Kong reverted to China.

2. In Imperial China the main forms of transport were unmechanized water carriage and road traffic. Where possible, trade took to the water, and much of it flowed on the backs of China's rivers. The east-to-west river systems served as the main arteries: the Yangtze in central China, the Liao River in Manchuria, and the West River in southern China. The Great Canal, from Beijing to Hangzhou at the lower Yangtze valley, was the only north-south inland connection, in addition to some coastal traffic. Unmechanized road transport was confined to light and valuable products. Land routes, however, did connect regions of China. The primitive nature of the transport system seriously limited the volume of trade and, in turn, the growth of production. Cities on the major arteries naturally became centers of trade and production; they included Beijing, Guangzhou, Hangzhou, Shanghai, and Wuhan.

3. China's field armies were perennially short of horses, which were sorely needed to maintain a suitably large and skilled corps of cavalrymen. To make up for the shortfall, border provinces were required to obtain horses through trade with the central Asian tribes. Once the latter had acquired a taste for tea and silk, the Chinese used these commodities to pay for the mounts they lacked (see Smith 1991).

4. In the late fourteenth and early fifteenth centuries, China possessed an ocean-going fleet of several hundred ships—some measuring 600 feet by 250 feet—with watertight bulkheads and, by the standards of the age, sophisticated rudders (see Levathes 1994). With this fleet China dominated trade routes all the way into the Indian Ocean. Under Zheng He, the eunuch admiral, a series of voyages in the first two decades of the fifteenth century made China's naval

presence widely felt and acquainted the Chinese with exotic products from far afield. Zheng He's fame and the cost of his voyages generated much intrigue between eunuchs and mandarins at the court of the Zhu De emperor of the Ming dynasty. In the end, the seafaring eunuchs and China's fleet suffered a crippling defeat at the hands of their opponents at the imperial court (see Levathes 1994). In fact, Zheng He's seven voyages were noted in barely 700 words in the 330 chapters of the Ming official history. The great admiral himself is described in just 30 words, and his fame rests on three books written by his subordinates (see Tsai 1996).

5. According to Skinner (1965), 63,000 basic markets existed in the early twentieth century grouped under eight market systems. Each comprised a hierarchy of interlinked towns, local cities, and central cities. These served as clearinghouses for trade in the locality, the province, and the region. They also funneled trade upward through the hierarchy, and the larger centers acted as channels for cross-provincial trade. At the apex of each marketing system stood the key urban center of the system, which served as the focus for commercial activity.

6. For a detailed account of Shanghai's history through the mid-nineteenth century, see Johnson (1995); for some striking snapshots of what Shanghai was like, warts and all, in the first three decades of the twentieth century, see Grayling and Whitfield (1994).

7. In all, the government established 19 arsenals and shipyards. Zeng Guofan and Li Hongzhang set up the arsenal in Shanghai in 1865, which was the largest of the lot. Li Hongzhang built the Nanjing arsenal in the same year (see Feuerwerker 1977).

8. Tianjin's early development owes much to Li Hongzhang, who was appointed governor-general of Zhili in 1890. He built up the infrastructure, sponsored the Kaiping Mines, built a shipyard and Tianjin's first railroad, and expanded the arsenal (which was destroyed during the Boxer uprising in 1900). See Hershatter (1986).

9. See Chao (1977) for a detailed account of the Chinese textile industry. Chao compares foreign-owned with Chinese mills, the latter being undercapitalized, lacking in reserves, and reliant on short-term working capital. As a result they were much more susceptible than foreign mills to economic fluctuations (as occurred in the 1920s). On the nature of China's industrial sector and its concentration in Shanghai, especially cotton spindlers, see Feuerwerker (1983).

10. China is planning to add around 5,000 miles (8,000 kilometers) of new rail lines in the second half of the 1990s, bringing its total network to more than 42,000 miles (67,200 kilometers). Even so, China's rail network is only about one-fourth of that in the United States, which is also backed by a superior network of roads.

11. China's natural resources are distributed unevenly across the country. The eastern region, where most centers of population and production are located, is generally some distance away from the major deposits of resources. For detail, see Dorian (1993).

12. Hankow consisted of three cities that straddled the Yangzi River: Wuchong, Hanyang, and Hankow—hence the name Wuhan by which it is now known (see Mackinnon 1996).

13. The *hukou* system began in 1951 with the initial intention of "maintaining peace and order," continued through the 1958 Regulations on Household Regis-

tration in the People's Republic of China, and went to full-scale implementation in 1960. See Cheng and Selden (1994); see also Chan and Xu (1985) and Bernstein (1977). In all, about 17 million urbanites were dispersed (see Naughton 1995a).

14. One of the effects of the Maoist strategy of spreading industry inland was to revive provincial capitals and other cities in the interior (see Chang 1994).

Chapter 3

1. Shanghai's GDP reached $30 billion at the end of 1995. All dollars are U.S. dollars; a billion is 1,000 million.

2. This mirrored the New Economic Policy introduced in the former U.S.S.R., which made cities the centers of production (see Colton 1995).

3. See chapter 6. On São Paulo and Rio de Janeiro, especially in the South Paraiba Valley, see Becker and Egler (1992). On the United Kingdom, see Freeman (1982).

4. See "German Carmakers Dominate in China," *Financial Times*, July 17, 1995. Also see "Volkswagen Set for a Windfall after China Ruling," *Financial Times*, June 24, 1994; "Volkswagen AG Plans to Boost Car Output in China to 700,000," *Wall Street Journal*, September 19, 1994; "Long March to Mass Market," *Financial Times*, June 25, 1997.

5. Harwit (1995); also known as Shanghai Car Plant, which is part of Shanghai Auto Industry Corp., the new plant is a modern facility but is located 25 miles from the city, and the access road is narrow and highly congested.

6. Tariffs on autos in 1993 ranged from 30 percent on buses to 220 percent on full-size sedans. Until the early 1990s government agencies or public bodies bought virtually all cars, and hence the scale of demand as well as prices could be regulated to fit plans. In recent years, private purchases have risen, but as of the end of 1995, no more than 3 percent of the 1.6 million autos were privately owned.

7. Foreign parts manufacturers that have entered into joint ventures include Shanghai Albthom Valve Co., a producer of engine valves, and Shanghai GKN, a source of universal joints.

8. Aside from the industrial deepening, just-in-time delivery, and reduced transport costs, the local manufacture of components embeds the low domestic wage costs into a higher proportion of the car; see Shaiken (1991) and Woodard and Zhu (1994).

9. This will result in an assembly plant capable of producing 100,000 midsize cars annually and an engine and transmission plant; see *China Digest News*, October 30, 1995. In 1995 Volkswagen introduced the Santana 2000, powered by the company's latest fuel-injected diesel engine. The car was formally unveiled on April 20, 1995. A second plant with a capacity of 100,000 came on stream in 1996 (Maxton 1994).

10. Since 1992 the number of workers in the textiles industry has been reduced to 365,000 as the result of layoffs and reduction in spindles. See *Far Eastern Economic Review*, August 29, 1996, p. 58.

11. Recent experience in the West suggests that collaboration between the manufacturers of synthetic fibers and downstream users has contributed fundamentally to the increasing popularity of blends and synthetics for high-value clothing. It has also helped to transform the nature of synthetic fibers by pro-

moting focused research. The ability to engineer synthetic fiber filaments has made it possible for nylons to breathe, has softened the appearance and texture of synthetic fibers, and has improved the drape ("A Taste for the Unnatural," *Financial Times*, April 15 and 16, 1995; "Nylon Spins a Good Yarn," *Financial Times*, March 9, 1995). Most recently, the rising cost of natural fibers has accelerated the use of nylon, viscose, and acrylic materials especially engineered to maximize comfort and provide the desired luster and draping characteristics.

12. Even in the United States, the apparel industry struggles on with labor-intensive sweatshops that depend on low wages, long hours, and niche marketing, but microchips and steel are the preferred weapons of the most competitive producers. Typical of the new breed of apparel producers is a factory producing Wrangler jeans in El Paso, Texas. In this plant, computer-guided slings hanging from overhead rails dump 144 pairs of jeans at a time into truck-size washers and dryers. Trunks, pumps, and pipes automatically feed in the right mix of chemicals for the specified finish; the 7-acre complex includes a warehouse that looks ready to run itself. Retail sales leave by satellite from the Wrangler headquarters in Greensboro, North Carolina, where computers supply a seasonally adjusted forecast of sales. Restocking signals bounce from there to the El Paso warehouse, where conveyor belts and electronic eyes do much of the sorting ("Jeans Makers Flourish on Border," *New York Times*, September 29, 1994, D1).

13. Shanghai's new breed of designers face three hurdles. First, the local market is tiny and not especially discriminating. Most women still commute on bicycles. Second, material is of variable quality, and special accessories are difficult to find. Third, competition from overseas designers remains very strong.

14. In some industrial subsectors, however, the role of foreign-invested enterprises in promoting exports has been growing in importance. For instance, such enterprises contributed more than half of Shanghai's exports of machinery and electronics in 1995.

15. The design and production strengths of large state-owned enterprises, the quality of their facilities, and the degree of vertical integration are nicely captured in "China's Technology and Manufacturing Base," *China Trade* 1 (1992).

16. The share of the state sector in industrial output fell to 43 percent in 1994 and is likely to drop by 2 or 3 percentage points each year. However, the concentration of state-owned enterprises in Shanghai means that the process will be slower here than in the country as a whole and the drain on the municipal budget will remain. For instance, the amount of subsidies for state-owned enterprises increased six times between 1987 and 1993. The 1993 sum of Y3.4 billion for such subsidies was in fact the largest category in the municipal budget (see Cheung 1996).

17. Water and sewerage facilities are inadequate, and building these at the requisite speed will be a considerable challenge. Most of Shanghai's water comes from an intake on the Huangpu River, but industrial development is compromising the quality of the water at that point. Hence the city is constructing a new intake 40 kilometers upstream from the existing one at Linjiang for a price of $406 million (Burley 1995). The problems of water shortages and water pollution will continue to place severe constraints on urban development.

18. Between 1990 and 1994 Shanghai constructed an average of 7 million square meters of floor space each year. More than 300,000 households have been relocated over the past few years (Leman 1995). City authorities plan to build 53 million square meters of housing so as to raise per capita living space to 9.7 square meters.

19. Another new mortgage scheme was introduced in Shanghai in early 1996. Individuals may open savings accounts in China Construction Bank's Shanghai Branch and may qualify for home mortgage loans. However, the rate schedule has not yet been worked out, and few loans have been actually taken out.

20. As a late starter, Pudong will not receive the advantages provided by severe economic distortions elsewhere in the country, which were the prime moving force behind creation of the early Special Economic Zones. Development of Pudong will depend primarily on its ability to offer genuine economic advantages to potential domestic and foreign investors.

21. Apart from Yaohan, which is using its Shanghai No. 1 Yaohan Department Store as a stepping-stone to establishing a chain of retail joint ventures throughout the country, other Japanese and foreign retailers, such as Isetan, Mihei, Parkson, and Seibu, are investing in Shanghai (see Matsudaira 1994). The problem of finding and leasing good locations and the constraints imposed by a consumer population of between 30 million and 50 million are described in "In Search of Fresh Pastures," *Financial Times*, December 8, 1995.

22. The price of industrial land was five times that of comparable plots to the west of the city in 1994, which claimed to offer similar tax incentives as Pudong (see Jacobs and Hong 1994).

23. S. Ho (1994), pp. 129–31. The retired engineers and technicians are known as *gaojia Laotou:* high-priced old men. Apart from retirees, many urban residents work in rural industries. Chinese estimates for the early 1990s put the number at 3 million. See Naughton (1995a); Jacobs and Hong (1994).

24. Shanghai hosts at least 266 independent research institutes (with 173 specializing in applied science and development) and more than 500 enterprises run by scientific research institutes (FBIS-CHI-93117, June 21, 1993, p. 60; FBIS-CHI-94096, May 18, 1994, p. 78). An effort was initiated in 1994 to reform the university system in Shanghai. Three universities—Fudan University, Shanghai Communications University, and Shanghai Foreign Language University—were selected as pilot projects for an experiment called joint development. The three universities will still be under the State Education Commission, but a dual leadership will be introduced. See FBIS-CHI-94096, May 18, 1994, p. 77.

25. FBIS-CHI-93171, September 7, 1993, p. 62. The city supported close to 2,600 research projects in 1991, of which about 1,045 are considered to be reaching or approaching international advanced levels. Shanghai also won 18 prizes for invention at the national level, the highest total among all provinces and cities.

26. Shanghai's research institutes, particularly those specializing in applied science and development, are beginning to develop some commercial linkages. Earnings from technical transfers, engineering services, and business operations rose to Y2.1 billion in 1992, almost three times the amount of government funding. In the five years prior to 1993 Shanghai also completed 14 key industrial R&D projects, including the Santana car, program-controlled telephone exchange board, fiber-optic telecommunications, thermal power equipment, nuclear power equipment, and color television tubes. After being put into operation, these projects generated an output value of Y17.2 billion in 1992 and earned foreign exchange worth $1 billion.

An even more encouraging phenomenon is the emergence of the nonstate-owned technological enterprises, which numbered about 5,650 by mid-1994. These firms are more entrepreneurial in turning research findings into new products and are becoming important players in Shanghai's science and technology sector. In 1993 they registered sales revenue of Y8.7 billion, compared with Y900 million earned by 2,000 such firms in 1992. See FBIS-CHI-93117, June 21, 1993, p. 60; FBIS-CHI-93079, April 27, 1993, p. 52; FBIS-CHI-094096, May 18, 1994, p. 78.

27. This is the descendant of a stock market set up around 1911 at the Beneficent Fragrance Tea House on the corner of Fuzhou and Daxin Roads. It traded stocks and bonds, securities for private Chinese companies, and securities for the state-owned railways. The stock market lasted through the 1940s, except during the four years of the war. Similar exchanges were established in Guangzhou and Tianjin in 1921. These too survived into the 1940s (Karmel 1994, p. 1106).

28. Even in more industrialized countries, stock markets are less important than usually perceived. They account for a small percentage of total corporate finance.

29. Interprovincial resource transfers accounted for a third of total investment in Shanghai during the first half of the 1990s, reflecting in part the pull of development in Pudong.

30. In particular, the value added from finance and insurance rose from Y8 billion in 1991 to Y14.1 billion in 1993 (FBIS-CHI-94086, May 4, 1994, p. 51).

31. The municipal Science and Technology Commission registered 1,271 consultancy organizations with nearly 10,000 employees during the period 1987–93. These organizations have completed more than 120,000 projects and produced a cumulative business volume of Y1.5 billion. By the year 2000 the revenue of consultancy services, which is expected to grow at an annual rate of 15 percent, will account for about 0.5 percent of local GDP. Other emerging services include foreign-funded insurance companies and accounting firms. For instance, the American International Group, founded in Shanghai before 1949, returned to the city ahead of others to try to reclaim its lost business. Deloitte & Touche, a large transnational accounting firm, also established an office in Shanghai in the early 1990s as soon as the Chinese government lifted the restrictions on foreign investment in services. See FBIS-CHI-94153, August 9, 1994, p. 59.

32. The macroeconomic situation and China's primitive regulatory system were two reasons why relatively few Western investors were drawn to Shanghai in the early 1990s. For further discussion, see "Bears in a China Shop," *Economist*, May 14, 1994, pp. 75–76.

33. Between 1950 and 1983 basic construction investment in Shanghai totaled Y35 billion, with the central government providing just Y14.8 billion, or 42 percent. This amount was less than the Y18 billion in revenue that Shanghai transferred to the central government in 1983 alone. See Jacobs and Hong (1994).

34. Leaf (1995, p. 150) notes that "inner city redevelopment is propelled not only by the need to upgrade existing residential conditions but by the recognition of inner city sites. . . . City governments are now beginning to understand how they can make money through the introduction of markets for long-term land leases."

35. In fact, the *Financial Times* (November 7, 1994) reported that in 1994 Shanghai ranked third, after Hong Kong and London, in net office rents, at around $800 a year. By 1995 these rankings had been modified, with Bombay surpassing all the other cities to achieve rents of $145 per square foot. Shanghai ranked fifth, after Beijing, with $80.27 per square foot ("Bombay Is World Capital of High Rents," *Wall Street Journal*, April 25, 1995, p. A17).

Chapter 4

1. The potential of Tianjin's textiles industry might be greatest in industrial textiles, including fabrics for construction and materials for agriculture and fishing, medical purposes, and personal protection. With its long history of basic textile production and a wide range of petrochemical facilities, Tianjin could remain competitive in these products.

2. To some extent this involved a shift of production from state-owned enterprises to collective-owned enterprises, which enjoy tax advantages and are less subject to the remaining plan directives. Hence state-owned enterprises have created these subsidiaries as profit centers and growth points.

3. The development of town and village enterprises around Tianjin is beginning to quicken, helped by investment in road transport and the rapid economic growth of nearby Shandong. One example of this is the county of Da Qin Zhuang, where 260 enterprises produce Y4 billion worth of animal feed, iron and steel products, chemicals, and electronics.

4. In fact, the competition now existing between Tianjin and a few cities in its hinterland, such as Shijiazhuang and Tangshan in textiles production, somewhat resembles what we call growth-diverting effects in chapter 1.

5. Under its activist mayor Bo Xilai, Dalian has campaigned actively for foreign direct investment. By the end of 1995 it had attracted $2.6 billion in Japanese investment alone. Investment has been mostly in manufacturing, some kinds of services, and transport infrastructure. Dalian is completing a large container terminal at Dayao Bay.

6. For instance, in Singapore a system called CITOS controls the movement of containers from the freight forwarding agent to the hold of the ship and, through a second system, called Tradenet, permits an agent to obtain customs approval electronically as well as to process other documents. Tradenet binds 12,000 companies to 20 government ministries, making it possible to obtain clearance in 15 minutes. See "All-Wired Island, Singapore," *Financial Times*, February 24, 1995, p. 7.

7. The new expansion has added an apron measuring 155,000 square meters, enough for 17 large and medium-size planes. The 3,000-meter runway is currently stressed for planes under 300 tons, and the airport's annual traffic-handling capability is 90,000 air movements. In 1993 the traffic consisted of 380,000 passengers and 270,000 tons of cargo.

8. The third group of products includes cut flowers and winter vegetables, which are flown into Japan and Western countries from long distances. It is a competitive market but a growing one. Tianjin has the land, the water, the farming skills, and the research base to make a success of greenhouse horticulture and hydroponic vegetables. Initially it will need to draw on research done elsewhere, but it is no more handicapped than producers in India and Zimbabwe, who are entering these fields.

9. An analysis of steel producers in the United States suggests that the presence of numerous workers who are on average older and have enjoyed long tenure can discourage a firm from adopting new work practices most directly by threatening layoffs and closures (Ichniowski and Shaw 1995).

10. The reasons underlying the shift of petrochemicals to Asia are the rapid expansion of the market, which is expected to exceed $500 billion by the end of the decade; the growth of downstream users in textiles, electronics, and auto

engineering; lower labor costs; and less stringent regulatory controls. According to the *Financial Times* (May 31, 1994), "The die is cast by growth and costs."

11. Firms getting started in Beijing's economic and technological development zone were given three years of tax exemption followed by three years of reduced taxes and generous foreign exchange retention privileges. In addition, firms received help with problems pertaining to visas, electricity supply, and red tape. Similar rules applied to the zones in Tianjin and outside Shenzhen (Solinger 1993).

12. The Personal Handy Phone System uses handsets that are far cheaper than the regular cellular phone and are anchored to small low-power base stations with an area coverage of 200 to 500 meters in diameter. A call cannot be switched from one cell to the next, and calls cannot be made from moving cars or public transport. However, the system is well suited for densely populated cities, as in China, and its cheapness and wide bandwidth make it highly attractive.

13. Sales of computers rose from 200,000 in 1992 to 700,000 in 1994. The value of the sales in 1995 was $7.4 billion. See "China Takes to Computers," *Financial Times*, February 27, 1995, p. 10; "China: Computer Market," Oxford Analytica, May 7, 1996.

14. Hanzification is the conversion of a keyboard designed for English language so as to input Chinese characters. There are three ways to do this at present: by using combinations of key strokes; by spelling (*pin yin*) characters; and by using an ASCI code designated by the International Standards Organization.

15. International experience suggests that microchip producers have a strong tendency to cluster in a few locations that provide the desirable infrastructure and have reliable utilities, plenty of water, clean air, and access to suppliers of the chemicals, equipment, and services demanded by manufacturers of semiconductors. Labor costs are secondary because they account for less than 10 percent of the costs of running a plant. A cluster begins forming when a company establishes a major chip-producing facility and begins to pull in suppliers and stimulate the development of the desired infrastructure. This reduces start-up costs and attracts other producers. Motorola's plans to build a facility could be the start of such a process.

16. "Silicon valleys" are built with human capital constantly nourished and replenished by major universities that are also important centers of research. Local governments and financiers have their own parts to play, but every constellation of technology-intensive firms revolves around one or several research-oriented universities with the strategic intent of sponsoring development and commercialization after the research is complete. The Massachusetts Institute of Technology, Stanford University, and Utah State University evolved and implemented ambitious plans using as building blocks their reputation for excellence, large volume of graduates, and faculty connections with the government to pull in lucrative contracts; modest investment in infrastructure to facilitate industrialization; and, on occasion, financial backing for start-ups. Each of the several university-centered industrial parks in the United States or Europe has depended on a mix of these ingredients. Having an established reputation as a major center of excellence for scientific research is perhaps a necessary condition.

17. Hunnewell (1994). Israel is a good example of a country that has used indigenous and immigrant scientists to develop high-technology industry, often in defense and related fields. Basic research is centered on seven universi-

ties, including Hebrew University in Jerusalem, the Weizmann Institute of Science, Tel Aviv University, and Technion at Haifa.

18. Several Korean and Taiwanese companies have found it advantageous to invest in U.S. electronics firms that can provide immediate access to product and process technology, impart training, and act as listening posts for gathering intelligence on new technological developments and trends in market demand. Hyundai and Samsung, which are the leading producers of memory chips in Korea, have used this strategy to narrow the technology gap and establish themselves as leading players in this competitive field, which is also a stepping-stone to more complex electronic products. Having sentinels in Silicon Valley can be one element of a longer-term strategy for penetrating international markets.

19. The Charade was priced at Y57,000, or $6,700, in 1994. Many automakers are pursuing the minicar/small family car market, and competition is bound to heat up in the future. Contenders include Porsche AG, Mitsubishi, and Peugeot-Citroën. The last assembles the bubble-back Citroën ZX from kits in Hubei Province, with full-scale production starting in 1995. Renault's Twingo is an example of future directions, as is the Smart, a project in which Mercedes has a large stake. "Renault Bucks the Global Auto Trend and Succeeds," *Wall Street Journal*, May 4, 1994; "Watchmaker's Car Silences the Skeptics," *Financial Times*, February 27, 1994 ; "Smart Image under Wraps," *Financial Times*, April 17, 1997.

20. The legacy of planning that lies heavily on China's state-owned enterprises has attracted frequent comment. Referring to the iron and steel industry, Franks (1988, p. 57) remarks that "the long history of interaction between economic and political planning structures had left enterprises and administrative authorities inexperienced in, and possibly ill-suited to, the effective management of new technology and of relations with business organizations outside the socialist system."

21. Toyota's association with Tianjin first began in 1938, when it established an assembly and repair plant with an investment of 10 million yuan. This became the Pei-Chin Automobile Company (see Hope and Jacobson 1989).

22. The old arrangement gave Tianjin sole claim to only 13 relatively minor local taxes. The city retained 47 percent of all other revenues, so its marginal retention rate was only half that of Shanghai then. See World Bank (1992a).

23. Mergers have a chance of succeeding—restoring the loss-making enterprise to profitability—if the lead enterprise is both profitable and dynamic. But even then hurdles remain.

24. Although Tianjin was historically linked with Japan, Dalian remains the favored location for Japanese investment in this region. Tianjin's relative proximity to Korea is also challenged by two coastal open cities in Shangdong—Qingdao and Yantai—which enjoy closer ties with Korea.

25. *Business China* rated the Tianjin Economic Development Area as the best-managed zone in China. Unlike Shanghai and Guangzhou, it has resisted the temptation to extract maximum revenues from land leases. A 50-year lease for industrial land costs around $40 per square meter, compared with around $100 in Shanghai's Minhang zone and Guangzhou's Huangpu zone. The infrastructure of Tianjin's Economic Development Area is also among the best in the country, particularly in terms of power supply, basic utilities, and rail connection. The zone's bureaucracy is perhaps the most efficient in the country: it even runs mandatory introductory courses for new workers at no cost to employers. By 1997 the zone had attracted $8 billion in FDI. Several of the leading multinationals have invested

in the zone with multimillion-dollar projects, with the main interest coming from U.S. companies. These include Motorola, Coca-Cola, Heinz, and Kraft Foods of the United States; Yamaha and Yazaki Auto of Japan; Dunlop and BOC of the United Kingdom; Wella of Germany; and Goldstar and Samsung of Korea. Several other large multinationals, including Honeywell, AST, Procter & Gamble, and British Petroleum, are in the process of setting up subsidiaries in the zone ("China: The Bohai Sea Rim," Oxford Analytica, May 29, 1997).

Chapter 5

1. For example, prior to 1979 the neighboring province of Fujian was one of the most poorly developed areas of the country, ranking 22 out of 29 in per capita GDP. It received no net injection of capital investment from the central government.

2. Shanghai, which topped the list, had a per capita net material product of Y1,918 compared with Guangdong's Y297. Tianjin was in third place with Y873 (see Denny 1991).

3. The difference in price levels means that the available data expressed in current prices overstate the size of Guangzhou's economy in relation to that of Shanghai and Tianjin. Taking into account the difference in price levels, it is likely that Tianjin's real GDP is still somewhat larger, although Guangzhou's industrial output may, on average, be of higher quality and more marketable. In 1995 Guangzhou's GDP was $14.9 billion, its per capita GDP was $2,333 (*Financial Times*, February 4, 1997).

4. A pattern of residential segregation by occupation is evident, largely as a result of workplace-related residence. Four groups of residents can be distinguished: cadres, intellectuals, factory workers, and farmers. For details, see Lo (1994).

5. A common problem facing many developing countries, migrant labor was never a concern in contemporary urban China because the strict household registration system prevented large-scale migration, particularly from rural to urban areas, until the early 1980s, when the system was significantly weakened.

6. The housing reform process has four major elements: a legal framework for property rights; a local regulatory environment and housing production reforms conducive to diversified sources of housing production; rent reforms and an accompanying, sharply targeted housing allowance program for severely disadvantaged households; and a viable financial intermediation system to make long-term finance for housing available on affordable terms.

7. The younger Ye has apparently made Guangdong his power base. He refused to take several promotions offered by Beijing after he became governor. He only agreed to accept the appointment as the vice chairman of the Chinese People's Political Consultative Conference in April 1991 on the condition that he would still spend most of his time in Guangdong.

8. The impact of the 1989 Tiananmen incident was the collapse of the pro-Guangdong group in the central government. The removal of Zhao Ziyang meant that Guangdong no longer had a close ally on the Politburo. For details, see Cheung (1994a).

9. Another factor that has contributed to Guangdong's autonomy is that a high proportion of senior officials in the government are from the province. In

1993 there were 26, including the governor and the six vice governors (see Goodman and Feng 1994).

10. Guangzhou Peugeot ran losses in 1994–95. In the first half of 1996 it produced just 1,748 sedans, although annual production capacity is 50,000 (Oxford Analytica, September 25, 1996).

11. Motorbike ownership ratios in China are a small fraction of those in Southeast Asia, even though income levels in cities have brought 100-to 150-cubic-centimeter motorbikes within reach of a sizable subset of households. In Malaysia, for example, a third of all adults own at least one motorbike. The market is certain to mushroom, but restrictions imposed by cities such as Beijing and Guangzhou could slow the growth rate.

12. In 1993, 36 percent of state-owned enterprises in the municipality incurred losses amounting to about Y3 billion. See FBIS-CHI-94095, May 17, 1994, p. 66. However, an estimate of productivity changes in a sample of 20 state-owned textile enterprises in Guangzhou indicates that reform is having a small but positive effect (see Mok 1996).

13. Guangdong, though, did set up a few pilot projects in various parts of the province, one of which is in the Shenzhen Special Economic Zone. After experimenting for about three years, in August 1992 Shenzhen finally adopted a temporary plan that covers a housing scheme, a retirement scheme, and a medical scheme. For details, see Yeung and Chu (1994).

14. In 1995 Matsushita entered into a joint venture with a local enterprise to produce 300,000 air conditioners and 1 million compressors annually.

15. The surge in development occurring in the delta region is brought into sharper relief by the widening disparity between it and the mountainous areas to the northwest. In 1980, personal incomes in the Pearl River delta area were five or six times higher. Ten years later the difference was tenfold (see Sawada 1992).

16. The impact was first on the 16 cities and counties in the Small delta, but it later embraced the 31 cities and counties of the Large delta centered on Guangzhou (Goodman and Feng 1994).

17. Guangdong's share in China's total exports was close to 30 percent in 1993, compared with only 9.5 percent of manufactured exports. Calculated from State Statistical Bureau, *Statistical Yearbook of China*, 1994, and *Statistical Yearbook of Guangdong*, 1994.

18. Compiled from World Bank (1994c) and *Taiwan Databook 1994*. The economies included in this accounting are Brunei, Cambodia, Hong Kong (China), Indonesia, Lao PDR, Malaysia, the Philippines, Taiwan (China), Thailand, and Vietnam.

19. Compensation trade refers to a type of agreement in which a foreign partner provides technology and equipment and a Chinese partner repays with goods produced with that equipment. The foreign partner markets the goods internationally.

20. The neighborhood effects arising from the Pearl River delta region are growth-creating for Guangzhou, but the challenge from such secondary cities as Foshan and Dongguan may eventually constrain the opportunities for growth.

21. In the early 1990s demand for electricity was outpacing supply, which itself was growing at the rate of 15 percent a year. The completion of a number of generating facilities (several by local authorities) during 1993–96 is helping to alleviate the problem (see Sung and others 1995).

22. The Beijing, Guangzhou, and Shanghai airports were expected to account for more than a third of all passengers in 1995, out of an estimated total of 95 million. A new airport at Zhuhai opened in 1990, the fourth in the Pearl River delta ("China Seeks Formula for Foreign Lending," *Aviation Week & Space Technology,* June 5, 1995). See Wang (1994).

23. Guangzhou stands to benefit from the intensive efforts under way to develop transport and communication infrastructure within the province and to strengthen transport links with neighboring provinces, particularly Hunan, as well as from investment in power generation inside Guangdong but also in Yunnan by way of collaborative deals (see Yukawa 1992). The number of ports being constructed or modernized is, however, a mixed blessing. Having three ocean-going ports in the vicinity of Hong Kong will spread freight very thinly. Over the medium term, only Hong Kong is likely to process the 1.5 million containers a year that would warrant frequent visits by ships plying international routes (Sung and others 1995).

24. By 1994, capacity in the delta area consisted of 158 berths that could handle ships of more than 1,000 tons. However, most vessels in use are much smaller, usually in the range of 16 TEUs. The facilities are between 100 and 1,000 meters in length, with the vast majority in the range of 100 to 300 meters. To many observers, and especially Hong Kong businessmen, increasing use of river transport is inevitable, and several Hong Kong companies are investing in the development of handling facilities.

25. The labor force in Guangdong was growing an estimated 2.9 percent during the second half of the 1980s (see Ash and Kueh 1993). This is a marked departure from the Maoist period, when even intraprovincial movement, especially to urban areas, was sharply curtailed.

Chapter 6

1. The government has ordered 2,000 state enterprises to engage in extensive restructuring during 1996–97 and is increasingly ready to allow some loss-making firms to close down.

2. According to Powell and Smith-Doerr (1994, pp. 371–76), "The open-ended relational features of networks, with their relative absence of explicit quid pro quo behavior, greatly enhance the transmission and acquisition of new knowledge." Networks disseminate information on jobs and are the basis of contacts providing access to capital, news about promising business locations, or the latest purchasing information. Movement of individuals between firms enfolded within the network and the presence of professional associations "contribute to the diffusion of standard solutions to organizational problems" and the acceptance of uniform standards.

3. However, Chinatron might be too large (25 percent of total electronics output) and too diffuse (everything from hospitals and schools to chip assembly and marketing) to be efficient. In fact, the corporation essentially resurrects the old Ministry of Electronics Industry, with much of its staff, responsibilities, and bureaucratic structure. The modern electronics corporation must be a nimble, innovative player in an exceedingly fast-moving market. Even if Chinatron manages to overcome the interprovincial conflicts of interest, its current structure and diffuse responsibilities will make it very difficult to frame a coherent strategy (see Frisbie 1992).

4. The Wanbao Corporation had a total workforce of 80,000 in 1992 and a value of gross output close to Y2 billion.

5. Venture capital is often defined as capital that is provided by institutional venture funds, including private venture capital limited partnerships and venture funds affiliated with banks, financial institutions, and large industrial corporations (see Florida and Smith 1992).

6. Even though small enterprises rely on their own resources in the early stages of emergence and growth, start-up of more technologically intensive enterprises, whose capital requirements can be lumpy, is problematic. In subsectors such as electronics, biotechnology, machine tools, and metallurgy, the equipment and facilities needed to achieve critical minimum scale, quality, and technical specifications are substantially larger; lacking access to the capital market or venture capital, individuals with good ideas but modest assets are finding the entry barriers difficult to overcome.

7. The bigger state enterprises are called social communities because they resemble small self-contained towns. Not only are they vertically integrated in terms of production but they also encompass a full range of services for their employees, from the growing of vegetables through the provision of bakeries and even hospitals and universities (see Stepanek 1991).

8. The greater emphasis on within-enterprise training is also related to the difficulties of "buying in" skills when the urban labor market is composed of a large number of enterprise-based internal labor markets.

9. Kyushu's recently acquired industrial strength was tested by the slowing of national growth in 1991–92, but the regional economy maintained its performance and attractiveness for industry. Quality of labor and cheapness of land were the two principal factors favoring the area.

10. Pittsburgh is an example of a city that did not succumb to such a vicious cycle after its steel industry went into eclipse. The city was able to diversify because its excellent universities enabled it to draw firms in fields such as health care, robotics, artificial intelligence, and computers. City authorities kept a grip on administrative and social service overheads while encouraging commercial development and promoting industrial ventures (Hochman 1992).

11. Ohashi (1992), MIT Commission on Industrial Productivity (1989); "The Big Threat to Big Steels' Future," *Fortune*, July 15, 1991, pp. 60–64. Recent advances that permit minimills to manufacture steel directly from iron ore (converted to iron carbide), rather than scrap, allow mills to compete with blast furnace–based operations. Likewise, advances in the quality of sheet steel will permit entry into the lucrative auto market.

12. Singapore may be an exceptional case among the newly industrializing countries because foreign investment has played a significant role in the economy (see Lim 1993).

13. A number of these have migrated to less costly suburban locations whose convenience has been enhanced by advances in communications technology (see Sassen-Koob 1986; Sassen 1991).

Chapter 7

1. Nonperforming loans constituted 17 percent of the total assets of China's specialized banks at the end of 1993 (see Wong 1995). These are unevenly divided across the four banks. For instance, the share of nonperforming assets in the portfolio of the People's Construction Bank of China is approximately 10 percent.

2. Voicing widely felt concerns that have been around for more than a decade, Japanese businesses have drawn pointed attention to the rising costs of doing business in China because of inflation, arbitrary levies, retrospective increases in fees for infrastructure facilities, an inadequate legal system for settling disputes, poorly developed infrastructure, and increasingly frequent labor disputes. These concerns require coordinated attention from the central and municipal authorities.

3. The bankruptcy law was passed in late 1986, but only 500 state-owned enterprises, out of a total of nearly 100,000, had been declared bankrupt and only 156 allowed to go under by the end of 1994 (see Wong 1995).

4. Compared with East European countries and those of the former U.S.S.R., China has made little effort to privatize even the small enterprises, which number more than 80,000 and account for a small fraction of the state sector's output.

5. The unemployment insurance system currently in place provides limited benefits and cannot support massive layoffs. In Dalian, where social security payments are relatively generous, the unemployed receive half pay for six months only.

6. The experience of the Polish economy in 1991–92 brought home the fact that successful enterprise reform depends on appropriate macroeconomic conditions.

7. Close to 1,000 Taiwanese engineers returned to Taiwan (China) in 1991 alone. A similar reflux of trained Koreans is helping Korean industry gain new skills. Engineers trained in the United States were instrumental in enabling Samsung to produce the 64-kilobyte chip and the 256-kilobyte DRAM in-house (see Hobday 1995).

8. Bernard and Ravenshill (1995, p. 183) have observed that an important characteristic of recent industrial trends is that "Malaysia, Thailand, and coastal China have all become linked to production in Northeast Asia so that we may now speak of regionalized manufacturing activity in a number of industries. A second permanent change is the shift from company to network as the locus of productive and innovative activity. It is the interaction between firms linked by chains of production, exchange, and distribution that now constitutes the basic organizational unit."

9. See "Comeback Kids: China's Prodigals Come Home to Prosper in Shanghai," *Far Eastern Economic Review,* August 7, 1997.

10. Korean firms are investing heavily in Jilin, Liaoning, and Shandong, with more than $500 million invested in Shandong alone by the end of 1994. See "S. Korea Discovers Joys of Investing in China," *Financial Times,* August 23, 1995.

11. Cartier 1995; "Singapore Looks for Beachheads," *International Herald Tribune,* July 20, 1995; "It's a Jungle Out There," *Far Eastern Economic Review,* April 25, 1996; "Suzhou Offers Singapore-Style Gate to the Chinese Market," *Financial Times,* January 9, 1996. One of the most successful technology parks in Southeast Asia is located at Hsinchu near Taipei. On the factors responsible for its success, see Castells and Hall (1994). A second, much larger industrial park, modeled on Jurong town in Singapore, is being developed outside Suzhou. This park had attracted $2.5 billion by early 1997—well below expectations, as initial enthusiasm has been tempered by a realization of the difficulties of transplanting an entire operating system from Singapore to China (*Financial Times,* May 27, 1997).

12. Fiat's project A178 is an example of an advanced technology venture tailored to the needs of developing countries. The company expects to produce the car in Argentina, Brazil, Poland, and Turkey.

Bibliography

The word "processed" describes informally reproduced works that may not be commonly available through library systems.

Current News Sources

Asiamoney
Aviation Week & Space Technology
Business China
Business Week
China News Digest
China Focus
China Trade
East Asian Executive Reports
Far Eastern Economic Review
Financial Times
Foreign Broadcast Information Service (FBIS)—China
Fortune
International Herald-Tribune
New York Times
Oxford Analytica
Ports and Harbors
Science
United Press International
Wall Street Journal

Other Sources

Admiraal, P. H., ed. 1991. *Merger and Competition Policy in the European Community*. Cambridge, U.K.: Basil Blackwell.

Ash, Robert F., and Y. Y. Kueh. 1993. "Economic Integration within Greater China: Trade and Investment Flows between China, Hong Kong, and Taiwan." *China Quarterly* 136(December):711–45.

Asian Development Bank. 1997. *Annual Report*. Manila.

Asian Population and Development Association. 1991. *Prospects of Urbanization in Asia*. Tokyo.

Australia, Department of Foreign Affairs and Trade, East Asia Analytical Unit. 1997. "China Embraces the Market: Achievements, Constraints, and Opportunities." Canberra.

Australian National University. 1995. *Asia Pacific Profiles*. Canberra: Asia Pacific Economics Group, Research School of Pacific and Asian Studies.

Ayal, Eliezer B. 1992. "Thailand's Development: The Role of Bangkok." *Pacific Affairs* 65(3, Fall):353–67.

Bairoch, Paul. 1988. *Cities and Economic Development: From the Dawn of History to the Present*. Chicago, Ill.: University of Chicago Press.

Bateman, Deborah, and Ashoka Mody. 1991. "Growth in an Inefficient Economy: A Chinese Case Study." World Bank, Industry and Energy Department, Washington, D.C. Processed.

Becker, Bertha K., and Claudio A. G. Egler. 1992. *Brazil: A New Regional Power in the World Economy*. Cambridge, U.K.: Cambridge University Press.

Bernard, Mitchell, and John Ravenshill. 1995. "Beyond Product Cycles and Flying Geese: Regionalization Hierarchy and the Industrialization of East Asia." *World Politics* 47(2, January):171–209.

Bernstein, Thomas P. 1977. *Up to the Mountains and Down to the Villages: The Transfer of Youth from Urban to Rural China*. New Haven, Conn.: Yale University Press.

Block, R. 1988. "Studies in the Development of the U.S. Aerospace Industry." Mimeo D850. Graduate School of Architecture and Urban Planning, University of California, Los Angeles. Processed.

Bramall, Chris. 1993. *In Praise of Maoist Planning: Living Standards and Economic Development in Sichuan Province since 1931*. Oxford: Oxford University Press.

Branbury, Katherine L., Anthony Downs, and Kenneth A. Small. 1982. *Urban Decline and the Future of American Cities*. Washington, D.C.: Brookings Institution.

Brandt, Loren. 1989. *Commercialization and Agricultural Development in East Central China 1870–1937*. Cambridge, U.K.: Cambridge University Press.

Brudvig, Lee A. 1993. "The Fifth Dragon." *China Business Review* 20(4, July–August):14–20.

Brusco, Sebastiano. 1989. "A Policy for Industrial Districts." In Edward J. Goodman and Julia Bamford, eds., *Small Firms and Industrial Districts in Italy*. London: Routledge.

Buck, David D. 1978. *Urban Change in China: Politics and Development in Tsinan, Shantung, 1890–1949*. Madison: University of Wisconsin Press.

Burley, Michael. 1995. "Quality Water for Shanghai." *Urban Age* 3(2, June):9.

Button, Kenneth J., and David W. Pearce. 1989. "Infrastructure Restoration as a Tool for Stimulating Urban Renewal—The Glasgow Canal." *Urban Studies* 26(2, December):559–71.

Calder, Kent E. 1988. *Crisis and Compensation*. Princeton, N.J.: Princeton University Press.

Capecchi, Vittorio. 1989. "The Informal Economy and the Development of Flexible Specialization in Emilia-Romagna." In Alejandro Portes, Manuel Castells, and Lauren A. Benton, eds., *The Informal Economy: Studies in Advanced and Less Developed Countries*. Baltimore, Md.: Johns Hopkins University Press.

Cartier, Carolyn L. 1995. "Singaporean Investment in China: Installing the Singapore Model in Sunan." *Chinese Environment and Development* 6(1–2):117–44.

Castells, Manuel, and Peter Hall. 1994. *Technopoles of the World*. London: Routledge.

Chan, Kam-Wing. 1994. "Urbanization and Rural-Urban Migration in China since 1982." *Modern China* 20(3, July):243–81.

Chan, Kam-Wing, and Xueqiang Xu. 1985. "Urban Population Growth and Urbanization in China since 1949: Reconstructing a Baseline." *China Quarterly* 104:583–613.

Chandler, Alfred. 1990. *Scale and Scope: The Dynamics of Industrial Capitalism*. Cambridge, Mass.: Harvard University Press.

Chang, Jui-te. 1993. "Technology Transfer in Modern China: The Case of Railway Enterprise 1876–1937." *Modern Asian Studies* 27(2):281–96.

Chang, Kyung-Sup. 1994. "Chinese Urbanization and Development before and after Economic Reform: A Comparative Reappraisal." *World Development* 22(4, April):601–13.

Chang, Sen-Dou, Xu-Wei Hu, and Jun-Jie Sun. 1992. "Tianjin: North China's Reviving Metropolis." In Yue-man Yeung and Xu-wei Hu, eds., *China's Coastal Cities: Catalysts for Modernization*. Honolulu: University of Hawaii Press.

Chao, Kang. 1977. *The Development of Cotton Textile Production in China*. Cambridge, Mass.: Harvard University Press.

Chen, Chung, Lawrence Chang, and Yimin Zhang. 1995. "The Role of Foreign Direct Investment in China's Post-1978 Economic Development." *World Development* 23(4, April):691–703.

Chen, Shengdong. 1990. "Major Issues in Transport Planning of Shanghai." *China City Planning Review* (September):17–26.

Chen, Xiangming. 1991. "China's City Hierarchy, Urban Policy, and Spatial Development in the 1980s." *Urban Studies* 28(3):341–67.

Chen, Yewei. 1991. "Renovation and Dispersion of the Old City in Shanghai." *China City Planning Review* (December):40–49.

Cheng, Tiejun, and Mark Selden. 1994. "The Origin and Social Consequences of China's Hukou System." *China Quarterly* 139:644–68.

Cheung, Peter Tsan-yin. 1994a. "The Case of Guangdong in Central-Provincial Relations." In Jia Hao and Lin Zhimin, eds., *Changing Central-Local Relations in China: Reform and State Capacity*. Boulder, Colo.: Westview Press.

———. 1994b. "Relations between the Central Government and Guangdong." In Yue-man Yeung and David K. Y. Chu, eds., *Guangdong: Survey of a Prov-*

ince Undergoing Rapid Change. Hong Kong: Chinese University Press.
———. 1996. "The Political Context of Shanghai's Economic Development." In Yue-man Yeung and Sung Yun-wing, eds., *Shanghai: Transformation and Modernization under China's Open Policy*. Hong Kong: Chinese University Press.

China–European Commission Management Institute. 1990. *The Management of Equity Joint Ventures in China*. Beijing.

Chu, David K. Y. 1994. "Challenges to the Port of Hong Kong before and after 1997." *Chinese Environment and Development* 5(3):5–23.

Colton, Timothy J. 1995. *Moscow: Governing the Socialist Metropolis*. Cambridge, Mass.: Belknap Press of Harvard University.

Conroy, Richard. 1992. *Technological Change in China*. Paris: Development Center, Organisation for Economic Co-operation and Development.

Cotterell, Brian, and Johan Kamminga. 1990. *Mechanics of Pre-Industrial Technology*. Cambridge, U.K.: Cambridge University Press.

Davis, Deborah. 1988. "Unequal Chances, Unequal Outcomes: Pension Reform and Urban Inequality." *China Quarterly* 114:223–42.

de Jong, Mark W. 1991. "Revitalizing the Urban Core: Waterfront Development in Baltimore, Maryland." In Joanne Fox-Przeworski, John B. Goddard, and Mark W. de Jong, eds. 1991. *Urban Regeneration in a Changing Economy: An International Perspective*. Oxford: Clarendon Press.

De Long, J. Bradford, and Andrei Shleifer. 1993. "Princes and Merchants: European City Growth before the Industrial Revolution." *Journal of Law and Economics* 36(October):671–702.

Denison, Edward F. 1967. *Why Growth Rates Differ: Postwar Experience in Nine Western Countries*. Washington, D.C.: Brookings Institution.

———. 1983. *The Interruption of Productivity Growth in the United States*. Washington, D.C.: Brookings Institution.

Denny, David. 1991. "Regional Economic Differences during the Decade of Reform." In *China's Economic Dilemmas in the 1990s: The Problems of Reforms, Modernization, and Interdependence*. Vol. 1: *Study Papers for the Joint Economic Committee, Congress of the United States*. Washington, D.C.: U.S. Government Printing Office.

Dittmer, Lowell, and Yu Shan Wu. 1995. "The Modernization of Factionalism in Chinese Politics." *World Politics* 47(4, July):467–94.

Dollar, David, and Kenneth Sokoloff. 1994. "Industrial Policy, Productivity Growth, and Structural Change in the Manufacturing Industries: A Comparison of Taiwan and South Korea." In Joel D. Aberbach, David Dollar, and Kenneth L. Sokoloff, eds., *The Role of the State in Taiwan's Development*. Armonk, N.Y.: M. E. Sharpe.

Donnithorne, Audrey. 1967. *China's Economic System*. New York: Praeger.

———. 1972. "China's Cellular Economy: Some Economic Trends since the Cultural Revolution." *China Quarterly* 52:605–19.

Dorian, James P. 1993. *Minerals, Energy, and Economic Development in China*. Oxford: Clarendon Press.

Downs, Anthony. 1979. *Urban Problems and Prospects*. Chicago, Ill.: Markham Publishing Company.

Drakakis-Smith, David. 1995. "Third World Cities: Sustainable Urban Development." *Urban Studies* 32(4-5):659–78.

Dyer, Jeffrey H., and William G. Ouchi. 1993. "Japanese-Style Partnerships: Giv-
    ing Companies a Competitive Edge." *Sloan Management Review* (Fall):51–63.
Eastham, Tony R. 1995. "High-Speed Rail: Another Golden Age." *Scientific Ameri-
    can* 273 (3):100–106.
Eisner, Marc Allen. 1991. *Antitrust and the Triumph of Economics: Institutions, Ex-
    pertise, and Policy Change*. Chapel Hill: University of North Carolina Press.
Enright, Michael J., Edith E. Scott, and David Dodwell. 1997. *The Hong Kong
    Advantage*. New York: Oxford University Press.
Etienne, Gilbert. 1990. *Asian Crucible: The Steel Industry in China and India*. Geneva:
    Modern Asian Research Center.
Etzkowitz, Henry. 1993. "Enterprises from Science: The Origins of Science-Based
    Regional Economic Development." *Review of Science, Learning, and Policy*
    31(3, Autumn):326–60.
Evans, Peter. 1995. *Embedded Autonomy*. Princeton, N.J.: Princeton University Press.
Fairbank, John K., ed. 1976. *The Cambridge History of China*. Vol. 10: *Late Ch'ing,
    1800–1911, Part 1*. Cambridge, U.K.: Cambridge University Press.
————. 1983. *The Cambridge History of China*. Vol. 12: *Republican China, 1912–
    1949, Part 1*. Cambridge, U.K.: Cambridge University Press.
Fairbank, John K., and Albert Feuerwerker, eds. 1986. *The Cambridge History of
    China*. Vol. 13: *Republican China, 1912–1949, Part 2*. Cambridge, U.K.: Cam-
    bridge University Press.
Fan, C. Cindy. 1988. "The Temporal and Spatial Dynamics of City-Size Distribu-
    tions in China." *Population Research and Policy Review* 7:123–57.
————. 1996. "Economic Opportunities and Internal Migration: A Case Study of
    Guangdong Province, China." *Professional Geographer* 48(1):28–45.
Faure, David. 1990. "What Made Foshan a Town: The Evolution of Rural-Urban
    Identities in Ming-Ching China." *Late Imperial China* 11(2, December):1–31.
Feuerwerker, Albert. 1977. *Economic Trends in the Republic of China, 1912–1949*.
    Ann Arbor: University of Michigan, Center for Chinese Studies.
————. 1983. "Academe in Contemporary China." *Michigan Quarterly Review*
    22(Fall):579–93.
Fewsmith, Joseph. 1994. *Dilemmas of Reform in China: Political Conflict and Eco-
    nomic Debate*. Armonk, N.Y.: M. E. Sharpe.
Fitzgerald, John. 1996. "Autonomy and Growth in China: County Experience in
    Guangdong Province." *Journal of Contemporary China* 5(11):7–22.
Florida, Richard, and Donald F. Smith, Jr. 1992. "Venture Capital's Role in Eco-
    nomic Development: An Empirical Analysis." In Edwin S. Mills and John
    F. McDonald, eds., *Sources of Metropolitan Growth*. New Brunswick, N.J.:
    Center for Urban Policy Research.
Forbes, Dean K., and D. Wilmoth. 1990. "Urban Problems and Planning in
    Tianjin." In G. J. R. Linge and D. K. Forbes, eds., *China's Spatial Economy:
    Recent Developments and Reforms*. Hong Kong: Oxford University Press.
Fox-Przeworski, Joanne, John B. Goddard, and Mark W. de Jong, eds. 1991. *Ur-
    ban Regeneration in a Changing Economy: An International Perspective*. Ox-
    ford: Clarendon Press.
Franks, Penelope. 1988. "Learning from Japan: Plant Imports and Technology
    Transfer in the Chinese Iron and Steel Industry." *Journal of the Japanese and
    International Economy* 2(1, March):42–62.
Freeman, Christopher. 1982. *The Economics of Industrial Innovation*. Cambridge,
    Mass.: MIT Press.

Friedman, John. 1989. "Restructuring an Old Industrial Region." Mimeo D891. Graduate School of Architecture and Urban Planning, University of California, Los Angeles. Processed.

Frisbie, John. 1992. "Chinatron: Ghost of MEI." *China Business Review* 19(1, January–February):30–35.

Fung, Ka-iu, Zhong-Min Yan, and Yue-Min Ning. 1992. "Shanghai: China's World City." In Yue-man Yeung and Xu-wei Hu, eds., *China's Coastal Cities: Catalysts for Modernization*. Honolulu: University of Hawaii Press.

Gardella, Robert. 1994. *Harvesting Mountains: Fujian and the China Tea Trade, 1757–1937*. Berkeley: University of California Press.

Gaubatz, Piper Rae. 1995. "Urban Transformation in Post-Mao China: Impacts of the Reform Era on China's Urban Form." In Deborah D. Davis, Richard Kraus, Barry Naughton, and Elizabeth J. Perry, eds., *Urban Spaces in Contemporary China: The Potential for Autonomy and Community in Post-Mao China*. New York: Woodrow Wilson Center.

George, K. D. 1991. "Lessons from U.K. Merger Policy." In P. H. Admiraal, ed., *Merger and Competition Policy in the European Community*. Oxford: Basil Blackwell.

Gerschenkron, Alexander. 1968. *Continuity in History and Other Essays*. Cambridge, Mass.: Belknap Press of Harvard University.

Glaeser, Edward L., Hedi Kallal, José Scheinkman, and Andrei Shleifer. 1992. "Growth in Cities." *Journal of Political Economy* 100(6, December):1126–52.

Glazer, Nathan. 1991. "The Lessons of New York City." *Public Interest* 104(Summer):37–49.

Goldstein, Sidney. 1990. "Urbanization in China, 1982–87: Effects of Migration and Reclassification." *Population and Development Review* 16(4, December):673–701.

Goodman, David S. G., and Feng Chongyi. 1994. "Guangdong: Greater Hong Kong and the New Regionalist Future." In David S. G. Goodman and Gerald Segal, eds., *China Deconstructs*. New York: Routledge.

Goodwin, Jason. 1991. *A Time for Tea*. New York: Knopf.

Gray, Jack. 1990. *Rebellions and Revolutions: China from the 1800s to the 1980s*. New York: Oxford University Press.

Grayling, A. C., and Susan Whitfield. 1994. *China: A Literary Companion*. London: John Murray.

Gui, Shixun, and Liu Xian. 1992. "Urban Migration in Shanghai: 1950–88: Trends and Characteristics." *Population and Development Review* 18(3, September):533–48.

Harral, Clell G., Peter Cook, and Edward Holland. 1992. *Transport Development in Southern China*. World Bank Discussion Paper 151. Washington, D.C.

Harris, Nigel. 1995. "Bombay in a Global Economy." *Cities* 12(3):175–84.

Harwit, Eric. 1995. *China's Automobile Industry: Policies, Problems, and Prospects*. Armonk, N.Y.: M. E. Sharpe.

Hayhoe, Ruth. 1988. "Shanghai as a Mediator of the Educational Open Door." *Pacific Affairs* 61(2, Summer):253–84.

Healey, Michael J., and Brian W. Ilbery. 1990. *Location and Change: Perspective on Economic Geography*. Oxford: Oxford University Press.

Heidhues, Mary F. Somers. 1974. *Southeast Asian Chinese Minorities*. Hawthorn, Australia: Longmans.

Henderson, Jeffrey. 1989. *The Globalization of High Technology Production: Society, Space, and Semiconductors in the Restructuring of the Modern World*. London: Routledge.

Henderson, Vernon. 1988. *Urban Development: Theory, Fact, and Illusion*. New York: Oxford University Press.

Henderson, Vernon, Ari Kuncoro, and Matt Turner. 1995. "Industrial Development in Cities." *Journal of Political Economy* 103(5):1067–85.

Hershatter, Gail. 1986. *The Workers of Tianjin, 1900–1949*. Stanford, Calif.: Stanford University Press.

Hill, Richard Child, and Kuniko Fujita, eds. 1993. *Japanese Cities in the World Economy*. Philadelphia, Pa.: Temple University Press.

Ho, K. C. 1994. "Industrial Restructuring, the Singapore City-State, and the Regional Division of Labor." *Environment and Planning* A26(1, January):33–51.

Ho, Lok-sang, and Tsui Kai-yuen. 1996. "Fiscal Relations between Shanghai and the Central Government." In Yue-man Yeung and Sung Yun-wing, eds. *Shanghai: Transformation and Modernization under China's Open Policy*. Hong Kong: Chinese University Press.

Ho, Samuel P. S. 1994. *Rural China in Transition: Nonagricultural Development in Rural Jiangsu, 1978–1990*. Oxford: Oxford University Press.

Ho, Y. P., and Y. Y. Kueh. 1993. "Whither Hong Kong in an Open-Door, Reforming Chinese Economy?" *Pacific Review* 6(4):333–51.

Hobday, Mike. 1994. "Technological Learning in Singapore: A Test Case of Leapfrogging." *Journal of Development Studies* 30(April):831–58.

———. 1995. "East Asian Latecomer Firms: Learning the Technology of Electronics." *World Development* 23(7, July):1171–94.

Hochman, Harold M. 1992. "New York and Pittsburgh: Contrasts in Community." *Urban Studies* 29(2, April):237–50.

Hope, Anne, and Marcus Jacobson. 1989. *China's Motor Industry: Risks and Opportunities to 2000*. Special Report 2008. London: Economist Intelligence Unit.

Hou, Chi-ming. 1965. *Foreign Investment and Economic Development in China*. Cambridge, Mass.: Harvard University Press.

Houseman, Susan N. 1991. *Industrial Restructuring with Job Security*. Cambridge, Mass.: Harvard University Press.

Howard, Maurice. 1990. "Industry, Energy, and Transport." In Terry Cannon and Alan Jenkins, eds., *The Geography of Contemporary China: The Impact of Dengxiaoping's Decade*. London and New York: Routledge.

Howard, Robert. 1990. "Can Small Business Help Countries Compete?" *Harvard Business Review* 68(6, November–December):88–106.

Howe, Christopher. 1981. *Shanghai: Revolution and Development in an Asian Metropolis*. Cambridge, U.K.: Cambridge University Press.

Howell, Jude. 1993. *China Opens Its Door*. Boulder, Colo.: Lynne Reinner.

Hughes, David W., and David W. Holland. 1994. "Core-Periphery Economic Linkage: A Measure of Spread and Possible Backwash Effects for the Washington Economy." *Land Economics* 70(3, August):364–77.

Hunnewell, Susannah. 1994. "Medical Industrial Complex." *Harvard Magazine* (January–February):34–37.

Hussain, Athar. 1990. *The Chinese Enterprise Reforms*. CP 5. London: London School of Economics, STICERD.

————. 1992. *The Chinese Economic Reforms in Retrospect and Prospect.* CP 24. London: London School of Economics, STICERD.

Hussain, Athar, Jean Olson Lanjouw, and Lei Li. 1990. *The Chinese Television Industry: The Interaction between Government Policy and Market Forces.* CP 9. London: London School of Economics, STICERD.

Ichniowski, Casey, and Kathryn Shaw. 1995. "Old Dogs and New Tricks: Determinants of the Adoption of Productivity-Enhancing Work Practices." *Brookings Papers on Economic Activity* (Microeconomics, 1):1–65. Washington, D.C.: Brookings Institution.

IFC (International Finance Corporation). 1996. *Emerging Stock Markets Fact Book 1996.* Washington, D.C.

Ikels, Charlotte. 1996. *The Return of the God of Wealth.* Stanford,Calif.: Stanford University Press.

Jacobs, J. Bruce, and Lijian Hong. 1994. "Shanghai and the Lower Yangzi Valley." In David S. G. Goodman and Gerald Segal, eds., *China Deconstructs: Politics, Trade and Regionalism.* New York: Routledge.

Jaffe, Adam B., Manuel Trajtenberg, and Rebecca Henderson. 1993. "Geographic Localization of Knowledge Spillovers as Evidenced by Patent Citations." *Quarterly Journal of Economics* 108(3, August):577–97.

Jefferson, Gary H., and Thomas G. Rawski. 1992. "Growth, Efficiency, and Convergence in China's State and Collective Industry." *Economic Development and Cultural Change* 40(2, January):239–66.

————. 1994. "Enterprise Reform in Chinese Industry." Research Paper Series CH-RPS 28. World Bank, Policy Research Department, Washington, D.C.

————. 1995. "How Industrial Reform Worked in China: The Role of Innovation, Competition, and Property Rights." In *Proceedings of the World Bank Annual Conference on Development Economics 1994.* Washington, D.C.: World Bank.

Johnson, Linda C. 1995. *Shanghai: From Market Town to Treaty Port: 1074 to 1858.* Stanford: Stanford University Press.

Kargon, Robert, and Stuart Leslie. 1994. "'Imagined Geographies': Princeton, Stanford, and the Boundaries of Useful Knowledge in Postwar America." *Minerva: A Review of Science, Learning, and Policy* 32(2, Summer):121–43.

Karmel, Solomon H. 1994. "Emerging Securities Markets in China: Capitalism with Chinese Characteristics." *China Quarterly* 140(December):1105–20.

Keating, Michael. 1995. "Local Economic Development: Policy or Politics?" In Norman Walzer, ed., *Local Economic Development.* Boulder, Colo.: Westview Press.

Kelliher, Daniel. 1992. *Peasant Power in China: The Era of Rural Reform, 1979–1989.* New Haven, Conn.: Yale University Press.

Kim, Sukkoo. 1995. "Expansion of Markets and the Geographic Distribution of Economic Activities: The Trends in the U.S. Regional Manufacturing Structure, 1860–1987." *Quarterly Journal of Economics* 110(4, November):881–908.

Kirkby, R. J. R. 1985. *Urbanization in China: Town and Country in a Developing Economy 1949–2000 A.D.* London: Croom Helm.

————. 1994. "Dilemmas of Urbanization: Review and Prospects." In Denis J. Dwyer, ed., *China: The Next Decades.* Essex, U.K.: Longman.

Kojima, Reeitsu. 1995. "Urbanization in China." *Developing Economies* 33(2, June):121–54.

Konvitz, Josef W. 1994. "The Crisis of Atlantic Port Cities, 1880 to 1920." *Comparative Studies in Society and History* 36(2, April):293–318.

Krugman, Paul. 1990. *Geography and Trade*. Leuven: Leuven University Press; Cambridge, Mass.: MIT Press.

———. 1991. "Increasing Returns and Economic Geography." *Journal of Political Economy* 99(3, June):483–99.

———. 1992. "A Dynamic Spatial Model." NBER Working Paper 4219. National Bureau of Economic Research, Cambridge, Mass. Processed.

———. 1993. "First Nature, Second Nature, and Metropolitan Location." *Journal of Regional Science* 33(2, May):129–44.

Kubuta, Hisashi, and T. Kidokoro. 1994. "Analysis of Bicycle-Dependent Transport Systems in China: Case Study in a Medium-Sized City." *Transport Research Record* 1441:11–15.

Kueh, Y. Y. 1992. "Foreign Investment and Economic Change in China." *China Quarterly* 131:637–90.

Kuo, Wen H. 1989. "Economic Reforms and Urban Development in China." *Pacific Affairs* 62(2, Summer):188–203.

Kuribayashi, Sumio. 1992. "Economic Development of the Yangtze River Valley." *JETRO China Newsletter* 100(September–October):2–8.

Lam, Kin-che, and Tao Shu. 1996. "Environmental Quality and Pollution Control." In Yue-man Yeung and Sung Yun-wing, eds., *Shanghai: Transformation and Modernization under China's Open Policy*. Hong Kong: Chinese University Press.

Landes, David S. 1969. *The Unbound Prometheus: Technological Change and Industrial Development in Western Europe from 1750 to the Present*. Cambridge, U.K.: Cambridge University Press.

———. 1991. "Introduction." In Patrice Higonnet, David S. Landes, and Henry Rosovsky, eds., *Favorites of Fortune*. Cambridge, Mass.: Harvard University Press.

Leaf, Michael. 1995. "Inner City Redevelopment in China." *Cities* 12(3):149–62.

Lee, Yok-Shiu F. 1989. "Small Towns and China's Urbanization Level." *China Quarterly* 120(December):771–86.

Leeming, Frank. 1993. *The Changing Geography of China*. Oxford: Blackwell.

Leman, Edward. 1995. "The Changing Face of Shanghai." *Urban Age* 3(2, June):8.

Levathes, Louise. 1994. *When China Ruled the Seas: The Treasure Fleet of the Dragon Throne*. New York: Simon and Schuster.

Lever-Tracy, Constance, David Ip, and Noel Tracy. 1996. *The Chinese Diaspora and Mainland China*. New York: St. Martins Press.

Li, Cheng. 1996. "Rediscovering Urban Subcultures: The Contrast between Shanghai and Beijing." *The China Journal* 36(July):139–53.

Li, Si-ming, and Siu Yat-ming. 1994. "Population Mobility." In Yue-man Yeung and David K. Y. Chu, eds., *Guangdong: Survey of a Province Undergoing Rapid Change*. Hong Kong: Chinese University Press.

Lichtenberg, Frank R. 1992. *Corporate Takeovers and Productivity*. Cambridge, Mass.: MIT Press.

Lim, David. 1994. "Explaining the Growth Performance of Asian Developing Economies." *Economic Development and Cultural Change* 42(4, July):829–43.

Lim, Linda Y. C. 1993. "Technology Policy and Export Development: The Case of the Electronics Industry in Singapore and Malaysia." Paper presented at the first conference of the United Nations University, Institute for New Technologies, Maastricht, The Netherlands. Processed.

Lin, Justin Yifu. 1992. "Rural Reform and Agricultural Growth in China." *American Economic Review* 82(1, March):34–48.

Lin, Justin Yifu, Fang Cai, and Zhou Li. 1994. "China's Economic Reforms: Pointers for Other Economies in Transition?" Policy Research Working Paper. World Bank, Policy Research Department,Washington, D.C. Processed.

Lin, Zhimin. 1994. "Reform and Shanghai: Changing Central-Local Fiscal Relations." In Jia Hao and Lin Zhimin, eds., *Changing Central-Local Relations in China: Reform and State Capacity.* Boulder, Colo.: Westview Press.

Linge, G. J. R., and D. K. Forbes, eds. 1990. *China's Spatial Economy: Recent Developments and Reforms.* Hong Kong: Oxford University Press.

Little, Daniel. 1992. *Understanding Peasant China: Case Studies in the Philosophy of Social Science.* New Haven, Conn.: Yale University Press.

Liu, Guoguang. 1989. "A Sweet and Sour Decade." *Beijing Review* (January):2–8.

Lo, C. P. 1994. "Economic Reform and Socialist City Structure: A Case Study of Guangzhou, China." *Urban Geography* 15(2, March):128–49.

Luger, Michael, and Harvey Goldstein. 1991. *Technology in the Garden: Research Parks and Regional Economic Development.* Chapel Hill: University of North Carolina Press.

Luk, Chiu-ming. 1994. "Transport and Communication." In Yue-man Yeung and David K. Y. Chu, eds., *Guangdong: Survey of a Province Undergoing Rapid Change.* Hong Kong: Chinese University Press.

Ma, Laurence J. C., and Chusheng Lin. 1993. "Development of Towns in China: A Case Study of Guangdong Province." *Population and Development Review* 19(3, September):583–606.

Ma, Laurence J. C., and Ming Fan. 1994. "Urbanization from Below: The Growth of Towns in Jiangsu, China." *Urban Studies* 31(10):1625–45.

Ma, Xia. 1994. "Changes in the Pattern of Migration in Urban China." In Lincoln H. Day and Ma Xia, eds., *Migration and Urbanization in China.* Armonk, N.Y.: M. E. Sharpe.

Mackerras, Colin. 1989. *Western Images of China.* Hong Kong: Oxford University Press.

Mackinnon, Stephen. 1996. "The Tragedy of Wuhan, 1938." *Modern Asian Studies* 30 (4, October):931–43.

Mann, Susan. 1984. "Urbanization and Historical Change in China." *Modern China* 10(1, January):79–113.

Markusen, Ann R. 1995. "Interaction between Regional and Industrial Policies: Evidence from Four Countries." In *Proceedings of the World Bank Annual Conference on Development Economics 1994.* Washington, D.C.: World Bank.

Matsudaira, Sudayuki. 1994. "Trends in Consumption and Foreign Retailers." *JETRO China Newsletter* 113(November–December):7–13.

Maxton, Graeme P. 1994. *The Automotive Sector of the Pacific Rim and China.* London: Economist Intelligence Unit.

Mills, Edwin S., and John F. McDonald, eds. 1992. *Sources of Metropolitan Growth.* New Brunswick, N.J.: Center for Urban Policy Research.

Ministry of Education. 1984. *Achievement of Education in China: Statistics 1949–1983.* Beijing: People's Education Press.

————. 1986. *Achievement of Education in China: Statistics 1980–1985.* Beijing: People's Education Press.

Mok, Vincent Wai-Kwong. 1996. "Industrial Productivity in China's State-Owned Enterprises: The Textile Industry in Guangzhou, 1979–93." *Journal of Contemporary China* 5(11):57–67.

Morris-Suzuki, Tessa. 1994. *The Technological Transformation of Japan.* Cambridge, U.K.: Cambridge University Press.

Moss, Mitchell L. 1997. "Technological Trends Affecting the Manufacturing Sector of New York City." *Economic Policy Review* 3 (1, February): 87–89.

Mowery, David C., and Nathan Rosenberg. 1989. *Technology and the Pursuit of Economic Growth.* Cambridge, U.K.: Cambridge University Press.

Mueller, Dennis, ed. 1983. *The Political Economy of Growth.* New Haven, Conn.: Yale University Press.

Murphy, Rhoads. 1980. *The Fading of the Maoist Vision: City and County in China's Development.* New York: Methuen.

Nanyang Commercial Bank, Ltd. 1992. *China's Economic Reform and Development Strategy of Pearl River Delta.* Hong Kong.

Naughton, Barry. 1988. "The Third Front: Defence Industrialization in the Chinese Interior." *China Quarterly* (September):351–86.

————. 1995a. "Cities in the Chinese Economic System: Changing Roles and Conditions for Autonomy." In Deborah Davis and others, eds., *Urban Spaces in Contemporary China.* Cambridge, U.K.: Wilson Center and Cambridge University Press.

————. 1995b. *Growing out of the Plan: Chinese Economic Reform, 1978–1993.* Cambridge, U.K.: Cambridge University Press.

Needham, Joseph. 1986. *The Shorter Science and Civilization in China.* Vol. 3, abridged by Colin A. Ronan. Cambridge, U.K.: Cambridge University Press.

Netzer, Dick. 1997. "The Outlook for the Metropolitan Area." *Economic Policy Review* 3 (1, February): 93–111.

Norris, Robert S. 1994. *British, French, and Chinese Nuclear Weapons.* Nuclear Weapons Data Bank, vol. 5. Boulder, Colo.: Westview Press.

OECD (Organisation for Economic Co-operation and Development). 1997. *Towards a New Global Age: Challenges and Opportunities.* Paris.

Ohashi, Nobuo. 1992. "Modern Steelmaking." *American Scientist* (November–December) 80 (6):540–55.

Oi, Jean C. 1993. "Reform and Urban Bias in China." *Journal of Development Studies* 29(4, July):129–48.

Olson, Mancur. 1982. *The Rise and Decline of Nations.* New Haven, Conn.: Yale University Press.

Pannell, Clifton W., and Lawrence J. C. Ma. 1983. *China: The Geography of Development and Modernization.* London: V. H. Winston and Sons.

Parish, William L. 1990. "What Models Now?" In Reginald Yin-Wang Kwok, William L. Parish, and Anthony Gar-On Yeh, eds., *Chinese Urban Reform: What Model Now?* Armonk, N.Y.: M. E. Sharpe.

Park, Sam Ock. 1993. "Industrial Restructuring and the Spatial Division of Labor: The Case of the Seoul Metropolitan Region, the Republic of Korea." *Environment and Planning* A25(1, January):81–93.

Park, Sam Ock, and Ann Markusen. 1995. "Generalizing New Industrial Districts: A Theoretical Agenda and an Application from a Non-Western Economy." *Environment and Planning* 27(1, January):81–104.

Pearson, Margaret M. 1991. *Joint Ventures in the People's Republic of China: The Control of Foreign Direct Investment under Socialism.* Princeton, N.J.: Princeton University Press.

Perkins, Dwight, and Shahid Yusuf. 1984. *Rural Development in China.* Baltimore, Md.: Johns Hopkins University Press.

Perlin, Frank. 1983. "Proto-Industrialization and Pre-Colonial South Asia." *Past and Present* 98(February):30–95.

Perry, Elizabeth J. 1993. *Shanghai on Strike: The Politics of Chinese Labor.* Stanford, Calif.: Stanford University Press.

Petrakos, George C. 1992. "Urban Concentration and Agglomeration Economies: Reexamining the Relationship." *Urban Studies* 29(8, December):1219–30.

Piore, Michael J., and Charles F. Sable. 1983. "Italian Small Business Development: Lessons for U.S. Industrial Policy." In John Zysman and Laura D'Andrea Tyson, eds., *American Industry in International Competition: Government Policies and Corporate Strategies.* Ithaca, N.Y.: Cornell University Press.

———. 1984. *The Second Industrial Divide: Possibilities for Prosperity.* New York: Basic Books.

Porter, Michael E. 1990. *The Competitive Advantage of Nations.* New York: Free Press.

Poston, Dudley L., Jr., Michael Xinxiang Mao, and Mei-Yu Yu. 1996. "The Global Distribution of the Overseas Chinese around 1990." *Population and Development Review* 20(September):631–43.

Powell, Walter W., and Laurel Smith-Doerr. 1994. "Networks and Economic Life." In Neil J. Smelser and Richard Swedberg, eds., *The Handbook of Economic Sociology.* Princeton, N.J.: Princeton University Press.

Poznanski, Kazimierz, ed. 1992. *Constructing Capitalism.* Boulder, Colo.: Westview Press.

Pratten, Cliff. 1991. *The Competitiveness of Small Firms.* Cambridge, U.K.: Cambridge University Press.

Pratten, Cliff, and Hermann Simon. 1992. "Lessons from Germany's Midsize Giants." *Harvard Business Review* 70(2, March–April):115–23.

Pyke, Frank, and Werner Sengenberger, eds. 1992. *Industrial Districts and Local Economic Generation.* Geneva: International Institute for Labor Studies; Beijing: China Statistical Information and Consultancy Service Center.

Rankin, Mary Backus. 1986. *Elite Activism and Political Transformation in China: Zhejiang Province, 1865–1911.* Stanford, Calif.: Stanford University Press.

Rappaport, Andrew S., and Shmuel Halevi. 1991. "The Computerless Computer Company." *Harvard Business Review* 69(4, July–August):69–80.

Rawski, Thomas G. 1989. *Economic Growth in Pre-War China.* Berkeley: University of California Press.

———. 1992. "Progress without Privatization: The Reform of China's State Industries." Research Paper Series CH-RPS 17. Policy Research Department, World Bank, Washington, D.C.

Redding, S. Gordon. 1990. *The Spirit of Chinese Capitalism.* Berlin: de Gruyter.

———. 1992. "Overseas Chinese Business Community in Asia." *RITT* 2:21.

Richardson, Nigel H. 1991. "Reshaping a Mining Town: Economic and Community Development in Sudbury, Ontario." In Joanne Fox-Przeworski, John B. Goddard, and Mark W. de Jong, eds, *Urban Regeneration in a Changing Economy.* Cambridge, U.K.: Oxford University Press.

Riskin, Carl. 1987. *China's Political Economy*. New York: Oxford University Press.

Rodwin, Lloyd. 1991. "European Industrial Change and Regional Economic Transformation: An Overview of Recent Experience." In Lloyd Rodwin and Hidehiko Sazanami, eds., *Industrial Change and Regional Economic Transformation: The Experience of Western Europe*. New York: Harper-Collins.

Romer, Paul M. 1989. "What Determines the Rate of Growth and Technological Change?" Policy Research Working Paper 279. World Bank, Policy Research Department, Washington, D.C. Processed.

———. 1990. "Endogenous Technical Change." *Journal of Political Economy* 98(5, pt. 2, October):S71–S101.

———. 1993. "Two Strategies for Economic Development: Using Ideas vs. Producing Ideas." In *Proceedings of the World Bank Annual Conference on Development Economics 1992*. Washington, D.C.: World Bank.

Rommel, Gunter, F. Bruch, R. Diederichs, J. Kluge, and R. D. Kempis. 1995. *Simplicity Wins: How Germany's Mid-Sized Industrial Companies Succeeded*. Cambridge, Mass.: Harvard Business School Press.

Ronan, Colin A. 1995. *The Shorter Science and Civilization in China*. Vol. 5. Cambridge, U.K.: Cambridge University Press.

Rotemberg, Julio J., and Garth Saloner. 1990. "Competition and Human Capital Accumulation: A Theory of Interregional Specialization and Trade." NBER Working Paper 3228. National Bureau of Economic Research, Cambridge, Mass. Processed.

Rowe, William T. 1984. *Hankow: Commerce and Society in a Chinese City, 1796–1889*. Stanford, Calif.: Stanford University Press.

Rozman, Gilbert. 1990. "East Asian Urbanization in the Nineteenth Century: Comparisons with Europe." In Ad van der Woude, Akira Hayami, and Jan de Vries, eds., *Urbanization in History: A Process of Dynamic Interactions*. Oxford: Clarendon Press.

Sako, Mari. 1990. "Enterprise Training in a Comparative Perspective: West Germany, Japan, Britain." World Bank, Industry Development Department, Washington, D.C. Processed.

Sassen, Saskia. 1991. *The Global City*. Princeton, N.J.: Princeton University Press.

Sassen-Koob, Saskia. 1986. "New York City Economic Restructuring and Immigration." *Development and Change* 17:85–119.

Sawada, Yukari. 1992. "Guangdong's Reforms and Their Impact on Society." *JETRO China Newsletter* 97(March–April):6–12.

Saxenian, Annalee. 1985. "The Genesis of Silicon Valley." In Peter Hall and Ann Markusen, eds., *Silicon Landscapes*. Boston, Mass: Allen and Unwin.

———. 1994. *Regional Advantage: Culture and Competition in Silicon Valley and Route 128*. Cambridge, Mass.: Harvard University Press.

Schmitz, Herbert, and Bernard Musyck. 1994. "Industrial Districts in Europe: Policy Lessons for Developing Countries?" *World Development* 22(6, June):889–910.

Scott, Allen J., and D. P. Angel. 1991. "The U.S. Semiconductor Industry: A Locational Analysis." Discussion Paper D868. Graduate School of Architecture and Urban Planning, University of California, Los Angeles. Processed.

Scott, Allen J., and Michael Storper. 1990. "Regional Development Reconsidered." Working Paper 1. Lewis Center for Regional Policy Studies, University of California, Los Angeles. Processed.

Seki, Mitsuhiro. 1994. *Beyond the Full-Set Industrial Structure: Japanese Industry.* Tokyo: International Library Foundation.

Serageldin, Ismail, Richard Barrett, and Joan Martin-Brown, eds. 1995. *The Business of Sustainable Cities: Public-Private Partnerships for Creative, Technical, and Institutional Solutions.* Environmentally Sustainable Development Series 7. Washington, D.C.: World Bank.

Shaiken, Harley. 1991. "The Universal Motors Assembly and Stamping Plant." *Columbia Journal of World Business* 26(2, Summer):124–37.

Shi, Peijun, Lin Hui, and Liang Jinshe. 1996. "Shanghai as a Regional Hub." In Yue-man Yeung and Sung Yun-wing, eds., *Shanghai: Transformation and Modernization under China's Open Policy.* Hong Kong: Chinese University Press.

Shirk, Susan. 1993. *The Political Logic of Economic Reform in China.* Berkeley: University of California Press.

Shue, Vivienne. 1988. *The Reach of the State.* Stanford: Stanford University Press.

Siebert, Horst. 1991. *The New Economic Landscape in Europe.* Oxford: Basil Blackwell.

Sigel, Louis T. 1993. "The Reform and Restructuring of the Guangzhou Economy: The Question of National Applicability." In George T. Yu, ed., *China in Transition: Economic, Political, and Social Developments.* Lanham, Md.: University Press of America.

Skinner, G. William. 1965. *Marketing and Social Structure in Rural China.* Tucson: University of Arizona Press.

Smil, Vaclav. 1996. "Environmental Problems in China: Estimates of Economic Costs." Special Report 5. East-West Center, Honolulu. April. Processed.

Smith, Paul J. 1991. *Taxing Heaven's Store House.* Cambridge, Mass.: Harvard University Press.

Solinger, Dorothy, ed. 1993. *China's Transition from Socialism: Statist Legacies and Market Reforms, 1980–1990.* Armonk, N.Y.: M. E. Sharpe.

State Statistical Bureau. 1990. *China: The Forty Years of Urban Development.* Beijing: China Statistical Information and Consultancy Service Center.

———. 1992a. *China: Foreign Economic Statistics, 1979–91.* Beijing: China Statistical Information and Consultancy Service Center.

———. 1992b. *Comparison of Population Information: Beijing, Tianjin, Shanghai, and Guangzhou.* Beijing: China Statistical Information and Consultancy Service Center.

———. Various years. *China: Population Statistical Yearbook.* Beijing: China Statistical Information and Consultancy Service Center.

———. Various years. *China: Urban Statistical Yearbook.* Beijing: China Statistical Information and Consultancy Service Center.

———. Various years. *Statistical Yearbook of China.* Beijing: China Statistical Information and Consultancy Service Center.

———. Various years. *Statistical Yearbook of Guangdong.* Beijing: China Statistical Information and Consultancy Service Center.

———. Various years. *Statistical Yearbook of Guangzhou.* Beijing: China Statistical Information and Consultancy Service Center.

———. Various years. *Statistical Yearbook of Shanghai.* Beijing: China Statistical Information and Consultancy Service Center.

———. Various years. *Statistical Yearbook of Tianjin.* Beijing: China Statistical Information and Consultancy Service Center.

———. Various years. *Yearbook of Industrial Statistics.* Beijing: China Statistical Information and Consultancy Service Center.

Stepanek, James B. 1991. "China's Enduring State Factories: Why Ten Years of Reform Has Left China's Big State Factories Unchanged." In *China's Economic Dilemmas in the 1990s: The Problems of Reforms, Modernization, and Interdependence.* Paper submitted to the Joint Economic Committee, U.S. Congress, Washington, D.C., April.

Storper, Michael, and Richard Walker. 1989. *Capitalist Imperative: Territory, Technology, and Industrial Growth.* New York: Basil Blackwell.

Sung, Yun-wing. 1991. *The China–Hong Kong Connection.* Cambridge, U.K.: Cambridge University Press.

Sung, Yun-wing, Pak-wai Lu, Yue-chim Richard Wong, and Pui-king Lau. 1995. *The Fifth Dragon: The Emergence of the Pearl River Delta.* Singapore: Addison Wesley.

Taiwan Databook 1994. Taipei.

Thompson, Ian B. 1995. "High Speed Transport Hubs and Eurocity Status: The Case of Lyon." *Journal of Transport Geography* 3(1, March):29–38.

Tian, Gang. 1996. *Shanghai's Role in the Economic Development of China.* Westport, Conn.: Praeger.

Todd, Daniel. 1994. "Changing Technology, Economic Growth and Port Development: The Transformation of Tianjin." *Geoforum* 25(3):285–304.

Tsai, Shih-Shan Henry. 1996. *The Eunuchs in the Ming Dynasty.* Albany: State University of New York Press.

Twitchett, Denis, and John K. Fairbank. 1976. *The Cambridge History of China.* Vol. 2: *Late Ch'ing, 1800–1911, Part 2.* Cambridge, U.K.: Cambridge University Press.

U.S. Congress, Office of Technology Assessment. 1987. *Technology Transfer to China.* Washington, D.C.: U.S. Government Printing Office.

———. 1995. *The Technological Reshaping of Metropolitan America.* Washington, D.C.: U.S. Government Printing Office.

Victor, F. S. Sit, ed. 1985. *Chinese Cities: The Growth of the Metropolis since 1949.* Oxford: Oxford University Press.

Vogel, Ezra F. 1989. *One Step Ahead in China: Guangdong under Reform.* Cambridge, Mass.: Harvard University Press.

Walder, G. Andrew. 1986. *Communist Neo-Traditionalism: Work and Authority in Chinese Industry.* Berkeley: University of California Press.

———. 1991. "A Reply to Womack." *China Quarterly* 126:333–39.

Wang, Xianping. 1994. "Chinese Airports: Opening the Door." *Airport Magazine* (May/June):1–4.

Wang, Ya Ping, and Alan Murie. 1996. "The Process of Commercialization of Urban Housing in China." *Urban Studies* 33(6, June):971–89.

Weitzman, Martin, and Chengang Xu. 1994. "Chinese Township Village Enterprises as Vaguely Defined Cooperatives." *Journal of Comparative Economics* 18(April):121–45.

Wheaton, William C., and Hisanobu Shishido. 1981. "Urban Concentration, Agglomeration Economics, and the Level of Economic Development." *Economic Development and Cultural Change* 30:17–30.

Williamson, Jeffrey G. 1992. "Macroeconomic Dimensions of City Growth in Developing Countries: Past, Present, and Future." In *Proceedings of the World Bank Annual Conference on Development Economics 1991.* Washington, D.C.: World Bank.

Wong, John. 1988. "Integration of China into the Asian-Pacific Region." *World Economy* 11(Summer):327–54.

———. 1991. "Economic Integration of Hong Kong and Guangdong." IEAP Internal Study Paper 2. Institute of East Asian Philosophies, Singapore.

———. 1995. "Assessing China's Economic Reform Progress in 1994." *JETRO China Newsletter* 114(January–February):8–14.

Wong, Linda. 1994. "China's Urban Migrants: The Public Policy Challenge." *Pacific Affairs* 67(3, Fall):335–55.

Wong, Sui-Lun. 1988. *Emigrant Entrepreneurs.* Hong Kong: Oxford University Press.

Woo, Edward S. W. 1994. "Urban Development." In Yue-man Yeung and David K. Y. Chu, eds., *Guangdong: Survey of a Province Undergoing Rapid Change.* Hong Kong: Chinese University Press.

Woodard, Kim. 1991. "Tianjin Comes of Age." *China Business Review* 18(1, January–February):20–25.

Woodard, Kim, and Wei Zhu. 1994. "Revved and Ready: Component Production Is Where the Real Opportunities Lie." *China Business Review* 21(2, March–April):24–30.

Woodside, Alexander B. 1971. *Viet Nam and the Chinese Model.* Cambridge, Mass.: Harvard University Press and the Council of East Asian Studies.

World Bank. 1981. *World Development Report 1981.* New York: Oxford University Press.

———. 1986. *China: Management and Finance of Higher Education.* Washington, D.C.

———. 1987. "Technical/Vocational Education for China's Development." Report 6789-CHA. East Asia and Pacific Regional Office, Washington, D.C. Processed.

———. 1990. *China: Between Plan and Market.* Washington, D.C.

———. 1991a. "China: Economic Development in Jiangsu Province." China and Mongolia Department, Washington, D.C.

———. 1991b. "China: Provincial Education Planning and Finance—Sector Study." Report 9222-CHA. China and Mongolia Department, Washington, D.C. Processed.

———. 1991c. "Impediments in China's Foreign Direct Investment Environment." Foreign Investment Advisory Service and International Finance Corporation, Washington, D.C. Processed.

———. 1992a. "China: Industrial Restructuring: A Tale of Three Cities." China and Mongolia Department, Washington, D.C.

———. 1992b. "Reforming Urban Employment and the Wage System." China and Mongolia Department, Washington, D.C. Processed.

———. 1992c. *Urban Land Management: Options for an Emerging Market Economy.* Washington, D.C.

———. 1993a. "China Southeast Coastal Region: Strategic Issues in Ports and Shipping Development." China and Mongolia Department, Washington, D.C. Processed.

———. 1993b. "China: Tianjin Industrial Development Project." Staff Appraisal Report. Washington, D.C. Processed.

———. 1994a. *China: Internal Market Development and Regulation.* World Bank Country Study. Washington, D.C.

————. 1994b. *World Development Report 1994: Infrastructure for Development.* New York: Oxford University Press.

————. 1994c. *World Tables 1994.* Baltimore, Md.: Johns Hopkins University Press.

————. 1996. *The Chinese Economy.* Washington, D.C.

————. Various years. *Social Indicators of Development.* Baltimore, Md.: Johns Hopkins University Press.

————. Various years. *World Development Report.* New York: Oxford University Press.

World Resources Institute. 1996. *World Resources: The Urban Environment, 1996–97.* New York: Oxford University Press.

Xu, Xue-qiang, and Li Si-ming. 1990. "China's Open Door Policy and Urbanization in the Pearl River Delta Region." *International Journal of Urban and Regional Research* 14(1, March):49–69.

Yamazawa, Ippei. 1990. *Economic Development and International Trade.* Honolulu, Hawaii: East-West Center.

Yang, Dali L. 1996a. *Calamity and Reform in China: State, Rural Society, and Institutional Change since the Great Leap Famine.* Stanford, Calif.: Stanford University Press.

————. 1996b. "Governing China's Transition to the Market." *World Politics* 48(3, April):424–52.

Yeh, Anthony Gar-On, and Xu Xueqiang. 1990. "Changes in City Size and Regional Distribution, 1953–1986." In Reginald Yin-Wang Kwok and others, eds., *Chinese Urban Reform: What Model Now?* Armonk, N.Y.: M. E. Sharpe,

Yeung, Yue-man. 1996. "Introduction." In Yue-man Yeung and Sung Yun-wing, eds., *Shanghai: Transformation and Modernization under China's Open Policy.* Hong Kong: Chinese University Press.

Yeung, Yue-man, and David K. Y. Chu, eds. 1994. *Guangdong: Survey of a Province Undergoing Rapid Change.* Hong Kong: Chinese University Press.

Yeung, Yue-man, and Xu-wei Hu, eds. 1992. *China's Coastal Cities: Catalysts for Modernization.* Honolulu: University of Hawaii Press.

Yeung, Yue-man, Yu-you Deng, and Han-xin Chen. 1992. "Guangzhou: The Southern Metropolis in Transformation." In Yue-man Yeung and Xu-wei Hu, eds., *China's Coastal Cities: Catalysts for Modernization.* Honolulu: University of Hawaii Press.

Yukawa, Kazuo. 1992. "Economic Cooperation between Guangdong and Inland Areas." *JETRO China Newsletter* 100(September–October):9–16.

Zhao, Songqiao. 1994. *Geography of China: Environment, Resources, Population, and Development.* New York: John Wiley.

Zhao, Xiaobin. 1996. "Spatial Disparities and Economic Development in China, 1953–92: A Comparative Study." *Development and Change* 27:131–63.

Zhao, Xiaobin, and Li Zhang. 1995. "Urban Performance and the Control of Urban Size in China." *Urban Studies* 32(4–5, May):813–46.

Zhou, Yixing. 1991. "The Metropolitan Interlocking Region in China: A Preliminary Hypothesis." In Norton Ginsberg, Bruce Koppel, and T. G. McGee, eds., *The Extended Metropolis: Settlement Transition in Asia.* Honolulu: University of Hawaii Press.

Index